D0919724

ENGLISH POETRY

A CRITICAL INTRODUCTION

ENGLISH POETRY

A CRITICAL INTRODUCTION

by

F. W. BATESON

LONGMANS, GREEN AND CO

LONDON · NEW YORK · TORONTO

LONGMANS, GREEN AND CO LTD
6 & 7 CLIFFORD STREET LONDON W I
ALSO AT MELBOURNE AND CAPE TOWN

LONGMANS, GREEN AND CO INC
55 FIFTH AVENUE NEW YORK 3

LONGMANS, GREEN AND CO
215 VICTORIA STREET TORONTO I

ORIENT LONGMANS LTD
BOMBAY CALCUTTA MADRAS

First published 1950

PRINTED IN GREAT BRITAIN
BY WESTERN PRINTING SERVICES LTD, BRISTOL

To

JAN

THE ANTI-ROMANTICS

So we are the music-unmakers, it seems—
Of Pastoral Park disinfecting your dreams,
At La Belle Sauvage the sardonic irregulars,
Of skylarks the scarers, the nobblers of Pegasus . . .

Treeless in their towns that acquisitive age
Filched the last foxglove from the prefigured ledge.
Unhappy those huntsmen! their hybridisation
Grew the Goliaths of a neurotic nation.

I have heard them hallooing in the guilty wood,
Father and Grandfather by the poltergeists pursued;
Green were the grasses under the weeping ashes.
But combine and crawler have settled the hashes

Of the Shires and their squires, the peaches in the
    pleasance;
Lucy and Lycidas must relearn their lessons:
'See, Science holds the Muse's ivory hand,
As golden Ceres re-assumes the land.'

Man makes the country. And gold made the town.
But devaluation melts Sir Midas down.
What in Whitehall meanwhile, much-waistcoated wandering,
Are the poemless persons now plotting and pondering?

ACKNOWLEDGMENTS

For permission to use copyright material I am indebted to the following: The author and Messrs. Faber and Faber Ltd. for 'Oxford' from *Another Time* by W. H. Auden; Messrs. George Allen and Unwin Ltd. for 'Oxford' from *Collected Poems* by Lionel Johnson.

CONTENTS

PART ONE

The Definition of Poetry

PART TWO

Applications of the Definition

CONCLUSION

If my criticism should seem sometimes harsh, that is, I believe, due to its being given in plain terms, a manner which I prefer, because by obliging the writer to say definitely what he means, it makes his mistakes easy to point out, and in this way the true business of criticism may be advanced.

ROBERT BRIDGES

Part One

THE DEFINITION OF POETRY

CHAPTER ONE

THE PRIMACY OF MEANING

I

For the last two hundred years or so the usual *non-critical* introduction to English poetry has been via the anthology.[1] And the imprint on the reader's consciousness left during adolescence by the *Elegant Extracts*, or *The Golden Treasury*, or the English Association's *Poems of To-day*, or whatever the particular selection was, is hardly ever entirely erased by later, more critical reading. Indeed, the whole adult attitude to poetry, what is expected from it as well as what is brought to it, can be unconsciously determined by the inclusions and exclusions of a school prize or an early birthday present. To anyone, therefore, who takes English poetry seriously and who is aware of the potential range of its social function to-day, the state of mind and methods of operation of the contemporary anthologist have a special importance. An anthology like the *Oxford Book of English Verse*, of which over half a million copies have already been sold, is really a sociological fact of the first significance. And, from this point of view, the editorial paraphernalia—the indication of a poem's historical context, the circumstances of its composition, the critical comments ventured or not ventured,

---

[1] The first English anthology in the modern sense, i.e. the first representative collection of English poems of all periods, arranged in approximately chronological order, was Elizabeth Cooper's *The Muses Library; or a Series of English Poetry, from the Saxons to Charles II* (1737). As well as the poems Mrs. Cooper provided 'the Lives and Characters of the known Writers, taken from the most authentic Memoirs.' Only a first volume (down to Samuel Daniel) was in fact published.

the explanatory notes, the glossaries, the biographical information, etc.—are almost as important as the poems themselves. They provide the spectacles through which the poems can be read. Without their assistance a poem's central point may be missed, the grammar may be misconstrued, the allusions may be misunderstood, and instead of a clear-cut, sharply focused experience the reader may only register a semantic blur, an emotional haze.

It is for this reason that a change that has come over anthologies of English poetry since the end of the nineteenth century assumes so sinister an aspect.[1] If you compare the *Oxford Book of English Verse*, which was originally published in 1900, with its eighteenth-century equivalents, such as Goldsmith's *Beauties of English Poetry* (1767) or Henry Headley's more ambitious *Select Beauties of Ancient English Poetry* (1787), and its nineteenth-century predecessors, such as Palgrave's *Golden Treasury* (1861), or the less familiar but much better *Household Book of English Poetry* (1868) of Archbishop Trench, you will find one startling difference. The *Oxford Book* is entirely without notes. Instead of the comments and explanations found in all these earlier anthologies, Quiller-Couch confined himself to a few marginal glosses on the obsolete words. And later anthologists have been equally uninformative. Even the more or less scholarly affairs, like the 'period' *Oxford Books*, Bridges's *Spirit of Man* and Norman Ault's admirable collections, rarely provide more than references to the sources of the texts used. Nor is this

[1] According to I. A. Richards (*Coleridge on Imagination* (1934), p. 193) it was round about 1900 that a deterioration in the capacity to read English poetry intelligently set in: 'The capacity to read intelligently seems undoubtedly to have been greater among educated men in Coleridge's time than it is to-day. . . . It was maintained—for modes of meaning close in structure to those in Wordsworth, Shelley or Keats—until towards the end of the nineteenth century. Then came a sudden decline in performance.'

state of affairs confined to the anthologies. The same editorial reticence is to be found in most modern reprints of the English poets. The 'Cambridge English Classics' and the 'Oxford Poets,' to cite only two standard series issued by their respective University Presses, contain no explanatory notes at all, though elaborate textual collations are included (which only one reader in a thousand ever looks at). This is in striking contrast with the eighteenth- and nineteenth-century editions of the English poetical classics; almost all of those which have any pretensions to scholarship provide either notes or a biographical-critical introduction, often both. I am not referring here to the *magna opera* like Zachary Grey's *Hudibras* (1744), or the Elwin-Courthope edition of Pope (1871–89), but to such more or less hack productions as Fenton's Waller (1729), Langhorne's Collins (1765), George Gilfillan's 'British Poets' (1853–60), or the 'Muses' Library' series issued by A. H. Bullen in the early 1890's. Apparently up to about 1900 or so readers of English poetry *expected* to have the obscure expressions and the literary and topical allusions explained to them. And then, apparently quite suddenly, the expectation ceased. Plain-text reprints and anthologies without notes, instead of being the cheap and nasty exception, became the rule over the whole published price-range from the private presses to 'The World's Classics' and 'Everyman Library.' With minor exceptions this is still the situation to-day. There have been plenty of reprints of Chaucer, Spenser, Donne, Milton, Dryden, Pope, Gray, Blake, Wordsworth, Coleridge, Shelley and Keats, and dozens of books and hundreds of articles *about* them, but with the exception of the de Selincourt-Darbishire Wordsworth and the 'Twickenham' Pope (the latter still incomplete), there has been no adequate English edition of *any* of these poets since 1912 (the date of Grierson's Donne). The Americans have recently come to our rescue with editions of Chaucer and Spenser, but for Keats we have still to rely on de Selincourt (1905), for Milton on Verity (1891-7), and for Dryden on Saintsbury's revision of Scott (1882-92). And of Gray, Blake, Coleridge and Shelley there are no satisfactory critical editions at all.

There seem to be two possible explanations of this anomalous situation. One is that the modern reader, unlike his grandfather and great-grandfather, always finds English poetry immediately intelligible. (In other words, he doesn't *need* notes.) The other is that the modern reader finds a detailed understanding of poetry inessential to its enjoyment. (In other words, he isn't *interested* in the kind of information that notes provide.)

The first of these two positions would seem to be that held by P. H. B. Lyon, until recently the Headmaster of Rugby School, who has committed himself to the proposition that 'Poetry is really a very simple affair, simpler than prose, very often much simpler than life itself.'[1] In saying this, Mr. Lyon may have been under the impression that he was only saying ditto to Milton, who once described poetry, it will be remembered, as 'less subtle and fine, but more simple, sensuous and passionate' than rhetoric.[2] But by *simple* Milton didn't mean *easy* so much as possessing 'that unity which enables one to think of the poem as a whole,' i.e. the quality that Coleridge was later to call 'esemplastic.'[3] He would have been the last person to think that poetry ought to be immediately intelligible to the man in the street. (For Milton nothing that was worth having in this life or the next could ever be achieved 'without dust and heat.') It is difficult, indeed, to

[1] *The Discovery of Poetry* (1930), p. 14. [2] *Of Education* (1644)
[3] See W. P. Ker, *Form and Style* (1929), p. 178.

believe that *anybody* could seriously maintain that the best poems of Shakespeare, Donne, Blake or Wordsworth, for example, are easy to understand. Sometimes there is, it is true, a delusive air of simplicity, but the 'silly sooth' of their songs and lyrics has a way of turning out to be particularly sophisticated.

Take that favourite anthology piece from Blake's *Milton* 'And did those feet in ancient time.' How many of the millions of men and women who chant these lines every year could really say what they are all about?

> And did those feet in ancient time
>> Walk upon England's mountains green?
> And was the holy Lamb of God
>> On England's pleasant pastures seen?
>
> And did the Countenance Divine
>> Shine forth upon our clouded hills?
> And was Jerusalem builded here
>> Among those dark Satanic Mills?
>
> Bring me my bow of burning gold!
>> Bring me my arrows of desire!
> Bring me my spear! O clouds unfold!
>> Bring me my chariot of fire!
>
> I will not cease from mental fight,
>> Nor shall my sword sleep in my hand.
> Till we have built Jerusalem
>> In England's green and pleasant land.

The poem originally came at the end of a prose preface in which Blake attacked the cult of 'Greek or Roman models,' and the phrase 'ancient time' apparently alludes to the legend, referred to by Milton himself in *Areopagitica*, that Pythagoras had derived his philosophical system from the British Druids. What Blake is saying, in effect, is that it is absurd for an Englishman to rely on classical models, as the culture of Greece and Rome was really based on that of primitive Britain. But how on earth can the modern reader realize this, unless it is explained to him in a note? And this is only one of the dark sayings in the poem. The 'Jerusalem' that we are to build in England is not, as the innocent reader might think, a Utopia of garden cities and national parks. 'Jerusalem' stands for something much more abstract, as a passage in a later Prophetic Book makes clear:

> Such Visions have appeared to me,
>   As I my order'd course have run:
> Jerusalem is nam'd Liberty
>   Among the sons of Albion.[1]

In particular, it would seem, 'Jerusalem' is sexual liberty.[2] Finally, the 'dark Satanic Mills' have nothing whatever to do with the Industrial Revolution. Another passage in *Milton* shows that Satan's mills are the altars of the Churches, on which the clergy of the eighteenth century were still plying their deadly Druidic trade:

> And the Mills of Satan were separated into a moony space
> Among the rocks of Albion's Temples, and Satan's
>   Druid Sons
> Offer the Human Victims throughout all the Earth.[3]

Blake's poem is now a popular hymn and is in process of becoming a sort of unofficial national anthem. No doubt it owes its popularity primarily to Parry's vigorous

[1] *Jerusalem*, f. 26. See Oxford Blake, ed. J. Sampson (1914), p. 389.
[2] Clouds are a recurrent symbol in the Prophetic Books of the Church's repression of the instinctive energies, and gold is generally a specifically sexual symbol.
[3] ff. 9, ll. 6–8, Oxford Blake, p. 371.

setting, but the adoption by the Churches and women's organizations of this anti-clerical pæan of free love is amusing evidence of the carelessness with which poetry is read to-day. Will no one tell them what they sing?

Blake's poem is perhaps an extreme case, but problems similar in kind, if not in degree, are raised by many familiar poems. Marvell's 'To his Coy Mistress,' for example, another standard anthology piece, ends with a metaphor that is far from easy to grasp:

> Let us roll all our strength and all
> Our sweetness up into one ball,
> And tear our pleasures with rough strife,
> Through the iron gates of life.

C. Day Lewis has commented on these lines in *The Poetic Image* (1947), where he says: 'If I try to visualize it, I see nothing but two lovers feverishly trying to squeeze an india-rubber ball through the bars of an iron gate.'[1] Obviously this won't do, and Day Lewis proceeds to try and explain away the incongruity by a theory that the images are 'abstract' and discourage visualization. I suspect myself that by 'ball' Marvell didn't mean a child's ball but a cannon-ball. The word is often used in the seventeenth century in this sense.[2] In that case there are not two detached images, as Day Lewis thinks, but a single image of a heavy cannon-ball crashing through the gates of a town or fort. If I am right, the passage surely *demands* a footnote. You cannot expect a modern reader to know the seventeenth-century meanings of 'ball' by the mere light of nature.

[1] p. 72. Tennyson also seems to have found the passage difficult. He told Palgrave 'that he could fancy *grates* would have intensified Marvell's image' (*Memoir by his Son* (1899 ed.), p. 843).

[2] In *Paradise Lost*, vi, 518, the apostate angels have 'their Engine and their Balls of missive ruin.'

And the case for notes goes further than this. 'I have eschewed notes,' Quiller-Couch wrote in the original preface to the *Oxford Book of English Verse*, 'reluctantly when some obscure passage or allusion seemed to ask for a timely word, with more equanimity when the temptation was to criticize or "appreciate." For the function of the anthologist includes criticizing in silence.' But does it? If the criticism is any good, it must surely be relevant. And, in practice, can a hard and fast line be drawn between interpretation and 'appreciation'?

Keats's 'Bright Star' is a good example of the poem that cannot be understood, except in the most superficial way, until it has been subjected to a critical analysis:

> Bright Star! would I were steadfast as thou art—
> Not in lone splendour hung aloft the night,
> And watching, with eternal lids apart,
> Like Nature's patient sleepless Eremite,
>
> The moving waters at their priestlike task
> Of pure ablution round earth's human shores,
> Or gazing on the new soft fallen mask
> Of snow upon the mountains and the moors:
>
> No—yet still steadfast, still unchangeable,
> Pillow'd upon my fair Love's ripening breast,
> To feel for ever its soft fall and swell,
> Awake for ever in a sweet unrest.
>
> Still, still to hear her tender-taken breath,
> And so live ever—or else swoon to death.

In this sonnet Keats, with his head resting on Fanny Brawne's breast, is comparing and contrasting his situation with that of the star, the octave providing pictures of the star shining down (*a*) on the sea, and (*b*) on snow-covered hills, and the sestet dealing with Keats himself and Fanny. He envies the star because, unlike himself, it is 'steadfast' and 'unchangeable,' the emotional temperature is constant. He would like to be, if not as distant and completely detached as the star, at least 'Half passionless' (the opening word of the poem's last line in the first draft). The structural heart of the poem is therefore the implied parallel between the 'pure and priestlike' seas and snows that the star is watching and Keats's own observation of his 'fair love's ripening breast.' (The repetition of 'soft-fallen mask,' l. 7, and 'soft fall and swell,' l. 11, clinches the parallel.) If only, in other words, he could infuse something of the same sexless purity into his relations with Fanny! The background to the poem is the old conflict between lust and love. Keats was trying to sublimate the sexual element in his feelings for Fanny. This is undoubtedly the central 'meaning' of the poem. But without an editor's assistance the common reader might easily miss it.[1]

The best comment on 'Bright Star' is the note that Keats entered in the margin of his copy of Burton's *Anatomy of Melancholy*:

> Here is the old plague spot; the pestilence, the raw scrofula. I mean there is nothing disgraces me in my own eyes so much as being one of a race of eyes nose and mouth beings in a planet call'd the earth who all from Plato to Wesley have always mingled goatish winnyish lustful love with the abstract adoration of the deity.[2]

[1] Uncommon readers have also missed it. In George Thomson's otherwise excellent *Marxism and Poetry* (1945), the poem is interpreted as Keats's response to the hypnotic swaying of the ship that was taking him to Italy, as it rode at anchor in Lulworth Cove. But it is now known that the sonnet was written in 1819 and not, as Lord Houghton thought, at Lulworth in 1820 (when Keats only *copied* it into the blank leaf of his Shakespeare's *Poems*).

[2] *Complete Works of John Keats*, ed. H. Buxton Forman, vol. iii (1901), p. 268. Keats's note is to Part 3, Sec. 1, Mem. 1, Sub. 2 of Burton ('*Loves* Beginning,

But, as far as I know, no editor of Keats has connected the two.

'And did those feet in ancient time,' 'To his Coy Mistress' and 'Bright Star' are three of the best-known English poems. They are in all the anthologies. But, as we have seen, the moment one starts looking at them at all closely, all sorts of problems arise. Any editor who is worth his salt must have been aware of some at any rate of the *cruces* I have been discussing in the last few pages; the Blake poem, in particular, cries out for editorial elucidation. It is obvious that these poems are not easy to understand. If anthologists have not provided the reader with the help, in the way of notes and introductions, that he manifestly needs, the reason must be that the anthologists do not think the difficulties matter. This is the desperate conclusion to which, it seems to me, one is driven by the logic of the facts. It means, in other words, that the second of the two hypotheses proposed at the beginning of this section is apparently the right one. Consciously or unconsciously the modern editor—who may be taken to represent responsible critical opinion—is in effect saying to his readers: 'Don't worry about the *meaning* of these poems. You can read them and re-read them, memorize them and recite them, if you like, but don't try to *understand* them.'

Is this reading too much into the editors' and anthologists' conspiracy of silence? One might have thought so,

Object, Definition, Division'). The note may have been made in September 1819 when Keats was reading Burton (*Letters*, ed. M. Buxton Forman, p. 404); it cannot have been made before 1819 as the copy is inscribed 'John Keats from Charles Brown 1819.' The sonnet is also dated 1819 in Brown's transcript, and a phrase resembling the last line is in the letter to Fanny Brawne of 25 July 1819: 'I have two luxuries to brood over in my walks, your Loveliness and the hour of my death. O that I could have possession of them both in the same minute.' The marginalia and the sonnet may therefore easily be more or less contemporary.

were it not for the fact that the same implications are to be read between the lines, and sometimes not only between the lines, of the critical pronouncements of many of the most reputable of modern poets and scholars. What more revered and representative figure could one find than Robert Bridges? But this is what Bridges had to say about poetic intelligibility in 1923 (it is at the end of an analysis of the diction in *Lycidas*):

> It might be urged that with Milton and Shelley, who were educated by Hellenic models and had come by reading and meditation to have panoramic views of History and Truth, it was natural to write at that height—their poetic diction may be the spontaneous utterance of their subconscious mind—but that it is nevertheless regrettable because common folk whom they might otherwise delight and instruct cannot understand it. This is a wrong notion. It was not Dr. Johnson's ignorance or deficient education that made him dislike *Lycidas*. It was his unpoetic mind that was at fault, and his taste in Music or Painting would probably have been at the same level. Moreover, children do not resent what they cannot understand in Poetry, and they generally have a keener sense for beauty than Dr. Johnson had—indeed, if he would have become again as a little child, he might have liked *Lycidas* very well.[1]

This is perhaps not an outright denial that poetry needs to be understood if it is to be worth reading, but it comes near it. The implication certainly seems to be that children and 'common folk' can respond to the beauty of *Lycidas* without understanding it, whereas Dr. Johnson, who understood the poem, could get nothing out of it because of his 'unpoetic mind.' In other words, the high road to culture was not more learning or a better educa-

---

[1] 'Poetic Diction,' *Collected Essays*, II, III (1928).

tion, but less of both. The way to appreciate Milton was not to consult introductions and notes but to 'become again as a little child.'

The significant thing about Bridges's *dicta* is their casualness. It is all taken so for granted. *Of course* the child's mind is more poetic than Johnson's. The explanation of this nonchalance is that Bridges was well aware that he was not saying anything very new. A hundred years or more before him Coleridge had been saying, 'Poetry gives most pleasure when only generally and not perfectly understood.'[1] And Bridges's criterion of poetic merit—*the spontaneous utterance of the subconscious mind*—would have been subscribed to by all the Romantic poets. It is the theory of 'inspiration,' that poetry, as Shelley put it, 'is not subject to the control of the active powers of the mind, and its birth and recurrence have no necessary connexion with the consciousness or will.'[2] As a protest against the narrow rationalism of eighteenth-century critical theory there was perhaps something to be said for 'inspiration.' But by Bridges's time the protest had outlived its usefulness. Instead, however, of curtailing its extravagances and retaining only the grain of truth that the theory contained (viz. that the conscious and subconscious parts of the mind should *co-operate* in the production of poetry) Bridges and his contemporaries pursued the premises of Romanticism to their perverse, if logical, conclusions.

Bridges, however, was one of the more restrained of the later Romantics. What is still only implicit in him becomes explicit in A. E. Housman. In Housman's Leslie Stephen Lecture *The Name and Nature of Poetry* (1933) Romanticism makes its last and most uncom-

[1] *Anima Poetæ* (1895), p. 5.
[2] *A Defence of Poetry* (1821).

promising bow. Here almost all meaning is banished from poetry. 'Take O take those lips away' is 'nonsense; but it is ravishing poetry.' 'Hear the voice of the Bard' is 'poetry neat, or unadulterated with so little meaning that nothing except poetic emotion is perceived and matters.' Perhaps the most significant passage in the lecture is the comment on a line from Milton's *Arcades*:

> But in these six simple words of Milton—
> Nymphs and shepherds, dance no more—
> what is it that can draw tears, as I know it can, to the eyes of more readers than one? What in the world is there to cry about? Why have the mere words the physical effect of pathos when the sense of the passage is blithe and gay? I can only say, because they are poetry, and find their way to something in man which is obscure and latent, something older than the present organization of his nature.

The pathos of Milton's six simple words obviously derives for Housman from the last two of them. As Shenstone had pointed out in the middle of the eighteenth century, 'the words "no more" have a singular pathos; reminding us at once of past pleasure, and the future exclusion of it.'[1] But Milton's injunction to the nymphs and shepherds was not, in fact, to stop dancing, but to 'dance no more By sandy *Ladons* Lillied Banks.' The nymphs were only to transfer their dances from Arcadia to Harefield in Middlesex (where an 'entertainment' was being presented to the Dowager Countess of Derby).[2] Housman's tears came from taking Milton's line out of its context and giving it a meaning it was never intended to

---

[1] *Works*, vol. ii (1764), p. 187.

[2] Housman's mistake has already been pointed out by Kenneth Muir. See 'Three Hundred Years of Milton's Poems,' *Penguin New Writing*, No. 24 (1945), p. 140.

have. By misreading Milton he has created what is essentially his own private poem.[1]

The procedure is typical of the egocentricity of Romantic criticism. What the poet intended is secondary to the adventures of the reader's soul among the masterpieces. Poetry ceases to be a *communication* from the poet; he is no longer a man talking to men, so much as a stimulator of the reader's subconscious mind. If all goes well, the result is 'ecstasy' or 'rapture.' An American professor has told us what it feels like:

A fine frenzy seizes the poet's heart and brain, transmits itself to his verse, passes through that medium into me, and, losing for the time being its creative quality, is transformed into that more or less passive state we call rapture. This is to me the supreme value of great poetry, that, more than anything else, with fewer draining demands upon my store of vitality, my time, my purse—in short, upon the essential me and my accessories—it lifts me higher toward heaven, opens my eyes more surely to the Beatific Vision, wraps me 'out of space, out of time,' transmutes me and transforms me more completely and ecstatically than any other transmuting and transforming agent of which I have knowledge.[2]

[1] A nice example of Housman hoist with his own petard is provided by Robert Graves in *On English Poetry* (1922), pp. 31-2. Housman's 'The Carpenter's Son' (No. xlvii in *The Shropshire Lad*) is an account of the Crucifixion in modern dress, as it were. Here, for example, is the fifth verse:

Here hang I, and right and left
Two poor fellows hang for theft:
All the same's the luck we prove,
Though the midmost hangs for love.

The whole point of the poem depends on the reader's recognition of the analogy. But when Graves asked a number of Housman enthusiasts 'how long it took them to realize what the poet is forcing on them,' he found that nine out of ten had actually missed the scriptural allusions altogether!

[2] W. P. Trent, *Greatness in Literature* (c. 1905), p. 228. Though no critic, Trent was a good scholar and did some useful pioneer work on Defoe.

This curious confession comes from a paper by W. P. Trent originally read before the Men's English Graduate Club of Columbia University in 1904. The date is perhaps significant. It confirms the evidence of a change of poetic taste at the turn of the century provided by the anthologies and the editions of the poets. But obviously to the advantages claimed for poetry by Trent as a saver of vitality, time and money, the economy of intellectual effort should have been added. If the poet's frenzy simply transmits itself in the act of reading to a passive recipient, questions of meaning need not arise at all. You simply sit back and gorge yourself with this inexpensive rapture.

The 1920's provided their own hard-boiled version of the theory of poetic ecstasy. But, although the tone of voice is very different, the fundamental doctrine is still the same. Here, for example, are some typical comments by the hero of Aldous Huxley's *Those Barren Leaves* (1925):

What is it that makes the two words 'defunctive music' as moving as the Dead March out of the *Eroïca* and the close of *Coriolan*? Why should it be somehow more profoundly comic to 'call Tullia's ape a marmosite' than to write a whole play of Congreve? And the line, 'Thoughts that do often lie too deep for tears'—why should its effect lie where it does? Mystery. This game of art strongly resembles conjuring. The quickness of the tongue deceives the brain. It has happened, after all, often enough. Old Shakespeare, for example. How many critical brains have been deceived by the quickness of *his* tongue? Because he can say: 'Shoughs, water-rugs and demi-wolves' and 'defunctive music,' and 'the expense of spirit in a waste of shame' and all the rest of it, we credit him with philosophy, a moral purpose and the most penetrating psychology.

C

And to-day there is Evelyn Waugh, who has a character-istic passage on pure poetry in *The Loved One* (1948):

> Dennis sat in one of the arm-chairs, put his feet on the trolley and settled himself to read. Life in the Air Force had converted him from an amateur to a mere addict. There were certain trite passages of poetry which from a diverse multitude of associations never failed to yield the sensation he craved; he never experimented; these were the branded drug, the sure specific, big magic. He opened the anthology[1] as a woman opens her familiar pack of cigarettes. . . . '*I wither slowly in thine arms,*' he read. '*Here at the quiet limit of the world,*' and repeated to himself: 'Here at the quiet limit of the world. Here at the quiet limit of the world' . . . as a monk will repeat a single pregnant text over and over again in prayer.

The three excerpts are reassuring as showing how Romantic 'ecstasy' has gone down in the world since 1904. What was then the Beatific Vision had become a conjuring trick in 1925, and a patent medicine in 1948. But Romanticism has been an unconscionable time dying. It lingers on in the English papers of the Higher and School Certificates, and the English Faculties of the Senior Universities. At Oxford, still the home of lost causes, Lord David Cecil and C. S. Lewis (who, however, wears his Romanticism with a difference) are keeping the flag flying, and at Cambridge the mantle of Housman and Quiller-Couch has descended to the exuberant and impenitent F. L. Lucas. Romantic poetry died of old age many years ago, and it is more than time that Romantic criticism also received its decent and final interment. Until that is done, I. A. Richards's charge that English

---

[1] It appears from chap. vi that Dennis's anthology was the *Oxford Book o. English Verse*. The lines quoted are from Tennyson's 'Tithonus.'

poetry is no longer read intelligently is likely to remain true. The editors, by refusing to supply notes, have made it extremely difficult for us to read the poets intelligently; the critics, going further, have unmistakably implied that it would be an æsthetic error in us to do so. Their prescription is a simple one—to become as little children. All we have to do is to lower our mental age.

II

What are the theoretic bases of the cult of poetic unintelligibility?

Two separate theories have been advanced by Romantic critics to justify the exclusion of meaning from poetry. One can be called the Suggestion Theory, the other the Pure Sound Theory.

According to the Suggestion Theory poetry is not concerned with what words mean but with what they suggest. Apparently a good poem should mean very little while suggesting a great deal. Housman's comment on Blake's 'Hear the Voice of the Bard' is: 'That mysterious grandeur would be less grand if it was less mysterious, if the embryo ideas which are all that it contains should endue form and outline, and suggestion condense itself into thought.'[1] It is essential, in other words, for the success of this poem that the ideas remain in embryo, so that its meaningless grandeur can 'work' upon the reader.

A standard example of the Suggestion Theory is Shelley's 'champak' in the 'Lines to an Indian Air':

> The wandering airs they faint
> On the dark, the silent stream—
> The champak odours fail
> Like sweet thoughts in a dream.

[1] *The Name and Nature of Poetry* (1933), p. 42. An attempt to disentangle the meaning of this poem of Blake's will be found on pp. 37-9 below.

A champac is a kind of magnolia with fragrant orange-coloured flowers. It is alleged that the knowledge of what a champac is spoils Shelley's poem. According to E. D. Snyder,[1] the 'peculiar effectiveness' of these lines derives from the reader not knowing *and not wanting to know* what the odours are. Unknown the 'champak' suggests mysterious illimitable possibilities; known the line contracts to a visit to a botanical garden.

There are only three comments that need be made on the Suggestion Theory. The first is that a word's connotation is as much a part of its meaning as its denotation. If Shelley thought of the champac vaguely as a fragrant Indian tree, that was its meaning for him, and it is all that the editor's footnote needs to detail. The indefiniteness of Romantic poetry is an essential part of its meaning, and to describe it as meaningless because it is imprecise is a misuse of words. A second objection to the Suggestion Theory is that a word's connotation is normally the product of its denotation. Unless he knows where Troy is and what happened there (Troy's 'meaning') the reader cannot respond to the 'suggestion' in such a passage as Shelley's

> O! write no more the tale of Troy,
> If earth Death's scroll must be.

Even words whose precise denotations the reader does not need to know, like the champac, or the 'sweet *Infanta*' of Herrick's 'The Primrose,' can only be used successfully in contexts in which all the other words are completely intelligible. Poets therefore like Swinburne, who suppress denotation in order to exploit connotation, are cutting the ground away from under their own feet. A blurring of 'meaning' inevitably entails a blurring of

[1] *Hypnotic Poetry* (Philadelphia, 1930), p. 45.

'suggestion' too. The third objection that the Suggestion
Theory invites is that though relevant as a *raison d'être* of
Romantic poetry, it can have no general application.
The central concept of Romanticism is the primacy of the
subconscious mind. The problem, therefore, that the
Romantic poet had to solve was how to establish a
relationship between the instinctive energy of his own
private subconscious mind, the Freudian *libido*, on the one
hand, and the system of communal conventional sounds
which constitutes language, on the other. To put it
crudely, the *libido* does not speak English. According to
the psycho-analysts, when the *libido* emerges into
consciousness, in dreams or under the influence of drugs,
it tends to express itself entirely in images, 'a picture
language whose meaning can only be discovered through
special methods of interpretation.'[1] The Romantic poets,
however, were more interested in exploiting than in inter-
preting the imagery of dreams and trances. They were
impressed and excited by the hints it gave of a reality that
was deeper and older than the communal life to which
they found themselves committed by the accident of
birth.[2] Intimations of immortality are the stuff of
Romantic poetry and 'suggestion' is the inevitable
vehicle of communication. It is impossible to translate
the language of the *libido* literally—accurate transcriptions
of dreams are either dull or ludicrous—and so the attempt

---

[1] J. Jacobi, *The Psychology of C. G. Jung* (1942), p. 39. I have lifted this
quotation from M. M. Lewis, *Language in Society* (1947), a most interesting
book which assembles most of the psychological and anthropological evidence.

[2] It is significant that the adjectives *deep* and *old* appear much more often in
Romantic than in earlier poetry. *Deep* is used by Shelley more often than any
other adjective except *sweet*; *old* is a favourite of Wordsworth's, only *good*
occurring more frequently. Other adjectives that are common in Romantic
poetry and relatively rare earlier are *bright* (common in Wordsworth and
Keats), *dark* (a favourite of Shelley's), and *long* (common in Tennyson).
I derive these facts from Josephine Miles, *Major Adjectives in English Poetry*
(Berkeley, 1946).

was made to render the *qualities* of dream-experience, its strangeness, its remoteness, its inexplicability. It is significant that Romantic poetry contains a much higher proportion of negative propositions than earlier or later poetry.[1] This is because the easiest way to define the activities of the subconscious mind is to say what they are *not*. The alternative is to convey the impression, by the use of vague imagery and a 'suggestive' vocabulary, that life in the *libido* is something like everyday life, only more intense and more rarefied. Shelley's odours ('like sweet thoughts in a dream') are prevented from becoming the real scents of an English garden by the interposition of the mysterious 'champak.' The word 'suggests' the grotesque and slightly sinister vegetation of the East, and the 'suggestible' reader registers at the back of his mind banyans, upas trees, and mandragoras.

The Suggestion Theory need not detain us any longer. It is clearly valid for the special purposes of Romantic poetry, but it has no general relevance and the meaning that it excludes, the precise, scientific, 'dictionary' meaning of words, is only a part of the semantic content of poetry.

The Pure Sound Theory is related to the Suggestion Theory—Poe's and Mallarmé's 'pure poetry' seems to be an amalgam of both—but there is much less to be said for it. It has four subdivisions which can be considered separately: (i) verbal music, (ii) melopœia (sound creating a meaning complementary to the sense), (iii) onomatopœia (sound creating a meaning that echoes the sense), (iv) hypnotic poetry.

Verbal music. The writing of poetry, according to this theory, consists in 'the conscious and deliberate construc-

---

[1] Spenser and Milton are also fond of negative adjectives, but they are both semi-Romantic poets.

tion, upon a theme in itself utterly indifferent, of a musical pattern of words which gives delight.' Its 'purity' lies in 'its absolute independence of subject.'[1] Poe's doctrine of 'sonorousness' was an earlier formulation of the theory.[2] It recurs as Article 7 of the *Imagist Manifesto*:

> Study 'cadences,' the finest that you can discover, preferably in a foreign language so that the meaning of the words may be less likely to divert your attention from the movement. Saxon charms, Hebridean folk-songs, Dante, and the lyrics of Goethe and Shakespeare (apart from their meaning) are especially recommended.[3]

It is odd that this kind of thing can ever have been taken seriously, but echoes of the theory can still be heard in French criticism and in that of English and American critics who have undergone French influence. From time to time too one comes across reports of children who have responded rapturously to poetry recited to them in a language they did not understand. It always transpires, however, that the reciter *did* understand the poems, and that the language in which they were written was cognate to the children's own language. To demonstrate the existence of verbal music, i.e. of beautiful word-sounds completely detached from meaning, the response must clearly be to a poem in a language that is (i) unconnected with the subjects' own language, and (ii) unknown to the

[1] J. Middleton Murry, 'Pure Poetry,' *Countries of the Mind*, 2nd series (1931), p. 19. Herbert Read is perhaps the foremost English exponent of the verbal music theory. In *Poetry and Anarchism* (1938), p. 37, Read says of English poetry, 'Its greatest beauty is inherent in its sound; it too is a kind of music.' A similar passage will be found in his *Collected Essays* (1938), p. 100.

[2] In 'The Raven' Pallas's bust was introduced because of 'the sonorousness of the word Pallas itself,' and the word *nevermore* was selected for the refrain because the long *o* is 'the most sonorous vowel' (*The Philosophy of Composition*).

[3] See H. P. Collins, *Modern Poetry* (1925), p. 160. 'The Manifesto' (by F. S. Flint and Ezra Pound) was published in *Poetry c.* 1913.

reciter. Otherwise there will always be the danger of some meaning sifting through. A phonetic transcription of a Chinese poem might provide the basis of such an experiment in this country. The fact that no such experiment has been recorded strongly suggests that there is no such thing as verbal music.[1] The illusion of its existence is attributable to the Suggestion Theory. Mallarmé had been one of the first to exploit methodically the connotations of words, and with the submergence of denotation it was easy to attribute the verbal associations not to the original meanings of the words but to their sounds. This is what Housman seems to have done. In *The Name and Nature of Poetry* he contrasts the 'suggestion' in Blake's poems with the 'thought' and the 'celestial tune' with the 'meaning,' as though each pair of terms was interchangeable. And his conclusion that poetry is 'more physical than intellectual' seems to confirm the confusion. Connotations are, of course, as intellectual as denotations. It is only 'pure sound' that is physical.

The theory of poetry as verbal music has been taken particularly seriously in America, perhaps because of the influence of Poe. R. C. Givler, an American psychologist, devoted no less than eight years to a scientific and statistical investigation of the problem, in which he measured phonetically and tabulated eighteen thousand lines of English poetry (principally Romantic poetry). His report on the experiments is an extraordinary document.[2] Thus in order to exclude any possible influence of meaning he 'transmogrified' the line 'One faint eternal eventide of gems' (*Endymion*, ii, 225) into

[1] Tennyson had been told about a Japanese poet who was deeply moved by *In Memoriam* without knowing any English. But apparently the poem had been read to him by an Englishman (*Memoir* (1899), pp. 757–8).

[2] *The Psycho-Physiological Effect of the Elements of Speech in Relation to Poetry* (Princeton, 1915).

Won fĕmz ē nānj ŏv dī năl tĕr ĕn tēev,

which was supposed to be a nonsensical rearrangement of the sounds in Keats's line. Not unnaturally the ideas, if any, that this suggested to his subjects were quite different from the effect produced by the original line. On the other hand, when Keats's 'The air was cooling, and so very still' (*I stood tip-toe*, 2) was rearranged as 'So cooling very still was and the air,' the impressions derived from the two lines were not unnaturally found to be practically identical. Givler's tentative conclusion that the 'tonal elements of the poetic line' have 'the power of arousing a mood congruous to that of the original poem, even when torn from their positions and their rhetorical anchorage, and recast' is only valid for experiments of this second type. To suggest, as T. C. Pollock has recently done,[1] that the experiments as a whole prove that the sounds of poetry have a value apart from their meaning is simply not true. All that they prove is (i) that sympathetic listeners will respond to the associations of words in ungrammatical or illogical contexts, and (ii) that if they meet a word they don't know and the context gives no clue to its meaning they will tend to equate it with the words that sound most like it. And this had already been demonstrated much more effectively in the Nonsense Rhymes of Lear and Carroll.

Melopœia. This is Ezra Pound's word for poetry 'wherein the words are charged, over and above their plain meaning, with some musical property, which directs the bearing or trend of the meaning.'[2] The claim, essentially, is that the sounds of the words create a meaning of their own simultaneous with and complementary to the sense of the poem. A simple example is provided by

[1] *The Nature of Literature* (Princeton, 1942), pp. 109-10.
[2] *How to Read* (1931), p. 25.

the opening words of the Chorus in *Samson Agonistes*,

> This, this is he; softly a while . . .

Here, according to Robert Bridges, 'the sibilants are hushing.'[1] An even simpler example is the line from *Macbeth*,

> To-morrow, and to-morrow, and to-morrow.

According to David Daiches, 'The drawn-out mournful "o" sound . . . helps to convey the emotion of quiet despair;'[2] he adds that the three words 'are 'three relentless tolling sounds; they tend to convey a mournful effect even apart from the meaning.'[3] Is there anything in melopœia? Or is it simply, as I suspect, a case of innocent self-deception? I cannot see that sibilants are particularly 'hushing.' Tennyson, who avoided them as far as he could, called them 'hissing.'[4] And in the lines on Camilla in the *Essay on Criticism* Pope uses the sibilants to suggest the *rapidity* of Camilla's running (like the 'whistling' of a projectile). Nor does 'to-morrow' strike me as a particularly mournful sound. In another context it might easily sound quite gay.[5]

Onomatopœia. This differs from melopœia in that the meaning that the sounds create is not apprehended by the reader until *after* the sense of the words has been grasped, whereas in melopœia, the two meanings are supposed to impinge simultaneously. In onomatopœia the repeti-

---

[1] *Milton's Prosody* (1901), p. 41.
[2] *The Place of Meaning in Poetry* (1935), p. 7.   [3] *Ibid.*, p. 18.
[4] *Memoir* (1897), vol. ii, p. 289.
[5] Let us imagine a poem entitled 'The Spendthrift's Resolution':

> I'm feeling as gay as the bird on the spray,
> A farewell I have said to my sorrow;
> I intend from to-day, instead of to pay,
> To borrow and to borrow and to borrow.

'To borrow' is phonetically almost identical with 'to-morrow.'

tion of sounds is, literally, an *echo* of the sense. It is only
the prior knowledge of the sense that makes possible the
recognition of a parallel in the sounds. This time-gap
between the sense and its echo reduces the poetic value of
the device. It is too easy for the reader, who has just
mentally translated the sounds of the poem into ideas, to
fail to realize that he is now expected to reverse the process
and to reconnect the ideas with the sounds. Pope, who
regarded onomatopœia as an indispensable epic property,
found it necessary to append an index, 'VERSIFICATION,
Expressing in the sound the thing describ'd,' to his translation of the *Iliad* to prevent this 'beauty' being overlooked.
And Tennyson, an indefatigable onomatopœist, went
further and warned his reader *in the text* when an onomatopœia was coming:

> the children call, and I
> Thy shepherd pipe, and sweet is every sound,
> Sweeter thy voice, but every sound is sweet;
> Myriads of rivulets hurrying thro' the lawn,
> The moan of doves in immemorial elms,
> And murmuring of innumerable bees.

Obviously here the only reason why we are twice told
that every sound is sweet is to prepare us for the sound-
effects in the last three lines. A more serious objection to
onomatopœia is that by breaking the thread of 'meaning'
to recall the reader to 'sounds' it tends to distract his
attention from what the poet is saying to the cleverness
with which it is being said. Words are stubborn things
and to make them ring like bells through a whole poem,
as Poe does, certainly evinces considerable ingenuity. But
I find it difficult to believe that tricks of this kind have
much to do with poetry. They are surely only the
literary equivalent of 'programme music' and *trompe*

l'œil paintings—ingenious but fundamentally perverse attempts to transcend the natural limitations of the medium. It is significant that there are next to no onomatopœias in Shakespeare.

Hypnotic poetry. This is a somewhat different matter. The device has been defined by Yeats in a characteristic passage:

> The purpose of rhythm, it has always seemed to me, is to prolong the moment of contemplation, the moment when we are both asleep and awake, which is the one moment of creation, by hushing us with an alluring monotony, while it holds us waking by variety, to keep us in that state of perhaps real trance, in which the mind liberated from the pressure of the will is unfolded in symbols. If certain sensitive persons listen persistently to the ticking of a watch, or gaze persistently on the monotonous flashing of a light, they fall into the hypnotic trance; and rhythm is but the ticking of a watch made softer, that one must needs listen, and various, that one may not be swept beyond memory or grow weary of listening.[1]

It is true that professional hypnotists often use the beat of a metronome at half-second intervals, or the ticking of a clock, as the physical stimulus of hypnosis. It is also true that in Swinburne's iambic metres, when the poems are read aloud with the appropriate sing-song, the stresses recur at exactly half-second intervals, and that in the anapæstic metres the stresses recur approximately every second. And there can be no doubt that Swinburne's exploitation of the hypnotic possibilities of verse induces in suitable readers a kind of trance, like that experienced by the Indian Yogi, 'in which the emotional sensitiveness

---

[1] *Essays* (1924), pp. 195–6. The quotation is from 'The Symbolism of Poetry,' and was written in 1900.

of the subject grows more and more intense, sometimes reaching the pitch of ecstasy, as his consciousness is concentrated on some one phase of life.'[1] But the fact that verse in which a heavy beat is combined with extreme regularity in the recurrence of the stresses can induce a mild condition of hypnosis is no justification of the device. Why is it *desirable* for the reader to be hypnotized? What is the poetic function of Swinburnian metrics?

The 'symbols,' in which, according to Yeats, the mind unfolds under the impact of hypnotic poetry, appear to be the counterpart of 'suggestion.' As the objective correlatives of subconscious forces they seem to provide obscure hints of the *libido*'s modes of operation. Hence their interest to the Romantic poet. But, unlike the symbolism of earlier Romantic poetry, that of Blake and Wordsworth, for example, the symbolism of hypnotic poetry is disappointingly elusive:

> Before the beginning of years
>   There came to the making of man
> Time with a gift of tears;
>   Grief with a glass that ran. . . .

As T. S. Eliot has pointed out: 'This is not merely "music"; it is effective because it appears to be a tremendous statement, like statements made in our dreams; when we wake up and find that the "glass that ran" would do better for time than for grief and that the gift of tears would be as appropriately bestowed by grief as by time.'[2] No doubt the Romantic reader was not supposed to 'wake up.' But even so Eliot's criticism is

---

[1] E. D. Snyder, *Hypnotic Poetry* (1920), p. 31. Snyder distinguishes between hypnotic poetry, semi-hypnotic poetry and intellectualistic poetry. Almost all his examples of the first two categories are drawn from the English and American Romantic poets.

[2] *The Sacred Wood* (1920), p. 135.

justified. For, unless the reader is sufficiently awake to respond to the specific associations of the separate words, it is difficult to see what he can derive from his reading of the poem except an emotional blur. The connotations of 'time' and 'grief' are not identical by any means, but the partial hypnosis blunts the reader's power of discriminating response.

The most that can be conceded to hypnotic poetry is that, when not carried to excess, the lulling of the critical faculty that it ensures assists the general suspension of disbelief and the release of 'suggestion' that even the best Romantic poetry requires. The rather mechanical rhythms of the *Ancient Mariner* might be justified on these lines.

III

So much, then, for the Pure Sound Theory. Verbal music and melopœia are, it seems to me, examples of metrical mythology with little or no basis in metrical fact. Onomatopœia and hypnotic poetry, on the other hand, though they are not mere figments of the prosodist's imagination, are of doubtful poetical utility. They can be best described as metrical perversions. In any case they provide no evidence whatever that poetry is meaningless. In onomatopœia the sound is the echo of the sense, and without the sense there would be nothing for the sound to echo. And the only possible justification of hypnotic poetry is not that it excludes meaning but that it modifies it, suppressing denotation and encouraging connotation.

The cult of poetic unintelligibility is based upon a misunderstanding of the nature of language. Language is not a system of sounds, but a system of *conventional* sounds. It is the meaning that a society agrees to attach to a specific noise that matters, and the kind of noise to which any one or more meanings is attached is of little importance. 'Dog,' 'hund,' 'chien' are very different sounds, though their meanings are virtually identical. Moreover sounds change—through spelling-pronunciations, class and regional influences, etc.—without the meanings necessarily being affected in any way, and the meaning of a word can be transformed without the sound being changed at all. With the exception of the small group of onomatopœic words ('murmur,' 'tomtom,' 'bomb,' 'cuckoo,' etc.) there is no umbilical cord which connects sound and meanings. The conclusion to which I find myself driven is that in language generally sound as such has little or no influence on meaning.

And if poetry is simply language at its maximum potency, 'the best words in the best order,' the rôle of sound in it may be expected to be equally subordinate. Such devices as rhyme, metre and alliteration are, I believe, primarily the servants of meaning rather than of 'music.' Their uses can indeed be reduced to three general modes of semantic reinforcement. (i) The main function of metre is simply to provide a recurrent pattern in the background of the poem, which will act as a continual reassurance to the reader.[1] 'Here is the cosmos of mind and not the chaos of phenomena.' (ii) In alliteration, assonance and rhyme the repetition of sounds provides a semantic pointer, emphasizing contrasts and underlining connections. Thus in Pope's line from the 'Epistle to Bathurst,'

> Die and endow a college or a cat,

the *d*'s hint that there is a subtle identity in the dying and the endowing (the only interest that the world takes in

[1] The individual 'rhythm' of a particular poet depends partly on his choice of metre, but is mainly a matter of the degree to which the rhythms of colloquial speech are subordinated to the prosodic pattern.

this particular death is in the testamentary endowments),
and the *c*'s point the contrast between founding colleges
and financing cats' homes. (iii) Vowel quantity and
the accumulation or avoidance of consonants serve as a
kind of punctuation, accelerating or slowing down the
reading of the poem. As Daniel Webb pointed out, in
Hamlet's

> And in this harsh world draw thy breath in pain

'The breast actually labours to get through this line.'[1] In
fact, the ten monosyllables and the twenty-one con-
sonantal sounds (the average for the iambic pentameter is
about sixteen) provide the equivalent of a stage direction.
They show how Shakespeare wanted this crucial line
spoken. This device—which Pope confuses with onomatopœia in the familiar passage in the *Essay on Criticism*—
has been used more effectively by Milton than by any
other English poet.[2]

The all-importance of meaning in poetry and the
comparative insignificance of sound can perhaps be
demonstrated by a brief technical analysis of the 'sublime
epitaph' (the phrase is Coleridge's) which Wordsworth
added, with three other poems about the mysterious
Lucy, to the second edition of the *Lyrical Ballads* (1800):

> A slumber did my spirit seal;
> I had no human fears:
> She seemed a thing that could not feel
> The touch of earthly years.

---

[1] *Remarks on the Beauty of Poetry* (1762), p. 46. Webb was also before his
time in realizing that alliteration always requires a semantic justification:
'it is a fault, to suffer any one letter to take possession of the ear, or to govern
entirely the sound of the verse: unless, where the alliteration is brought in
aid of the sense; in which case, it may sometimes become a beauty' (p. 29).

[2] See Robert Bridges, *Milton's Prosody* (1901), pp. 41–3, for an analysis, on
these lines, of *Samson Agonistes*, ll. 115–31.

No motion has she now, no force;
 She neither hears nor sees;
Rolled round in earth's diurnal course,
 With rocks, and stones, and trees.

The structural basis of the poem is clearly the contrast between the two verses. Verse one deals with the past (there are no less than four verbs in a past tense—*did, had, seem'd, could*). Lucy had been such a vital person that the possibility of her growing old or dying had not crossed Wordsworth's mind. Verse two concerns the present (in addition to the *now* in the first line there are three main verbs in the present tense—*has, hears, sees*). Lucy is dead. The invulnerable Ariel-like creature is now as lifeless and immobile as stocks and stones. And the contrast is emphasized by the repetition of *earth*: Lucy, who had seemed immune from the passage of *earthly years*, must now submit to *earth's diurnal course*. So far from escaping the *touch* of years she is now undergoing a daily contact with the earth. The use of the solemn Latinism *diurnal*, the only three-syllable word in this mainly monosyllabic poem, completes the contrast. But the final impression the poem leaves is not of two contrasting moods, but of a single mood mounting to a climax in the pantheistic magnificence of the last two lines. How then is the surface conflict reconciled? The metre certainly makes its contribution. The identity of the metrical pattern in the two verses—which is paralleled by the virtual identity of the word-order (l. 5 repeats l. 1, abstract noun + verb + pronoun + abstract noun, l. 6 repeats l. 2, and l. 8 and l. 4 both have nouns but no verb)—suggests an underlying identity of mood. The gap between the two verses is also bridged by the negatives. There are no less than six negatives in the first six lines. Indeed, as the first line

really means 'I was not mentally awake,' all the sentences
are essentially negative propositions, until we reach the
tremendous positive of the last two lines. Finally, the
description of the living Lucy as a mere *thing* has prepared
the transition to the dead Lucy who is passively *roll'd*. The
rhymes have no special significance, as far as I can see,
but the alliterations should not be overlooked. The
initial *s*'s in l. 1. do not seem to me of much interest (it is
much the weakest line in the poem), though they may be
intentional, but the *r*'s in ll. 7-8 are masterly. There are
no less than three initial *r*'s and four internal *r*'s in the last
twelve words,[1] and they provide a kind of cohesive
cement to the lines. The implication is that the pantheistic
universe is solidly *one*. The parallel lines in verse one are
without alliteration, and its absence confirms the suggestion of fragility in the living Lucy (a *thing* who can only
be described in negative terms).[2]

In the famous 'Observations' that Wordsworth
prefixed to the edition of the *Lyrical Ballads* that included
'A slumber did my spirit seal' he justified metre as
providing a kind of sedative to the excitements of poetry
by 'the co-presence of something regular.' This is
essentially the semantic theory of metre that is being
advocated here. It is not denied, of course, that the disembodied 'tunes' of the prosodists—the Italian canzone, for

---

[1] The *r*'s in *earth's diurnal course* are not sounded in modern English. Wordsworth, however, certainly sounded them. Hazlitt had found 'a strong tincture
of the northern *burr*' in his voice when they first met in 1798 (the year before
'A slumber did my spirit seal' was written). See Hazlitt's 'My First Acquaintance with Poets.'

[2] I have not attempted more than a technical analysis of the poem. A full
critical discussion would need to go into the question of Lucy's identity. I
have no doubt that Lucy is in some sense Dorothy Wordsworth. It is surely
time the veil was withdrawn from the quasi-incestuous relationship between
Wordsworth and his sister, which almost certainly lies behind this poem.
Stones and trees, of course, had a special mystical virtue for Wordsworth
(cf. *Prelude*, iii, 124-6, 161-2, in 1805 text), and in associating Dorothy with
them he was satisfying the two central emotions of his life.

example, or the trochaic tetrameter, whose respective fortunes W. P. Ker used to delight in tracing from Dante to Arnold and from Bede to Browning—have an objective existence. So has the paper on which treasury notes are printed. But you don't collect treasury notes because of their paper, and to isolate metre from its context of meaning is at least as wrong-headed.

The importance that the Romantics ascribed to rhythm was part of their general disparagement of the reason. As John Foster put it in the admirable essay 'On the Application of the Epithet Romantic' (1805), they thought they had discovered 'something sublimer than thinking.' And unfortunately, as the nineteenth century progressed, the part played by thinking in poetry diminished. A minor poet of the period, who was later to become a distinguished novelist, has described the situation in an illuminating passage:

> For a great number of years I could not read 'poetry.' I wanted to; but I could not. I used to put that down to the fact that rhymes, accent, stresses, assonances, alliterations, vowel colourings, and the other devices of poets, embarrassed me as a reader. But this was not the case. The real fact is that—the dog it was that died. I have discovered this for myself from my own practice in verse. I found that as soon as I came to write a 'poem' I automatically reduced my intelligence to the level of one purely childish. And, looking one day through the Collected Edition of my own poems that some misguided publisher issued some years ago I was appalled. It was not so much that the stuff was rhetorical. It was just silly—with the silliness of a child of a bad type. There is hardly a poet of to-day or yesterday who ever, in his matter, his ideas and his verbal texture, attempts to soar above the level of the intellect of scarcely adolescent

pupils in young ladies' seminaries. Poets in fact, once they put on their laurel crown, divest themselves of every shred of humour, irony, incisive knowledge of life as it is lived.[1]

It cannot be said that the twentieth century has yet re-established the rule of reason in poetry. Even T. S. Eliot, the type almost of the cerebral critic, has not been able to resist an occasional fling at 'meaning'—'The chief use of the "meaning" of a poem,' he writes in *The Use of Poetry and the Use of Criticism*, 'may be to satisfy one habit of the reader, to keep his mind diverted and quiet, while the poem does its work upon him.'[2] Eliot does not explain how a poem can 'do its work' upon the reader without coming to have some sort of a meaning for him. If it is not absorbed through the consciousness, how is it absorbed? The *libido*, as we have seen, does not speak English. Nor can it read English. Probably all that Eliot meant was, as he puts it later in the same book, that a poem tends to have several 'levels of significance.'[3] While the reader is concentrating on the surface-meaning (the narrative element, or the 'moral') the other meanings are enriching and complicating his impressions of the primary meaning without his fully realizing what is occurring.

Eliot's own verse raises its own problems. At its best the attentive reader should not find a meaning impossible to unravel, but there are certainly a few passages from which the essential links and pointers seem to have been omitted. It is better, I think, to admit that these passages are among Eliot's failures than to accede to the logical contortions which his admirers sometimes adopt. F. R. Leavis, for one, has compared the looseness of structure

[1] F. M. Hueffer (Ford), *Thus to Revisit* (1920), pp. 132–3. He adds that none of his volumes of verse sold more than 200 copies!
[2] p. 151.   [3] p. 153.

and apparent absence of logic in *Ash Wednesday* with
certain obscurities in Blake's 'Hear the Voice of the Bard'
(which, it will be remembered, Housman also found
unadulterated with meaning). He prints Blake's poem in
a long note in *Revaluation* and, after a cursory examination
of some of the ambiguities, virtually throws up the
sponge:

> Interpretation is not a matter of deciding, here and there,
> which of two or more possible readings gives the right
> sense. Blake, by his own poetic means, which essentially
> disdains the virtues of prose, is defining his own peculiar
> intuition of evil, disharmony and a general fall.[1]

This is, I think, unfair to Blake, and it misrepresents the
poem's intentions. The poem is not particularly obscure
when it is read, as it should be, in conjunction with its
sequel 'Earth's Answer.' It will be worth re-examining,
if only to demonstrate that Blake's verse is susceptible to
exactly the same process of analysis as Wordsworth's. If
Eliot's is not—and in general, of course, it is—so much
the worse surely for Eliot. Here, then, is Blake's poem:

> Hear the voice of the Bard,
> Who present, past and future, sees;
> Whose ears have heard
> The Holy Word
> That walked among the ancient trees,
>
> Calling the lapsèd soul,
> And weeping in the evening dew;
> That might control
> The starry pole,
> And fallen, fallen light renew!

[1] pp. 141-2. René Wellek challenged Leavis's interpretation in *Scrutiny*,
(March 1937), but he too failed to take 'Earth's Answer' into account and his
own paraphrase is clearly on the wrong lines. Leavis's reply to Wellek does
not take the problem much further.

'O Earth, O Earth, return!
Arise from out the dewy grass!
Night is worn,
And the morn
Rises from the slumberous mass.

'Turn away no more;
Why wilt thou turn away?
The starry floor,
The wat'ry shore,
Is giv'n thee till the break of day.'

Leavis begins by asking 'whether it is the Holy Word or the Bard that is calling the "lapsèd soul".' The obvious answer is that it is the Holy Word (the God of Genesis). Otherwise there would be nothing for the ears of the Bard (Blake) to hear. Leavis continues:

> There is clearly a reference to the voice of God in the Garden calling Adam, but is it God who is weeping in the evening dew? And is it God that *might* control the starry pole?—though it could hardly be the Soul (an interpretation permitted by punctuation and syntax) that might? And surely 'fallen light' is Lucifer? When we find in the next two lines that Earth has fallen too we cannot help associating her with Lucifer though she is clearly the 'lapsèd soul,' and is also associated by the 'dew' ('dewy grass'—'evening dew') with the Holy Word (or the Bard); and by then it has become plain that prose paraphrase is an inappropriate enterprise.[1]

In spite of the final surrender, this is clearly on the right lines. The 'lapsèd soul' is certainly Adam (mankind) and the 'fallen light' must be Lucifer ('How art thou fallen from heaven, O Lucifer, son of the morning,' Isaiah xiv, 12). But 'Earth's Answer' makes it clear that it

[1] *Revaluation* (1936), p. 141.

must be God who is weeping (in 'Earth's Answer' he is also 'Weeping'), and who *might*, but won't, 'control the starry pole' (which is associated with 'Jealousy' in 'Earth's Answer'). And the Earth (mankind) must, I feel, be identified with the 'lapsèd soul' rather than Lucifer, as 'dewy grass' and 'Night' certainly refer back to the 'evening dew' of Eden. The general meaning of the poem is made clear by 'Earth's Answer.' Blake's God is the jealous deity of the Old Testament and eighteenth-century respectability who binds love in the bondage of marriage, and the poem is an invitation to his contemporaries to resist the blandishments of conventional religion. I cannot find any basis for Leavis's 'intuition of evil, disharmony and a general fall.'[1]

The conclusion to which this chapter has been leading can now be stated in unequivocal terms. It is simply that poetry *is* meaning. Poetry *qua* poetry must be completely intelligible. The contribution that each word, image or rhythm makes to the poem must be primarily explicable in rational terms. The difficulties of poetry are not due to an irrational element attracted to or imbedded in the meaning provided by the words, but to the concentration and complexity of the particular poetic statement. Poetry differs from prose and everyday speech mainly because it says so much more in the same number of words. But it is a difference of degree, not of kind. In analysing and paraphrasing a poem we are not transposing it into a wholly different medium. Meaning, like peace, is indivisible. As in any other purposive use of speech, the units of meaning in a poem are words and sentences. And

---

[1] A detailed study of the poem would entail an excursion into Blake's symbolic system. The trees, stars and watery shores are recurrent symbols in the Prophetic Books and are always associated with the repressive conventional religion which is the continuous object of Blake's righteous indignation. Their presence in this poem confirms its anti-religious nature.

words and sentences have only one proper function—the communication of 'thought' (using the word in the widest sense).

The slogan, then, is 'The meaning, the whole meaning, and nothing but the meaning.' Sound may have a small non-semantic contribution to make in English poetry, but it is so small that it can be safely neglected in a work that only professes to be an *introduction* to its critical discussion.[1] The dangers of underemphasis are at any rate less serious than those of overemphasis. It can't do a boy, or a girl, any harm to ask him what a particular poem *means*. But to encourage the analysis of verbal 'texture,' the repetition and contrasts of vowels and consonants, *is* to open the floodgates of nonsense. Any teacher of literature who is honest with himself will confirm this. Not here, O Apollo! are haunts meet for thee.

The next step in the process of definition, to which Part One of this book is committed, will be to discuss how and in what sense poetic meaning differs from prosaic meaning. For, though there is the common basis in speech, there obviously *are* differences. The greater concentration and complexity of the poetic statement, to which reference has just been made, require an explanation. By limiting the discussion to meaning it is, I believe, possible to take the old poetry-prose problem a stage nearer solution.

[1] I have not discussed the anthropological theory of poetry that is fashionable to-day, especially among the Marxists. It was expounded by Geoffrey Grigson in the first talk in the Third Programme's 1949 series 'The Art of Poetry.' According to this theory, 'music' and 'magic' are the bases of poetry because the first poems were the almost meaningless chants improvised by dancers at the tribal feast. This appears to be a gross example of the fallacy of origins. Modern poetry may derive from the primitive combination of speech, music and dance, but it is not the same thing. The process of specialization that the speech-element has undergone has created something different. The modern scientist descends from the witch-doctor, but it would be absurd to treat their respective techniques as identical. There is no harm, of course, in the drawing of *analogies*.

CHAPTER TWO

POETIC MEANING AND THE POET'S AUDIENCE

I

THE meaningless 'ecstasy' experienced by the Romantic reader of poetry was a corollary of the irrational 'inspiration' of the Romantic poet. The undefinable cause had produced an undefinable effect. And if the reader were rash enough to ask why certain words in a certain order caused him to experience 'ecstasy' or 'rapture,' whereas other words in other orders didn't, or didn't to the same degree, a third undefinable was introduced. This was 'magic.' This word, with its synonyms and derivatives, comes up again and again in Romantic discussions of poetry. In Coleridge's famous description of the poet 'in ideal perfection' in *Biographia Literaria*[1] a 'magical power' is specifically ascribed to the poetic Imagination. And 'natural magic' was, of course, one of Matthew Arnold's principal critical counters. Moreover the two words Arnold uses to define the 'romantic element' in modern poetry in *On the Study of Celtic Literature*[2] are 'magic' and 'charm.' Tennyson's tribute to Keats—'there is something magic and of the innermost soul of poetry in almost everything which he wrote'[3]—suggests that if he had attempted a formal definition of poetry it too would have been in terms of 'magic.' Indeed, in 'Merlin and the Gleam'—the poem intended as Tennyson's literary

[1] At the end of chap. xiv. [2] Chap. vi.
[3] *Memoir by his Son* (1899 ed.), p. 127.

autobiography—he uses Merlin's magic as the basis of the allegory.

Though not definable 'magic' was exemplifiable. And from the instances and specimens—hardly ever more than two or three lines long—provided by the Romantic critics it is clear that 'magic' was a quality of poetic style rather than of poetic structure. According to Lascelles Abercrombie, 'magic'—or, as he prefers to call it, 'incantation'—is the basic element or *sine qua non* of *all* poetry. In *The Idea of Great Poetry*, a discussion of the long poem, Abercrombie begins by asking what the irreducible poetic minimum is:

> What is the first thing which we require of all poetry —not merely in order to be great, but to exist at all? I will call it, compendiously, 'incantation': the power of using words so as to produce in us a sort of enchantment; and by that I mean a power not merely to charm and delight, but to kindle our minds into unusual vitality, exquisitely aware both of things and of the connexions of things.'[1]

Here we seem to be on the threshold of a definition. In the final phrase the metaphors look for a moment as though they were condensing into a generalization. But it is as far as Abercrombie gets. Instead of defining 'incantation' he talks round it. We are told, for example, that the poet

> must, out of the subtly adjusted sound and sense of words, contrive such a texture of intensities and complexities of meaning, of unsuspected filaments of fine allusion and suggestion, as will enable these gossamers to capture and convey into our minds just those fleeting, gleaming qualities of experience which elude the hold of every-day straightforward language.[2]

[1] *The Idea of Great Poetry* (1925), p. 18.   [2] *Ibid.*, p. 23.

But to be told, as Abercrombie tells us here in effect, that 'incantation' is the quality that differentiates the language of poetry from the language of everyday use is not really very helpful. We want to know *how* the differentiation is effected. How is the sound adjusted to the sense? How do the allusions and suggestions operate?

Abercrombie, both as poet and critic, was one of the later Romantics. In the heyday of Romanticism the questions that he raised—even if he did not find answers for them—would have seemed impertinent and irrelevant. To the Victorian critics, with their implicit confidence in the inspiration of the subconscious mind, anything approaching *technical* criticism of poetry was abhorrent. Ideally, for them, a poem wrote itself—like 'Kubla Khan.' The conscious intervention of the poet was limited, according to Shelley, to the 'artificial connexion of the spaces between [the inspired passages] by the intertexture of conventional expressions.'[1] It is not surprising, therefore, to find E. S. Dallas, one of t⟨...⟩ and sensitive of the mid-ninet⟨...⟩ writing as follows:

> Among the systematic ⟨...⟩om Scaliger downwards, crit⟨...⟩ed to questions of language ⟨...⟩gures of speech and varieti⟨...⟩are for the weightier points ⟨...⟩nner, character, moral and inte⟨...⟩ and metaphor, in rhyme and r⟨...⟩een rules and measures, and they ha⟨...⟩art of expression to a system

[1] *A Defenc⟨...⟩s MSS. throw a curious light on this avowal. In *Epipsychidi⟨...⟩*, the original draft has many lines that are completely blank exce⟨...⟩rhymes. See C. D. Locock, *An Examination of the Shelley Manuscripts in* ⟨...⟩*Bodleian Library* (1903), pp. 3–13.

as easy as grammar; but they have not sought to methodize
the poet's dream, they have not cared in their analysis to
grasp his higher thought.[1]

Dallas had not realized that a poet's higher thoughts
are not detachable, like the roof of a house, and can only
be grasped *through* the figures of speech, etc., in which
they are expressed. Hence, in spite of his intelligence, the
obscurity into which his treatise has fallen. It is at two
removes from reality—not about particular 'poems' but
about what 'poetry' is *supposed to be about*. If during the
last thirty years or so there has been a partial return, if
not to Scaliger, at least to that detailed discussion of
particular poems and passages that is to be found in the
best neo-classic critics, it is because we now know too
much about the subconscious mind to accept the Divine
Right that the Romantics accorded to it. The subconscious mind *can* do wrong, in poetry as in life. Its magic
may be black magic. And it is surely of the first importance to the reader of poetry, as to the critic of poetry, to
know the answer—however general and tentative its
formulation may have to be—to the question Lascelles
Abercrombie raised. What is the quality that poetry
must have 'not merely in order to be great, but to exist at
all'? What is it that creates the dividing line between
poetry and verse, between the poet and the poetaster?

If the argument of the preceding chapter was valid,
our answer must be capable of statement in terms of
meaning and not of sound. As a first step towards the
definition of poetic meaning it will be worth while taking
a good look at the six examples Abercrombie provides of
'incantation' in *The Idea of Great Poetry*. Here are six
short passages that a competent critic has guaranteed to

[1] *The Gay Science* (1866), vol. i, pp. 26–7.

be poetry. Is there a single principle common to all of them? If so, what is it?

Abercrombie's first example is from 'The Knight's Tale.' It is a line (italicized in the following quotation) from the account of Arcite's funeral pyre. Chaucer is employing the rhetorical figure *occupatio* (a refusal to describe or narrate) and has just said that he will not go into details about the trees that were felled for the pyre:

> Ne how the goddés ronnen up and doun,
> Disherited of hire habitacioun,
> In whiche they wonéden in reste and pees,
> Nymphés, fawnés, and amadriadés;
> Ne how the beestés and the briddés allé
> Fledden for feré, whan the wode was fallé;
> *Ne how the ground agast was of the light,*
> That was nat wont to seen the sonné bright.[1]

It is clear, I think, that the 'incantation' in the italicized line derives from the metaphor *agast* (terrified). The ground, no longer shaded by the trees, is exposed to the full glare of the sun, and Chaucer makes us see it recoiling in terror, like a denizen of the night in the rays of a lantern. The grotesque image is accepted by the reader because it is the natural climax to a catalogue of man's disturbances of nature. It was a *living world* into which Theseus's woodmen had penetrated. The ground is unobtrusively assimilated with the exiled dryads and the frightened birds and beasts. The effectiveness of *ground agast* (note the connective alliteration) is surely due to the delighted surprise with which the reader accepts this reconciliation of apparently unconnected units of meaning. Nothing could *seem* more unemotional than the land-surface in a forest. The gap that the metaphor had

[1] ll. 2925–32.

to bridge was a wide one; its memorability derives from the fact that it has succeeded in a peculiarly difficult act of synthesis.

Abercrombie's second example of 'incantation' was the first stanza of Herrick's 'Upon Julia's Clothes':

> Whenas in silks my Julia goes,
> Then, then (me thinks) how sweetly flowes
> That liquefaction of her clothes.

Although Abercrombie does not say so, it is fairly clear, I think, that the poetic magic is concentrated here in the word *liquefaction*. And the source of the word's effectiveness in this context is not really very obscure. Like *vibration* (a term from physics), which performs a similar function in the second stanza of the poem, *liquefaction* was a technical term in Renaissance science. It is essentially a 'learned' word, and the contrast between its polysyllabic latinity and the Anglo-Saxon monosyllables and disyllables of the rest of the passage, by concentrating the reader's attention on it (he is brought up sharp and compelled to linger over the word), brings into special prominence the metaphor already introduced in *flowes*. We are compelled to visualize the silks, and when we do so they become, as it were, a semi-transparent liquid in which Julia, a naked water-nymph, is floating. The sensuous paganism, always latent in Herrick, makes its impact *through* the verbal wit. Parallel to the integration of a scientific term in a context of love-compliment is the integration of primitive instincts within the framework of a seventeenth-century social occasion (a dance perhaps, or a stroll in one of the public 'gardens').

Abercrombie's remaining examples—one from *Julius Cæsar* (Casca's lion 'Who glazed upon me and went surly by'), one from Keats's *Hyperion*, and two from

Giles Fletcher—are of a similar character. He did not give examples of 'disenchanted' verse to oppose to the specimens of 'incantation,' but other Romantic critics have done this. The Abbé Brémond, who achieved a short-lived notoriety in the early 1930's by identifying poetry with prayer, made a great deal of play in his argument for pure poetry with the difference between the first line of *Endymion* in its original (though perhaps legendary) form,[1]

> A thing of beauty is a constant joy,

and the revision,

> A thing of beauty is a joy for ever.

The latter, according to the Abbé, has 'magie,' the former has not, though the two lines are notionally indistinguishable. It is clear, however, that the words *constant* and *for ever* are not strictly synonymous. *Constant* is a

---

[1] There is no authority in the MSS. of *Endymion* for 'constant joy.' The phrase derives from Henry Stephens, a fellow medical-student and a close friend of Keats's. According to Sir B. W. Richardson (*The Asclepiad* (April 1884), pp. 148–9), Stephens as an old man used to recount the following anecdote about Keats: 'In a room, Mr. Stephens told me, he was always at the window peering into space, so that the window-seat was spoken of by his comrades as "Keats's place." Here his inspiration seemed to come most freely. Here, one evening in the twilight, the two students sitting together, Stephens at his medical studies, Keats at his dreaming, Keats broke out to Stephens that he had composed a new line:

'"A thing of beauty is a constant joy."

'"What think you of that, Stephens?"

'"It has the true ring, but is wanting in some way," replies the latter, as he dips once more into his medical studies.

'An interval of silence, and again the poet:

'"A thing of beauty is a joy for ever."

'"What think you of that, Stephens?"

'"That it will last for ever."'

Richardson only knew Stephens from 1856 to 1864 (when Stephens died), and so an interval of some forty years must separate the actual occurrence of the episode, if it did occur, from its relation to Richardson. And Richardson did not *record* the anecdote until twenty years after Stephens's death.

rather drab latinism, meaning here not much more than *continuous*, whereas the two words *for ever* are highly charged with emotional associations from romance ('for ever and a day') and the services of the Church ('for ever and ever, Amen'), and mean *always*. Keats is saying two different things in the two versions. The second version is better because it is bolder, and effects a synthesis across a wider semantic gap—on the one hand, *joy* (short-lived, laughing, pagan), on the other, *for ever* (eternal, solemn, Christian).[1]

In the preceding examples 'magic' has proved, under analysis, to be nothing more mysterious than the successful collocation of contrasted or conflicting 'meanings.' The process is essentially, I suggest, one of *semantic synthesis*. Two or more detached units of human experience have been symbolized in language in such a way that the final impression left on reading the poem is of a wider unity which has included and absorbed the separate items.

What is essentially the same point, though more vividly phrased, is made by T. S. Eliot in his essay on 'The Metaphysical Poets':

When a poet's mind is perfectly equipped for its work, it is constantly amalgamating disparate experience; the ordinary man's experience is chaotic, irregular, fragmentary. The latter falls in love, or reads Spinoza, and these two experiences have nothing to do with each other, or with the

---

[1] Two well-known passages by Pope and Tennyson also exploit the associative values of *for ever*:

> The meeting Points the sacred Hair dissever
> From the fair Head, for ever and for ever!
>
> *Rape of the Lock*, iii, 153–4.

> But not by thee my steps shall be,
> For ever and for ever.
>
> *A Farewell*.

noise of the typewriter or the smell of cooking; in the mind of the poet these experiences are always forming new wholes.[1]

The notion is, indeed, one of the commonplaces of criticism. Its history seems to begin with Aristotle's discussion of metaphor in the *Poetics*[2]—'a good metaphor,' in Bywater's translation, 'implies an intuitive perception of the similarity in dissimilars.' It reappears in Hobbes's definition of 'fancy' in *Leviathan*,[3] from which Dryden derived his theory of 'imagination' or 'wit.' And Dr. Johnson's *discordia concors* is only a variant of the same doctrine. Its most elaborate statement, however, is the passage on the Imagination in Coleridge's *Biographia Literaria* that has already been referred to because of the use there of the word 'magical.' Familiar though it is the passage is perhaps worth quoting in its entirety:

> The poet, described in ideal perfection, brings the whole soul of man into activity, with the subordination of its faculties to each other according to their relative worth and dignity. He diffuses a tone and spirit of unity, that blends, and (as it were) *fuses*, each into each, by that synthetic and magical power, to which I would exclusively appropriate the name of Imagination. This power, first put in action by the will and understanding, and retained under their irre- missive, though gentle and unnoticed, control, *laxis effertur habenis*, reveals itself in the balance or reconcilement of opposite or discordant qualities: of sameness, with difference; the individual with the representative; the sense of novelty and freshness with old and familiar objects; a more than usual state of emotion with more than usual order; judgment ever awake and steady self-possession with

---

[1] *Homage to John Dryden* (1924), p. 30.
[2] Chap. xxii.   [3] Chap. viii.

enthusiasm and feeling profound or vehement; and while it blends and harmonizes the natural and the artificial, still subordinates art to nature; the manner to the matter; and our admiration of the poet to our sympathy with the poetry.[1]

In the phrase 'the balance or reconcilement of opposite or discordant qualities' Coleridge made a crucial addition to the earlier definitions. By distinguishing between 'balance' and 'reconcilement' on the one hand and 'opposite' and 'discordant' on the other, Coleridge pointed the way to a differentiation of degrees of synthesis. The more 'balance' approximated to 'reconcilement,' i.e. the more the separate units of meaning are fused together, the more *complete* the synthesis would be; the nearer the 'discordant' units of meaning came to being 'opposite' the more *valuable* the synthesis would be. The second criterion might be called the Principle of the Semantic Gap. Although Coleridge was, I believe, the first to relate it to the theory of poetic synthesis, the principle itself was an old one. John Hoskins, a sixteenth-century poet and critic, had formulated it as follows: 'you shall most of all profit by inventing matter of agreement in things most unlike, as London and a tennis court: for *in both all the gain goes to the hazard.*'[2] In other words, the more heterogeneous and unassimilable the two 'meanings' appeared on the surface to be, the greater the poetic triumph if a synthesis could be achieved. And Hoskins's example provides an exact parallel to the specimens of 'incantation' already analysed. It was because of the gap in meaning between the soil in Theseus's forest and the human emotion of fear that Chaucer's *ground agast* was so triumphantly 'incantatory.' And a

[1] Chap. xiv.
[2] *Directions for Speech and Style*, ed. H. H. Hudson (1935), p. 18.

similar gap explained the effectiveness of Herrick's *liquefaction* and Keats's *for ever*.

It follows from the two criteria of 'reconcilement' and 'opposition' that the Principle of the Semantic Gap can be transgressed in two ways. On the one hand, the gap can be too wide to be easily synthesizable. According to Dr. Johnson this was what was wrong with the Metaphysical Poets; and it is a criticism that has been made in our own time of Jules Laforgue,[1] and of Laforgue's poetic disciples in English—especially Ezra Pound and T. S. Eliot.[2]

On the other hand, the gap may be too narrow. The reconcilement in this case will not be difficult enough, because the qualities are insufficiently discordant, the 'meanings' too much *in pari materia*. Poetry that one tends to dismiss as merely graceful, pretty or pleasant—that of the minor Victorians, for example, or such Georgians as W. H. Davies or John Freeman—will generally be found to suffer from a narrowness of the semantic gap. As T. S. Eliot has put it in a comparison between some lines in Cowley's *Davideis* and Dryden's parody of them in *Macflecknoe*: 'The passage from Cowley is by no means despicable verse. But it is a commonplace description of commonly poetic objects; it has not the element of *surprise* so essential to poetry, and this Dryden provides.'[3] The evocation of *surprise* in the reader is not, of course, the only symptom of a successful observation of the Principle of the Semantic Gap. Its engenderment, indeed, tends to show that the gap has only just been bridged. The surprise is the product of a feeling of relief that all is still well, the chain of meaning unbroken. In

---

[1] See G. M. Turnell, *Scrutiny* (Sept. 1936).
[2] See John Sparrow, *Sense and Poetry* (1934).
[3] *Homage to John Dryden* (1924), p. 16.

the masters of Semantic Synthesis—Chaucer, Shakespeare or Keats, for example—exaltation rather than surprise is the predominant accompaniment. In Acts IV and V of *Antony and Cleopatra*—the highwater mark perhaps of English poetry—the unpredictable connections are made with such assurances and such success that the grain of scepticism implicit in 'surprise' is no longer warranted.

II

The reduction of Verbal Magic to Semantic Synthesis carries with it a further implication. If poetry is only a form of synthesis, there can be no difference of kind between the poet and the non-poet. Synthesis, with its opposite analysis, is after all a normal function of thought. At almost every moment of our lives we are either abstracting from the *data* of experience (analysis) or building up our abstractions into a new unity (synthesis). Unless the syntheses of the poets can be shown to have no more than a formal resemblance to the syntheses of everyday experience, another critical tenet of the Romantics will be imperilled. This is the theory of the Genius: *poeta nascitur, non fit.* A fundamental assumption of Romanticism was that poets, the inspired agents of the divinity within us, were not as other men. The undefinability of poetry was the complement of the poets' essential superiority to other human beings. 'Magic' implied the magician.

But, like 'pure poetry' and 'incantation,' the theory of the Genius will not stand up to close examination. Recent attempts to rehabilitate it have been on the lines of attributing a 'reality' to the visions of the poet that the abstractions of the scientists and philosophers do not possess. C. S. Lewis has summarized the argument with his usual clarity:

The difference between scientific or philosophical language and poetical language is emphatically not that the first utters truths and the second fancies. On the contrary everything that is concrete is real, and some suspect that everything real is concrete. The abstractions used by science and philosophy may or may not be the names of universals which are timeless realities as Plato thought; but they are not the names of 'real things' in the popular sense—things that occur in space and time. In space and time there is no such thing as an organism, there are only animals and vegetables. There are no mere vegetables, only trees, flowers, turnips, etc. There are no 'trees,' except beeches, elms, oaks, and the rest. There is even no such thing as 'an elm.' There is only *this* elm, in such a year of its age at such an hour of the day, thus lighted, thus moving, thus acted on by all the past and all the present, and affording such and such experiences to me and my dog and the insect on its trunk and the man a thousand miles away who is remembering it. A real elm, in fact, can be uttered only by a poem.[1]

A somewhat similar point of view has also been elaborated by T. C. Pollock who distinguishes three uses of language: (i) Phatic Communion ('How do you do?' and similar almost meaningless social gestures), (ii) Referential Symbolism (the abstract language of science), (iii) Evocative Symbolism (the communication of private experience in its concrete actuality).[2] The danger of such distinctions is that they attribute to poetry 'something sublimer than thinking'—in this case a mystical *photographic* capacity to reproduce phenomena in their original complexity. No linguistic medium can possibly do this. Lewis's elm may be a less general term than tree, vegetable

[1] C. S. Lewis and E. M. W. Tillyard, *The Personal Heresy* (1939), pp. 109-10.
[2] *The Nature of Literature* (Princeton, 1942).

or organism, but it is just as much an abstraction. His hypothetical poet is not only restricted to abstractions by the nature of his medium (basically all words are abstract), but the experience he is communicating, the isolation of this particular elm from the flux of his sense-impressions, is itself an abstraction. It is only indeed by a process of abstraction that the poet can give meaning, a scale of social values, to the chaos of individual experience.

The syntheses of poetry, then, are essentially the same as the syntheses of our everyday intellectual life. The difference between the poem and ordinary conversation is due (i) to the rarity in poetry of the complementary process of analysis, and (ii) to their different social functions. The first of these characteristic *differentiæ* determines the *form* of poetry, the second explains its *content*.

The spoken language is the vehicle of the two-way intellectual traffic (analysis and synthesis) of practical social life. Although both analysis and synthesis have tended to develop a special vocabulary (the language of science and 'poetic diction'), most of the words and virtually all the word-combinations that they use derive from colloquial speech. The special linguistic problem of their practitioners, therefore, has been to protect themselves and their readers from the incursion of the opposite faculty, from synthetic implications in works of pure analysis and analytic implications in works of pure synthesis.

The danger to poetry has come primarily from grammar. Grammar is a codification of the analytical (logical) forces in the spoken language. Instead of the synthetic unity of the poetic statement grammar tends to prefer a step-by-step syllogistic process. In the sentence 'The cat is eating the mouse' the grammarian distinguishes three separable semantic elements (i) cat, (ii) eating, (iii) mouse, whereas for the poet, there is a single complex image of cat-eating-mouse. Many of the formal devices of poetry seem to derive from the necessity for a defensive strategy against grammar. Inversion in poetry is usually simply an anti-grammatical gesture. ('You have been warned that this is not prose or the language of conversation.') It is therefore particularly frequent at the beginning of poems, as in these opening lines of a sonnet by Drummond of Hawthornden:

> With flaming horns the Bull now brings the year;
> Melt do the horrid mountains' helms of snow;
> The silver floods in pearly channels flow;
> The late-bare woods green anademes do wear.

The word-order in the second line might have been expected to be:

> The horrid mountains melt their helms of snow.

Grammatically this is better, because the sentence-structure will now be parallel in the four lines, but it is certainly no improvement poetically.

The positive function of the various formal devices of poetry—metre, alliteration, metaphor, verbal repetition, etc.—is to ensure that the poem achieves a unity of impression. They are all fundamentally 'esemplastic,' to use Coleridge's word. The continuous verbal links, interconnections and references back (i) prevent the reader from relegating to his memory the beginning of the poem before he has reached its end, and (ii) are continual reminders that each sentence in the poem must be read against a background of awareness of the whole poem in all its semantic complexity. Without realizing what is happening we find ourselves forced, in fact, to retain the whole poem in our consciousness all through the process of reading.

The sense in which poetry is opposed to science should be clear in the light of the preceding discussion. One way of putting the difference between the step-by-step processes of analysis and the comprehensive unity of synthesis would be to say that science collaborates with time whereas poetry is a continuous struggle to abrogate time. In the sentence 'Tom hits John' the grammatical order of the words is the same as the temporal sequence of events. First of all one has the mental picture of Tom, as it were, in repose. This is followed by a picture of Tom striking the blow (the fist, as it were, in mid-air). Finally, a fraction of a second later, the blow impinges on John. To the poet, on the other hand, the whole episode is a single event, involving Tom, John and the delivery and reception of the blow *simultaneously*. Poetically it makes no difference if the word order is 'Tom hit John' or '(it was) John Tom hit,' or 'John (was) hit (by) Tom,' though grammatically these distinctions can be all-important.

This *simultaneity* of poetry may explain the relative unimportance of stanza-order in many poems. Wotton's 'You meaner beauties of the night' is a poem which survives in a number of different printed and MS. texts.[1] In the version printed in most anthologies the second verse is the one beginning

> You curious chanters of the wood.

There is, however, equally good authority for making this the third verse and printing as the second verse the one beginning

> You violets that first appear.

[1] See J. B. Leishman, *The Library* (Sept., Dec. 1945), pp. 99-121.

As poetry one version is as good as the other. Both verses are needed in the poem, but the order in which they appear doesn't really matter.[1]

The same point could perhaps be made in connection with Landor's 'Rose Aylmer.' Does it really make any appreciable difference to the poem as poetry if the order of the two verses is reversed, and we read:

> Rose Aylmer, whom these wakeful eyes
>   May weep, but never see,
> A night of memories and of sighs
>   I consecrate to thee.
>
> Ah what avails the sceptred race,
>   Ah what the form divine!
> What every virtue, every grace!
>   Rose Aylmer, all were thine.[2]

Shelley seems to have been feeling his way to some such conclusion in *A Defence of Poetry*:

A poet participates in the eternal, the infinite, and the one; as far as relates to his conceptions, time and place and number are not. The grammatical forms which express the moods of time, and the difference of persons, and the distinction of place, are convertible with respect to the highest poetry without injuring it as poetry; and the choruses of Aeschylus, and the Book of Job, and Dante's Paradise, would afford, more than any other writings,

[1] In Nashe's poem suggested by the 1593 plague, which includes the famous stanza beginning 'Beauty is but a flower,' the verses, according to F. P. Wilson (*Elizabethan and Jacobean* (1945), p. 57), 'are linked together not by argument but by mood and theme, so that the six stanzas might be rearranged without destroying the poem.'

[2] Another two-stanza poem in which the order of the stanzas can be reversed without any essential loss is Congreve's 'Song,' beginning

> False though she be to me and Love.

No doubt there are other examples.

examples of this fact, if the limits of this essay did not forbid citation.

Some of the incidental implications of these conclusions will be explored later in this book in the discussion of individual poems. In the meantime it will be desirable to say something about the opposition between poetry and prose. The distinction between the poetic statement and the prose of science is clear, but what about poetry and the novel or the drama in prose? These are obviously in some sense synthetic *genres*, but their individual sentences are generally indistinguishable formally from the prose of science and philosophy.

Two differences between poetry and fiction or the drama have often been remarked upon. One is that poetry is virtually untranslatable. The only poems that can be successfully translated into the poetry of another language are those with a large 'story' element. Most poems, satires and philosophical poems as well as lyrics, when translated into the poetry of another language, become not only bad poems but to all intents and purposes new poems. On the other hand, most novels and plays can be translated with little or no loss. The second difference is that poetry is very much easier to memorize than prose. This is as true of blank verse, and even of so-called 'prose poetry'—Whitman's *Leaves of Grass*, for example—as of rhyming or metrical verse. Poetry seems to *want* to be remembered, whereas prose as such *wants* to be forgotten.

The two differences are perhaps different sides of the same thing. It is what is untranslatable in poetry that sticks in the memory. And, on the other hand, the quality that makes prose easy to translate is exactly what makes it easy to forget.

Poetry has, indeed, been defined as 'memorable words.'

But this is to put the emphasis in the wrong place.
Memorability cannot be made the criterion of poetic
merit. If the best poem was the most memorable poem
a jingle like Peacock's 'The War-song of Dinas Vawr'
or Poe's 'Bells' would be preferred to Keats's odes or
Milton's sonnets. The primary function of the various
poetic devices and figures of speech is not mnemonic,
though their secondary effects often are. What the poet
qua poet is trying to do is to 'synthesize,' i.e. to say several
things at the same time. The things, though apparently
disconnected and even contradictory, are really related,
and it is their interrelationship that is the point of the
poem. The poet's problem is to get the reader to think
of several separate things all at once, and not one by one,
in a temporal and logical sequence. The mnemonic
devices make this possible, *positively*, by linking the
different stanzas, sentences and words together in a
variety of ways, so that in Stanza III the reader is continually being called back to Stanzas I and II, and *negatively*,
by reminding the reader from time to time that this is
not prose and that he must hold in abeyance for the
moment the thought-processes that prose has encouraged
him to apply to written words. Memorability, therefore,
is only a by-product of poetry. All the poet requires is
the reader's retention of the poem in his consciousness
during the process of reading. Once that is completed
the ability to repeat the poem parrot-wise has no special
point. Indeed it might be argued that exceptional facility
in quotation, the Macaulay kind of memory, is a symptom
of mental indigestion. The mind when functioning
properly absorbs experience selectively, rejecting from
the total impression left by a poem whatever is not
relevant to its own requirements. The healthy response
to the mental experience provided by the conscientious

reading of a good poem is not to be word-perfect in it but to make it something of one's own. This incorporation of the poem into one's own consciousness is to 'criticize' it. By 'criticize' I do not, of course, mean 'find fault,' nor do I wish necessarily to suggest a formal stocktaking in the manner of Dr. Johnson. The right reaction to a poem will often be a single phrase, like Arthur Symons's description of Clare's songs of childish humour, 'made out of bright laughing sound,'[1] or Tennyson's admirable comment on Shelley's 'Life of Life'—'He seems to go up into the air and burst.'[2]

The reason why poetry is so difficult to translate will now be clearer. The translator has to find the equivalents in another language not only of the words of the poem, with their special associations (which may derive from a connection of *sound* with other words), but also of the incidental alliterations, the more important verbal and grammatical repetitions, and the deliberate deviations from a prose vocabulary or sentence-structure. Prose, on the other hand, is fairly easy to translate because it is 'analytic.' The separate statements are detached and complete in themselves. There are no complicated inter-relationships between one sentence and another, and it is not in the least necessary to help the reader to retain the whole of a chapter in his consciousness while he is reading it. Prose is difficult to memorize because there is no point in doing it. Once an episode is completed all that it is necessary to retain in the memory is a skeletal summary of it. The actual words in which the episode has been described have fulfilled their function when the reader

[1] *Poems by John Clare* (1908), p. 24.
[2] This raises the whole question of the teaching of English poetry. At present most examinations in English literature, including the Final Schools at the Universities, are essentially an invitation to the candidates to quote, quote, quote.

has translated them into 'ideas.' All that need be remembered is the synthetic element in the novel or play, and that is generally embodied in the plot and characterization rather than in the individual words and sentences.

Poetry, therefore, is always 'the best words in the best order'; prose, on the other hand, though it begins in words, loses its verbal envelope in the process of reading, until it impinges on the consciousness simply as a mental picture. In a good novel or a good play the actual words should be absorbed by the reader or spectator almost without being noticed. In a poem, on the other hand, the words must be in the forefront of the reader's consciousness all the time. There are, therefore, two different arts of reading, and the difficulty of combining them when reading aloud or reciting is what makes Shakespeare's plays so disappointing on the stage. In the study it is possible to pass from Hamlet the 'character' to Hamlet the speaker of poetry, and back again, in the course of a single line. But only the greatest of actors can achieve a similar agility. The broadcasting of an epic or narrative poem raises the same problem. Almost inevitably either the prose elements or the poetry will be overemphasized.

A rough-and-ready definition of the novel (or play) might be analytic form plus synthetic content. A poem, on the other hand, is synthetic in both form and content (which tend to be more closely identified in poetry than in fiction). The invention of printing has helped to differentiate the two *genres*. During the Middle Ages the memorability of verse was an economic asset. Owing to the rarity of manuscripts and readers a story that was not in verse was at a competitive disadvantage and could only achieve a limited circulation. Hence the multiplication of romances, alliterative and tail-rhymed, in which the verse has a mnemonic function only. Poetry benefited by the invention of printing, because the diffuseness that the prospect of recitation imposed was no longer a necessary evil. The listener only hears a line once—unless the metrical scheme requires its repetition, as significantly in many medieval forms like the rondeau, the rondel and the triolet—and, if he is to carry it in his mind until the end of the poem (as he must, on our definition of poetry, if the poem is to succeed), the line must not be too tightly packed with meaning. With the printed poem the reader can stop and look back at an earlier line if he has a momentary difficulty in remembering it. This permits a greater concentration of meaning and the opportunity for subtler verbal effects (such as the elaborate rhetorical figures so dear to the Renaissance). The decreasing diffuseness of sixteenth-century poetry can be attributed very largely to the growth of a *reading* public, which had only been made possible by Caxton and his successors. The long-term trends have also been in the same direction. With negligible exceptions novels and plays are no longer written in verse, and the long poem is becoming rarer, the epic being apparently extinct. The complexity of modern poetry may not be entirely attributable to the fact that it is rarely read aloud, but it is certainly one of the relevant factors.

III

A fourth undefinable factor in Romantic poetic theory was *taste*. *De gustibus non disputandum erat*. To the Romantics, with their predilections for 'ecstasy' and 'magic,' poetic preferences were necessarily reduced to a matter of private, personal taste. There could be no *theoretic* basis for any critical standards at all. On one man the 'magic' worked; on another it didn't. But the only way to decide if it was the man who was at fault or the 'magic' was to count heads—a procedure that can be applied fairly easily to the poetry of the past but that it is impossible to apply to poetry that has just been written. Homer's 'magic' was guaranteed by the fact of the *Iliad*'s and the *Odyssey*'s survival. But what about Blake's or Clare's? Palgrave and Tennyson (who assisted him in the selection of the poems) played for safety by leaving them both out of *The Golden Treasury*.[1]

At no period in the history of literature has the poet, as distinguished from the poetaster, had a harder struggle to achieve recognition than in the nineteenth century. There will be no need to recite more than one or two of the familiar facts. Thus in spite of the reviews and counter-reviews Keats's poems *made no impression whatever*, as poems, on the contemporary reading public. When Rossetti 'discovered' Keats in 1845 he supposed he had found an unknown writer. So did Holman Hunt, who found a copy of the 1820 *Poems* in a book-bin labelled 'This lot 4d.' about the same time.[2] Even Tennyson, the poetic best-seller, 'was so far persuaded that the English people would never care for his poetry, that, had it not been for the intervention of his friends, he declared it not unlikely that after the death of Hallam he would not have continued to write.'[3]

But in the poetical slump versifying boomed. Scott's and Byron's narrative poems sold like hot cakes. Tom Moore was paid £3,000 for the milk and water of *Lalla Rookh*. And Tennyson's sales were equalled or excelled by Martin Tupper's *Proverbial Philosophy*, Sir Lewis

[1] The 1890 edition—in which Palgrave again acknowledges 'the advice of that distinguished Friend, by whom the final choice has been so largely guided' —adds Blake, Campion, Darley, the Earl of Essex, Lyte, Henry Norris, Quarles and Smart, but not *inter alios* Skelton, Donne, King, Crashaw, Rochester, Beddoes or Clare.

[2] See G. H. Ford, *Keats and the Victorians* (1944), p. 94.

[3] *Memoir by his Son* (1899), p. 83.

Morris's *The Epic of Hades,* and Sir Edwin Arnold's *The Light of Asia.* At no other time has the bad poet 'got away with it' so successfully. Essentially, as we can see now, the Victorian poetasters wrote prose disguised as poetry. In terms of meaning their mode of progression is analytic rather than synthetic. The verse form is an irrelevant trimming to the narrative or ethical content. But their success, which was by no means confined to the 'Mudie' public, was the inevitable consequence of Romantic poetic theory. Without objective critical standards it had become as difficult to reject the fake poem as to acclaim the original poem. In their absence, by an æsthetic Gresham's Law, the bad poetic money drove out the good.

A standard of poetic taste can only be maintained in a society where the poet and his audience are in direct and intimate contact with each other. The Principle of Semantic Synthesis works both ways. It assumes a reader prepared to respond to the poet's stimulus as well as a poet with the wish to stimulate. And the units of meaning that are to be synthesized must not only be intelligible to the reader but must assume in the process of reading the same order of importance that they have to the poet. Finally the width of the semantic gap must be implicitly agreed between them as well as the methods necessary for its bridging. It might almost be said that the reader must be the poet's *alter ego.* He must be sufficiently like the poet to think, feel and see as he does, and yet sufficiently unlike him for the act of communication involved in the writing of the poem to be worth while.

The fulfilment of these conditions was made difficult and often impossible during the nineteenth century by the increasing individualism of the period. In its final

Paterian form Romanticism shivers on the brink of solipsism. Unless the world is your creation, what *right* have you to burn in it with a hard gemlike flame? But the trend is there from the first. It is no doubt a literary counterpart of the political liberalism and *laissez-faire* capitalism of the nineteenth century. The Romantic poet was not the spokesman of the social group so much as its martyr (Shelley), its exile (Blake), its victim (Coleridge), or its prisoner (Tennyson). Wordsworth is sometimes cited as the exception. But, with all his social consciousness, Wordsworth's sense of social reality was erratic in the extreme. He was fond of distinguishing between the 'public' and the 'people,' the 'public' being the middle classes, Arnold's Philistines, who wouldn't buy his poems, whereas the 'people' were the peasantry, among whom, as he told Wrangham, he hoped his poems would circulate in chap-book form.[1] In fact 'We are Seven' was the only one to achieve this distinction, and Canon Rawnsley found that his humbler Westmorland neighbours had never read Wordsworth at all. 'Well you see, blessed barn, there's pomes and pomes, and Wudsworth's was not for sich as us.'[2] In the end it was the 'public' from whom the Wordsworthians were recruited, but the initial isolation was as complete in his case as in that of the other Romantic poets.

Poetry, in any of its normal manifestations, involves four factors: (i) the poet, (ii) his readers or auditors, (iii) a common language, and (iv) a literary tradition shared by the poet and his readers. Remove any one of the four factors and poetry ceases to be possible. Upset the balance

---

[1] Letter of 5 June 1808.
[2] *Trans. Wordsworth Soc.* (1884), vi. Rawnsley was quoting the ex-garden boy at Rydal Mount. The ex-page's verdict was even more devastating : 'There's no doubt but what he was fond of quality, and quality was very fond o' him.'

F

between them and poetry, though possible, becomes more difficult to achieve. The Romantics, in their theories at any rate, consistently overlooked these elementary considerations. Obsessed by individualism they concentrated their attention either on the poet alone (Coleridge and Shelley) or on the reader alone (Pater and Symons), although it is in the poet-reader *relationship* that the essence of poetry lies. To Coleridge, for example, 'What is poetry?—is so nearly the same question with, what is a poet?—that the answer to the one is involved in the solution of the other. For it is a distinction resulting from the poetic genius itself which sustains and modifies the images, thoughts, and emotions of the poet's own mind.'[1] This means that if you can define what goes on in the poet's mind, you will have defined poetry. Coleridge then proceeds to give his definition of the poet 'in ideal perfection,' which has already been quoted. In this definition Coleridge only once refers to the reader's share in poetry. (I presume the *we* implied in 'our admiration of the poet' and 'our sympathy with the poetry' is the poet's readers, though it is not clear why a reader would find the two things necessarily opposite or discordant.) But without some much fuller indication of the reader's rights and responsibilities a definition of poetry is obviously seriously incomplete. It is the reader who must fuse *his* separate faculties and reconcile the qualities that *he* would normally find discordant. Without the reader's co-operation the poem might just as well not exist. A comprehensive definition of the poet's function *must* include a summary of the processes by which he secures that co-operation. The first thing the poet must know is whom he is writing for. Until he has located his audience the question of the modes and *media* of communication

[1] *Biographia Literaria*, chap. xiv.

cannot arise. But did Coleridge know whom he was
writing for? Would any of the Romantics have been
able to identify that ghostly 'gentle reader' they are so
fond of addressing?

Take the case of Keats, the greatest probably of the
Romantic poets. At one period he was writing apparently
for the mere sake of writing. 'I feel assured,' he wrote to
Woodhouse in October 1818, 'I should write from the
mere yearning and fondness I have for the beautiful even
if my night's labours should be burnt every morning,
and no eye ever shine upon them.' And Lord Houghton's
account of Keats's habits in 1819 confirms this. 'Shorter
poems were scrawled, as they happened to suggest themselves, on the first scrap of paper at hand, which was
afterwards used as a mark for a book, or thrown any-
where aside.'[1] We may say that these poems were
written for *nobody*. At an earlier stage Keats had been
writing primarily for Leigh Hunt and the Hampstead
coterie, but by 1819 he had become ashamed of this
dependence. 'I have done nothing,' he wrote to Haydon
in October, '—except for the amusement of a few people
who refine upon their feelings till anything in the
un-understandable way will go down with them—people
predisposed for sentiment.' Later it was apparently
posterity that he was addressing. '"If I should die," said
I to myself, "I have left no immortal work behind me—
nothing to make my friends proud of my memory—
but I have lov'd the principle of beauty in all things, and
if I had had time I would have made myself remember'd."'[2] It is clear that the posterity he has in mind here
is not a remote one, because his friends are expected to be
still alive when he is 'remember'd.' Presumably it was

---

[1] *Life and Letters of John Keats*, World's Classics ed., p. 176.
[2] To Fanny Brawne, Feb. 1820.

the mid-nineteenth-century reading public, who, as it turned out, were to read Keats with more ardour than any of his contemporaries. (The 1850's were the turning-point in his reputation.[1]) For the reading public of his own day Keats expressed loathing and contempt. 'The more I know what my diligence may in time probably effect; the more does my heart distend with Pride and Obstinacy—I feel it in my power to become a popular Writer—I feel it in my strength to refuse the poisonous suffrage of a public.'[2] But this is not the only note. On one occasion he told Haydon: 'I have no cause to complain because I am certain any thing really fine will in these days be felt.'[3]

Keats's contradictions and confusions can be paralleled in all the other nineteenth-century poets. Rossetti only melodramatized their uncertainty when he buried the MSS. of his poems in his wife's coffin in 1862 and dug them up again in 1869. With Flecker, a typical late Romantic, who dedicated his poems 'To a Poet a Thousand Years Hence,'

> O friend unseen, unborn, unknown,
>   Student of our sweet English tongue,
> Read out my words at night, alone:
>   I was a poet, I was young.

we may contrast Dryden's dedications 'To the Right Honourable the Earl of Abingdon, etc,' 'To His Grace the Duke of Ormond,' 'To the Most Honourable John, Lord Marquis of Normanby, Earl of Mulgrave, etc., and Knight of the Most Noble Order of the Garter,' etc. The seventeenth and eighteenth centuries were free from the doubts and difficulties which beset the nineteenth and twentieth centuries. The Augustan poets knew exactly

---

[1] See G. H. Ford, *Keats and the Victorians* (1944).
[2] To Reynolds, 24 Aug. 1819.   [3] To Haydon, 3 Oct. 1819.

whom they were writing for. They knew that 'the Readers of Poesie,' as Hobbes put it, 'are commonly Persons of the best Quality,'[1] and their eyes were firmly fixed, during the process of composition, on the 'great,' the 'polite world,' the 'best companies,' the 'people of fashion,' 'upper life,' and the 'beau monde' (to quote some of their synonyms for their ruling class). Their difficulties arose not from any uncertainty who their audience was, but from an internal contradiction in that audience itself.[2]

Criticism has not paid sufficient attention to this problem of the poets' audiences. As it is fatally easy to hypostatize 'poetry,' it will be safer to limit this discussion to 'poems.' The first point, then, that must be made is that a poem only becomes a poem, in the ordinary sense of the word, when it is read. Up to that stage it is only so many black marks on a piece of white paper. (The psychological processes inside the poet as a result of which the black marks are on the paper include so much that is not recorded there that they cannot be equated with the poem, though they are, of course, related to it.[3]) The actual process of reading falls into four stages: (i) the reader translates the black marks into words (meaningful

[1] 'To the Reader concerning the Vertues of an Heroique Poem,' *Homer's Odyssey* (1675).

[2] The Augustan philosophy of life was based on 'common sense,' the rational faculty that is shared by all human beings except children and lunatics. But this egalitarianism was contradicted by the rigid class-divisions that the aristocracy imposed upon eighteenth-century society. See p. 173 below.

[3] See, e.g., Robert Graves's account of the composition of 'The General Elliott' in *On English Poetry* (1922), pp. 55–62, or the equally illuminating passage in *Poetry for You* (1944), pp. 35–9, by C. Day Lewis, which describes the genesis of his poem beginning

> Children look down upon the morning-gray
> Tissue of mist that veils a valley's lap.

Both accounts include a variety of personal experiences and reminiscences that are quite irrelevant to the appreciation of the completed poem. See also the detailed 'Birth of a Poem' by Robert Nichols (appended to Rosamond E. M. Harding's *An Anatomy of Inspiration*, 2nd ed. [1942]). The poem in question is Nichols's own 'Sunrise Poem.'

sounds); (ii) the separate words are combined into phrases or detached statements (units of meaning); (iii) the associated phrases and statements are linked up so as to form a complex statement or sentence (the poetic unit); (iv) the various complex statements or sentences are connected together in the mind and *their* interrelations worked out (the composite meaning which is the poem).

Of the four stages the third is clearly the complement of the poet's Semantic Synthesis ('magic' in the terminology of the Romantic critics) that was discussed in the preceding section. In the line, for example, that Abercrombie quoted from Chaucer,

> Ne how the ground agast was of the light,

the reader has in effect to repeat the poet's bridging of this particular semantic gap. There are already two phrases or units of meaning in his mind, (i) the ground exposed to the light, (ii) 'agast' (the emotion of fear), and by synthesizing them the reader *recreates* Chaucer's metaphor.

An identical process of synthesis operates, in fact, at all the four stages. In the first two stages habit, i.e. continuous practice, has made the process almost wholly unconscious, though any unusual spelling or unfamiliar word that threatens to interrupt the synthetic continuity will always bring it back into the full light of consciousness. These two stages are, of course, common to the reading of prose and poetry. It is only at the third stage that the two modes of statement-response diverge. Opposed to the 'esemplastic,' synchronous synthesis of phrases characteristic of poetry is the analytic temporal sequence of phrases in prose.[1] The fourth stage is not met by the reader of

[1] For Coleridge's 'homely definitions of prose and poetry; that is, prose = words in their best order;—poetry = the *best* words in the best order' (*Table-Talk* [12 July 1827]), I would like to substitute the following equally homely definitions: *Prose is saying one thing after another; poetry is saying two (or more) things at the same time.*

science or philosophy, but the reader of fiction or the spectator of drama goes through it in much the same way as the reader of poetry. If a metaphor, such as that of 'ground agast,' is typical of the third synthetic phase, the fourth phase is typified by the literary resolution of a psychological conflict. The synthesis in this final stage may be, in the case of poetry, *formally* of poetic units (such as metaphors), but *materially* it is made up of items of human experience (such as the sense-impression, in the example from Chaucer, of the treeless wood and the emotion of fear). It must therefore necessarily have much in common with any other synthesis of human experience based upon speech, such as the catharsis of Greek tragedy or the 'happy ending' of a sentimental novel. A fuller discussion of the fourth phase must await the treatment of the content of poetry in the next chapter. On the whole, in this phase, considered in critical isolation, matter predominates over manner, whereas in the third phase poetic manner (style) tends to predominate over poetic matter. For most purposes, indeed, the third phase can be identified with the 'figures of speech' of rhetoric.

At each of the four stages the possibility of variant interpretations arises. A letter may be misprinted, a word may be understood in more than one way (e.g. the 'ball' in Marvell's 'Coy Mistress'), a phrase may be construed in a variety of senses (e.g. Blake's denunciation of the 'dark Satanic Mills'), and there may be several interpretations not only of the separate poetic units (e.g. the relevance of a 'metaphysical' metaphor), but also of the whole poem considered as a semantic entity (e.g. Thomson's reading of the 'Bright star' sonnet and mine; see p. 11 above). Such problems cannot always be resolved because the conclusive evidence is not always available. But the principle involved is a simple one, though its implications are far-reaching. It bases itself on *the inter-connectedness of the four synthetic stages*. In the case of a disputed word, for example, the reader will tend to prefer the interpretation that is most compatible with the meaning of the rest of the poem. If the rest of the poem is in English, a sense the word bears in English will be preferred to that which it has in French or Latin. If the rest of the poem is in English of the mid-seventeenth century a sense the word had then will be preferred to one it has acquired later. And if the poem is addressed to the 'Persons of the best Quality' of that period a sense that was current in Charles II's court will be preferred to one only found among his seamen. Similar considerations, though they are necessarily more complex, apply to the third and fourth synthetic stages. Such familiar poetic devices as metaphor, simile, paradox and symbolism have in fact very different functions at different periods.[1]

In other words, the better the poem is and the more there is felt to be 'in it' (i.e. the more *meaningful* it is), the closer the modern reader will unconsciously tend to try to identify himself with the poet's original readers. (Bad poems can generally be seen through without all this trouble because they are fundamentally *meaningless*, i.e. nothing is synthesized.) The ultimate criterion, therefore, in poetic interpretation is not 'what the poet meant' *tout court*, i.e. what was going on inside the poet during the composition of the poem (which is largely either unknowable or irrelevant), but 'what the poet meant to his contemporaries,' i.e. the way his poem would have been understood by the particular social group to whom it was primarily addressed:[2]

[1] See Part Two of this book.
[2] The point could be made in a number of ways. Rosemond Tuve has recently demonstrated—in *Elizabethan and Metaphysical Imagery* (1947)—that Renaissance imagery is rooted in the training in rhetoric and logic that the

It takes two people to say a thing—a sayee as well as a sayer—and by parity of reasoning a poem's original audience and environment are integral parts of the poem itself. Poem and audience are as *ego* and *non ego*; they blend into one another. Change either, and some corresponding change, spiritual rather than literal, will be necessary in the other, if the original harmony between them is to be preserved.[1]

This conclusion has a number of important consequences. The first is its delimitation of the information about a poet's personal life that the modern editor needs to give in his notes. Since poetry only exists in the poet-reader relationship, and the ideal reader approximates as closely as possible to one of the more intelligent of the poet's original readers, all that it is necessary for us to know about the poet is the personal information that he could take for granted in his contemporaries. In the case of a Byron or a Pope that was, of course, considerable. Most poems, however, are quasi-anonymous to their original readers and the question of the personality and even the identity of their authors often hardly arises. Such works therefore as *The Road to Xanadu*, or B. I. Evans's detailed investigation of what was in Keats's head when he wrote the sonnet 'On First Looking into Chapman's Homer'[2] (a beautiful bit of detective work), fall outside the province of strict criticism. They are contributions of great interest to the psychology of literary creation, but they have only incidental *critical* value. This is not neces-

---

schools and universities then provided. Nineteenth- and twentieth-century criticism of Sidney and Donne, overlooking this, has been in continual danger of misreading their poems. The writing of Latin verse at school had a similar influence on Augustan poetry that has not yet been properly documented.

[1] Samuel Butler, *The Iliad of Homer Rendered into English Prose* (1898), Preface.

[2] *Essays and Studies*, English Association (1930).

sarily to decry 'source-hunting.' A proper understanding of a poem must entail an appreciation of the literary allusions that the ideal contemporary reader would have detected. To go further than this, however, is to desert literary criticism proper for the history of ideas. A similar caveat must be made against the investigators of the authorship of anonymous or disputed work with their paraphernalia of metrical tests and verbal clues. Occasionally the successful attribution of an anonymous poem to a known author or the bringing together of evidence that a certain poem has been misattributed may effect a reorientation of our views on who its original readers were, but more often the new factual information makes no poetic difference. The game of attribution, as played by J. M. Robertson, Charles Crawford, Dugdale Sykes, etc., in the field of minor Elizabethan and Jacobean drama, is an enjoyable sport, with its own elaborate rules, but it should not now be mistaken for criticism.

A second critical corollary that follows from the general principle of the primacy of 'what the poet meant to his contemporaries' is that the modern editor's initial duty is to identify the audience for whom a poem or group of poems was originally intended. The more precise the identification, the easier it will be for the modern reader to recapture the meaning of a poem in its pristine totality. But for this to be achieved more is required than a mere descriptive label of the individuals or the social group to whom the poem was, explicitly or implicitly, originally addressed. We need to know a good deal about this audience's habits and assumptions at each of the stages that reading involves. What were the *words* that they expected to meet in a poem, and what meanings did they attach to those words? What were the kinds of *statement*, or combination of words, that they looked for in poetry?

Finally, what sort of general *relationships* between the separate statements were they accustomed to find in poetry? In reading a modern poem such questions hardly arise, because the poem is addressed to *us* and it naturally conforms to *our* semantic habits and *our* literary tradition. But we cannot take such a conformity for granted in the poems of the past.

The history of English criticism includes a series of Awful Warnings—Rymer on *Othello*, Johnson on Milton's sonnets, Macaulay on Restoration comedy, Eliot on Hobbes,[1] Leavis on *Samson Agonistes*,[2] C. S. Lewis on Donne.[3] These and similar *gaffes* were not failures of taste so much as *misreadings*, condemnations based on misinterpretations. And in each case the root of the error has been the isolation of a body of writings from its original context—in other words, the neglect of the 'reader' element in the original poet-reader relationship. The wise man will follow Sainte-Beuve's advice and humbly try to cultivate 'cette faculté de *demi-métamorphose*, qui est le jeu et le triomphe de la critique, et qui consiste à se mettre à la place de l'auteur et au point de vue du sujet qu'on examine, à lire tout écrit *selon l'esprit qui l'a dicté*.'[4] That at any rate remains the ideal. How exacting it can be, how difficult of attainment, Sainte-Beuve himself has unconsciously demonstrated in this very passage. The quotation with which he ends is an adaptation of Pope's famous couplet in the *Essay on Criticism*:

> A perfect Judge will read each work of Wit
> With the same spirit that its author writ.

[1] *For Lancelot Andrewes* (1928).   [2] *Revaluation* (1936), pp. 64–7.
[3] *Seventeenth-century Studies presented to Sir Herbert Grierson* (1938), pp. 64–84.
[4] 'Diderot,' *Causeries du Lundi*, ser. 3. Sainte-Beuve would certainly have included the original reading public in the *point de vue du sujet qu'on examine*.

Pope, however, did not in fact mean to recommend a *sympathetic* reading, but, as the quotation from Quintilian in his note on the passage proves,[1] a *careful* reading ('spirit' meaning *energy, vivacity*). Without realizing it, therefore, Sainte-Beuve has committed the very error against which he is warning others—in this case, of making Pope speak the language of nineteenth-century relativism.

A continuous alertness is certainly necessary. Some knowledge of the history of the language is virtually indispensable. An acquaintance with social and economic history is highly desirable. The 'perfect Judge' will not make the mistake of thinking poetry simple. But some signposts can be erected for his guidance. We have already discovered one criterion of semantic relevance. The meaning of a poem is the meaning that it had for the ideal representative of those contemporaries of the poet to whom the poem, implicitly or explicitly, was originally addressed. But this is only a first stage in the enquiry. The next step will be to consider the *content* of poetry.

---

[1] Dilgenter legendum est, ac pæne ad scribendi sollicitudinem: nec per partes modo scrutanda sunt omnia, sed perlectus liber utique ex integro resumendus.

CHAPTER THREE

POETRY AND SOCIETY

I

IT will be as well at this point to try and summarize the course of the argument in the two preceding chapters. Chapter One, it will be remembered, was devoted to a demonstration of the primacy of meaning in poetry. It was not denied that the spoken word is sounded, or that the sounds of poetry can be utilized by the poet either as a mimetic echo of the sense or as a mild form of hypnotism. But in poetry, as in language generally, sound is always *primarily* semantic. Words, like bank-notes, are in general use in the civilized world because they are convenient symbols. In both cases their social utility does not derive from their physical properties, but from what they symbolize. A word is 'an intellectual thing,' and to fail to recognize this elementary fact is as irrational as to imagine that the value of a bank-note lies in the paper that it is printed on.

Poetry, then, is meaning. But poetic meaning is not the only kind of meaning. In Chapter Two it was suggested that *formally* a poem is a verbal synthesis, a complicated, simultaneous, unified whole, and that the familiar technical devices, such as rhyme and metaphor, should all be considered the agents of poetic meaning, either defeating the reader's temptations to divagate into analysis or reinforcing the synthetic habits that he or she carries over from everyday life. The last question to be asked was 'Meaning to whom?' In the final section of Chapter Two the suggestion was made that a poem only comes to have meaning in the poet-reader relationship. Although the poet need not be fully conscious of it, the fact is that his poems are only written with a view to being read. The readers, therefore, that the poet is implicitly addressing *determine* to a considerable degree the kind of poem that he is writing. It follows that to understand a poem's meaning to-day we need to be able to identify ourselves as far as possible with its original readers, the poet's contemporaries, whose ideal response to the poem in fact constitutes its meaning.

Poetry, finally, represents a specialization of normal speech. It is an act of communication, and so far from being restricted to the inspired few, is always, as Wordsworth insisted, 'a selection of the language really spoken by men.' The basis of the selection is not, however, the exclusion from poetry of certain allegedly non-poetic words,[1] but the mitigation of the word-order of grammar with its rigid syllogistic patterns.

It now remains to consider the *content* of poetry. What are the meaningful elements that are synthesized in the poem? How many of such elements will there normally be? What relation, other than that of mere juxtaposition, will the separate elements bear to each other?

The content of poetry is often said to be coextensive with the range of human interests, *quidquid agunt homines*. To Wordsworth, as long as they concern us 'as enjoying and suffering beings,' poems could be about almost anything:

---

[1] This is the *negative* theory of poetic diction. The earlier Augustan critics, such as Hobbes, Dryden and Dennis, had merely tried to ban technical terms and words with vulgar associations. The *positive* theory of poetic diction—that certain words are poetical in themselves—is implicit in Collins and explicit in Goldsmith and Shenstone. Both theories are defensible in certain special circumstances, but neither has any general validity.

The remotest discoveries of the Chemist, the Botanist, or Mineralogist, will be as proper objects of the Poet's art as any upon which it can be employed, if the time should ever come when these things shall be familiar to us, and the relations under which they are contemplated by the followers of these respective sciences shall be manifestly and palpably material to us as enjoying and suffering beings.[1]

But the Wordsworthian formula of 'enjoying and suffering beings' is unsatisfactory. Two objections immediately suggest themselves:

(i) Do purely *physical* pleasures and pains, however intense or prolonged, ever form the basis of major poetry? Poems are not, in fact, written about toothaches or Parisian cooking. Even the poetry of intoxication derives its essential *élan* from the thirst that from the soul doth rise.

(ii) Is poetry limited to enjoyment and suffering, as the words are ordinarily understood? Wordsworth has surely overstressed its emotional elements. Much of his own poetry, for example, is contemplative rather than emotional. Such admirable things as the 'Cumberland Beggar' and 'Peter Bell' do not provoke the smile or the lump in the throat so much as the reflection 'How odd, how very odd, human beings are!'

I am inclined to believe that the content of poetry is best defined as *human nature in its social relations*. The purely private emotion and reflection cannot get into poetry, because the use of language necessarily involves a socialization of individual experience. All poems are therefore in the last analysis public poems. And, other things being equal, the poems that seem to 'come off' best with their original readers, those with the maximum

---

[1] 'Observations' prefixed to *Lyrical Ballads* (1802).

semantic exchange-value, tend to be those where a large amount of common ground is shared by the poet and the reader. This is another way of saying that the constituents of poetry tend to be

> What oft was thought but ne'er so well express'd.

It follows that the contribution of the poet is limited to 'expression,' i.e. the selection and synthetic arrangement of the social units of meaning.

By 'a social unit of meaning' I mean a social attitude, i.e. one of the series of relations that one human being can take up, or find himself in, or be forced into, *vis à vis* one or more other human beings. In most poems the theme, content or subject-matter turns out under analysis to consist of the juxtaposition of *two* contrasted or conflicting social attitudes. This is true at both the third and fourth stages of poetic synthesis (as distinguished in the preceding chapter). At the fourth stage the concept becomes a particularly useful critical tool. The typical poem can be thought of at this stage as a miniature drama in which two 'sides' meet, come into conflict and are eventually reconciled.[1] In Wordsworth's 'A slumber did my spirit seal' (see p. 32 above) the two 'sides' could perhaps be labelled 'humanism' (Wordsworth *ought* to have had 'human fears') and 'pantheism' (the mysticism of 'rocks, and stones, and trees'). The vague living-Lucy of this poem is opposed to the grander dead-Lucy who has become involved in the sublime processes of nature. We put the poem down satisfied, because its last two lines succeed in effecting a reconciliation between the two philosophies or social attitudes. Lucy is actually more

---

[1] I derive this metaphor from Cleanth Brooks who has elaborated it in *Modern Poetry and the Tradition* (1939) and *The Well Wrought Urn* (New York, 1947).

alive now that she is dead, because she is now a part of the life of Nature and not just a human 'thing.'

The two contrasted social attitudes need not be -isms. In the following poem, in which a great deal of meaning is condensed into the four lines, the opposition is at a less abstract level:

> Western wind, when wilt thou blow,
> The small rain down can rain?
> Christ, if my love were in my arms
> And I in my bed again![1]

Here ll. 1–2, addressed to the west wind, are a prayer for rain for the growing crops, and ll. 3–4, addressed to Christ (the exclamation has the effect of a vocative), are a prayer for the return of the lover. And the parallelism of form overcomes the contrast of content. The effect is to suggest that the lover whose return is desired so passionately is also involved in the natural cycle of the seasons. In spite of appearances to the contrary spring will eventually come again, and the speaker tries to attribute a similar certainty to the return of the lover. By a blasphemous implication Christ is in effect assigned the rôle of a fertility spirit. The 'sides' in this poem are therefore (*a*) the non-human processes of growth, and (*b*) human self-fulfilment in sexual love. To define the content of the poem in more abstract terms would be to distort its meaning.

The Principle of the Semantic Gap assumes a peculiar importance at this final level of synthesis. However

[1] The MS. in the British Museum that has preserved the only text of this anonymous poem includes pieces by William Cornish and other professional musicians at Henry VIII's Court. The lines, however, are so different in style that they suggest an earlier date and a popular origin. E. K. Chambers has recently suggested that the poem is a fragment—perhaps a variant first verse of the well-known ballad 'The Unquiet Grave' (*English Literature at the Close of the Middle Ages* (1945), p. 157).

G

brilliant the details no poem can be considered a good one unless the basic social attitudes implied or expressed are genuinely 'opposite' or 'discordant.' It is the absence of any fundamental conflict of human attitudes that accounts for the emptiness of many nineteenth-century anthology pieces. I seem to detect just such a deficiency in the familiar lines that Landor prefixed to *The Last Fruit off an Old Tree* (1853):

> I strove with none, for none was worth my strife.
> Nature I loved, and, next to Nature, Art;
> I warmed both hands before the fire of Life;
> It sinks, and I am ready to depart.

The arrogance surely is oversimplified. The social attitude struck in the first line is maintained too consistently, so that Landor seems guilty of attitudinizing. The love of Nature and of Life which might have provided the counter-attitude is not developed sufficiently. It was for his own selfish gratification, we feel, that he loved them. The image of warming the hands before the fire, though vivid, is too reassuring, emphasizing, as it does, the agreeable sensation felt by the hands rather than the mysterious forces of the fire and the surrounding blackness.

A poem that can be compared with Landor's because of the similiarity of form and content, and that 'comes off,' it seems to me, whereas his just doesn't, is Herrick's 'The comming of good luck':

> So Good-luck came, and on my roofe did light,
> Like noyse-lesse Snow; or as the dew of night:
> Not all at once, but gently, as the trees
> Are, by the Sun-beams, tickel'd by degrees.

The contrast that gives this poem its attractively idiosyncratic flavour is between the beneficiary of Good Luck, the jolly Devonshire clergyman whom we know, and Good Luck itself, a curiously impalpable figure. But the contrast operates at two separate levels. In the four lines we are told five things about Good Luck:

(i) it is personal, something with a purposive existence of its own (it *comes* and *lights*, instead of being brought or dropped);

(ii) it is a natural phenomenon, like dew, snow or sunbeams;

(iii) it insinuates itself gradually, noiselessly and when there is nobody about—like snow or dew at night, or the early morning sunshine (*tickel'd* implies the rays of the sun *under* the leaves and twigs);

(iv) it is beneficent, refreshing and enlivening what it touches;

(v) it is local, lighting upon the house instead of the occupier of the house.

Good Luck, it is clear, is not a Robin Goodfellow so much as a semi-supernatural semi-natural being like Will-o'-the-wisp, and, although there is a faint suggestion of *lares et penates*, it is primarily an English deity unconnected with the Goddess Fortuna. The initial contrast between Herrick and Good Luck, i.e. between human and non-human nature, is therefore *duplicated* in the complexities of Good Luck's own make-up. As compared with Landor's poem Herrick's is much more 'meaningful.'

An additional requirement is that the two social attitudes be more or less equally matched. A poem of which the outcome is a foregone conclusion, in which one of the 'sides' is manifestly a man of straw, cannot engage the reader's interested co-operation to the same degree. Perhaps another four-line poem, Prior's 'The Lady Who Offers her Looking Glass to Venus,' may be held to exemplify this social lopsidedness:

> Venus, take my Votive Glass:
> Since I am not what I was;
> What from this Day I shall be,
> Venus, let Me never see![1]

The poem gets its effectiveness from the contrast between what the lady says and the poet's implied comment on it. At first we take the lady at her word and accept her logic. Yes, as the sight of her wrinkles distresses her, she will be well advised to get rid of the mirror. In this way she will be able to bring the march of time to a halt. But a moment's reflection reminds us that this is really a *non sequitur* and we swing over to Prior's side. Unfortunately getting old is not just a matter of seeing oneself do it. The lady's gesture is a futile one. The comedy of the poem derives from the contrast between the lady's apparently perfect logic and its real fallacy. Like the great comic figures—for example, her own contemporary Lady Wishfort in Congreve's *Way of the World* (1700)—she exposes herself by what she herself says, and not as the result of what other people say about her. But the comedy borders on farce because there is not even a suggestion of pity for the lady's very human failing. The poem might have been a better one if it had not been so heavily weighted against her.

The attempt here made to restrict the content of poetry to human nature in its social relations has received some confirmation in recent investigations into the way children learn to speak. M. M. Lewis, who is the Director of the Institute of Education at University College, Nottingham, has now demonstrated that the incentives to linguistic

[1] Text from *Poems on Several Occasions* (1718). The poem is a translation from an epigram attributed to Plato which is reprinted in Johnson's *Rambler*, No. 143. A reference to the poem in 'Cloe Jealous' suggests a date in the late 1690's, when the majority of Prior's poems to 'Cloe' (Jane Ansley) were written.

communication can be either 'manipulative' (serving the practical activities of society and its members) or 'declarative' (in which the social response is an end in itself):

The child uses speech manipulatively when it is an instrument to secure the satisfaction of his primary needs: to remove discomfort, to obtain pleasant experiences or to prolong them once they have begun. At the beginning the child in discomfort vaguely strives to rid himself of it; the contortions of his body, the thrusting out of his arms and legs, and not least his cries—these are all of them different ways in which his striving shows itself.[1] Then, as he comes to recognize that the possession of a particular object, for instance food, relieves his discomfort, his vague striving may change into a directed reaching-out to secure this object. In the same way, catching sight of some plaything, for instance a bright ball dangling from his cot, he gurgles with pleasure and reaches out towards it. But it is of course a long time before he is physically capable of achieving his intention; this is when the group intervenes to help him. His cry is heard and food is brought to him. Or his mother hears his gurgle of delight, and her sympathetic hand swings the ball towards him. Thus his utterance becomes the instrument of achieving his intention, an instrument used blindly and fumblingly at first, but with a clearer understanding of its use as time goes on. It is a social instrument —a means by which, instead of directly manipulating his physical environment, the child manipulates his social environment, which in turn manipulates his physical environment for him.

In its declarative function language plays a different part. Often it is evident that the child is not so much attempting to seize hold on some portion of his physical environment

[1] This is Darwin's account of the origin of expression in *Expression of the Emotions* (1872).

as simply to express its effect on him, and that his satisfaction comes from securing an appropriate expressive response from someone else. For instance, the child lying in his cot and gurgling with pleasure at the dance of light and shade on the ceiling becomes happier still when his mother points to the dancing pattern and also expresses her delight. Soon it is clear that he is intentionally trying to secure this response from her, that he declares his pleasure in order to enhance it by effective communion with her. In this declarative use of speech the child seeks to obtain from others, not some manipulation of his physical environment, but simply an expressive response. Speech is still a social instrument, but now it is directed, not to secure some change in the physical environment, but social response as an end in itself.[1]

In terms of adult life, the 'manipulative' function of language is especially prominent in business, politics and science, whereas the 'declarative' function ranges from 'phatic communion' (talk about the weather, etc.) to the art of literature.

The relevance of Lewis's distinctions to the definition of poetry will be clear. Poetry is obviously the declarative function in its purest and most concentrated form. Poetry makes no attempt to manipulate the physical environment; hence the futility of didactic poetry and the inferiority of partisan political verse. In its essence it is simply the expression in language of the sense of social solidarity, the linguistic equivalent of flags, national anthems and emblems, or symbolic figures like Saint George, John Bull and the reigning constitutional monarch. *Das folk dichtet*—the formula of ballad-origins attributed to Jacob and Wilhelm Grimm—can be applied to poetry generally

[1] *Language in Society* (1948), pp. 23–4.

in the sense that a social group, by virtue of its possession of a special highly developed instrument for its own internal communication in language or dialect, is the indispensable precondition for the composition of poetry. Without the group you cannot have a living language; without a living language you cannot have poetry. Poetry, however, is something more than an alternative outlet of the herd-instinct. Because of the intimate interconnections between language and thought it is at its best the herd-instinct at its point of maximum consciousness, the synthesis of a particular social order, in which that society achieves its most significant self-expression—and ultimately its historic meaning. Andrew Fletcher of Saltoun's 'wise man,' who 'believed if a man were permitted to make all the ballads, he need not care who should make the laws of a nation,' was making the same point in more homely terms. In the long run, and by a curious paradox in spite of their untranslatability, it is by its poems above all that a country is remembered by the rest of the world. And it is right that this should be so. As man, the political animal, is most himself in a selfless service to the community, so the community fulfils itself most completely, not in war or commerce or religion or science (impermanent and transient occupations infected by the physical environment, soon lost in the mist of time), but in that assertion of its own *idea*, which constitutes poetry.

II

In the light of the foregoing considerations the old problem of the *utile* and the *dulce* can be seen to be a quarrel between half-truths. Instruction can never be poetry's primary purpose, because the impartment of instruction is a practical activity, involving a use of language that is 'manipulative' rather than 'declarative.' Poetry is only useful in the sense that it is not self-regarding, a disinterested activity. In its essence it is simply a part, in some respects a culmination, of the process of social living, one of those things, like law-abidingness and politeness, voting at a General Election, or reading the newspaper, that life in a human community necessarily involves, and it is no more useful, strictly speaking, than any other purely social activity. On the other hand, it is equally misleading to insist on the delightfulness of poetry. No doubt most poetry does incidentally delight both its writers and readers, but to make delight the basis of poetry is as wrong-headed as making happiness the basis of virtue. Delight is generally a by-product of poetry, just as happiness is generally a by-product of virtue. But you do not live a good life in order to be happy, and you should not write or read poetry primarily because of the pleasure it will give you.[1] Poetry has a more honourable function than the titillation of the æsthetic sense. It is written or read because one is a member of a social group, because one is expected to do so by the group, because it enlarges one's consciousness of the group and one's relations with it, because in the last analysis the operation of the herd-instinct in oneself makes it impossible not to. The reading and writing of poetry is, in fact, a natural function of man the political animal. To insist on its delighting us as individuals, as the Romantics did with their demand for 'ecstasy,' is a kind of perversity comparable to perversities of the natural function of sex.

The reading of poetry and the writing of poetry are *both* social duties, essential acts of citizenship. The two

[1] Cf. I. A. Richards (*Principles of Literary Criticism* (1930), pp. 96–7): 'Pleasure and impleasure are complicated matters arising in the course of activities which are directed to other ends. . . . It is the form in which we should be interested, not in a by-product of having managed successfully to read it.'

things are complementary. A proper reading of poetry is not possible unless one is at least a writer of poetry *in posse*. The process of verbal synthesis that is demanded of the reader of poetry differs only in degree from the synthesis of poetic creation. To claim, as Ben Jonson and others have done, that 'To judge of poets is only the faculty of poets; and not of all poets, but the best,'[1] is to mistake the function of criticism, which is the formulation of the *reader*'s reaction in the poet–reader relationship. Poets are not necessarily the best readers of poetry, not even of the poems they have written themselves. And they may well be unaware of the *social* element in criticism. How important that is can be gauged from Sainte-Beuve's note on the French reading public:

> Car en France, notez-le bien, on ne veut pas surtout s'amuser et se plaire à un ouvrage d'art ou d'esprit, ou en être touché, on veut savoir si l'on a eu droit de s'amuser et d'applaudir, et d'être ému; on a peur de s'être compromis, d'avoir fait une chose ridicule; on se retourne, on interroge son voisin; on aime à rencontrer une autorité, à avoir quelqu'un à qui l'on puisse s'adresser dans son doute, un homme ou un corps.[2]

In Sainte-Beuve's time the English reader had not got beyond 'knowing what he liked.' Even to-day, there is a prejudice against 'knowing what one ought to like,' though Arnold, Eliot, and Leavis, and some other propagandists for criticism, have done much to break it down. But the desirability of there being somebody

[1] *Timber: or, Discoveries* (1641), p. 129. Landor thought that 'Great poets are the only judges of poets' (*Imaginary Conversations*, 'Lord Chesterfield and Lord Chatham'), and T. S. Eliot has made a similar claim in the English Association's *Essays and Studies* for 1936. Dryden's position is more plausible: 'Poets themselves are the most proper, though I conclude not the only critics' (preface to *All for Love* [1678]).

[2] *Causeries du Lundi*, vol. xiv, p. 209.

about to guide the amateur reader to the best poets is, one would imagine, obvious. And the poets themselves usually have other things to do.

Such a guide *must* base his operations upon the contemporary poets of his own social group. The usual thing to-day is to start by introducing the beginner to the poets of the past. He has then to work his way slowly and painfully up to his own contemporaries. But this is to put the cart before the horse. The dead poets did not write for us but for their own countries and their own generations. A process of mental adjustment is needed before we can understand what it is exactly that they are saying. With our own contemporaries, however, such problems do not arise to the same degree. They are talking to us in our own language about the things that we too are interested in. If they are any good at all—and the proportion of good poets is more constant than is often thought[1]—they must have things to tell us that we need to hear. Relations between poet and reader of the same generation and the same social group—what Wordsworth meant to Mill, what Pope meant to Horace Walpole, what Auden means to us—are necessarily far more intimate and stimulating than any contacts between the living and the Mighty Dead can ever be. And they are the only possible base from which to conduct raids into the Dantes and Shakespeares. The man who is not prepared to understand the poetry of his own time *must* be incompetent to appreciate that of the past. This may seem a desperate conclusion, but are not many even of the best academic critics of to-day and yesterday—men like Oliver Elton, W. P. Ker, H. W. Garrod, F. L. Lucas, J. Dover Wilson, and F. P. Wilson—a standing proof that learning and a lucid prose style are not enough?

[1] See p. 259 below

The essential connection between the literature of the present day and the literature of the past was pointed out by T. S. Eliot in the now famous passage in 'Tradition and the Individual Talent';

> No poet, no artist of any art, has his complete meaning alone. His significance, his appreciation is the appreciation of his relation to the dead poets and artists. You cannot value him alone; you must set him, for contrast and comparison, among the dead. I mean this as a principle of æsthetic, not merely historical, criticism. The necessity that he shall conform, that he shall cohere, is not one-sided; what happens when a new work of art is created is something that happens simultaneously to all the works of art which preceded it. The existing monuments form an ideal order among themselves, which is modified by the introduction of the new (the really new) work of art among them. The existing order is complete before the new work arrives; for order to persist after the supervention of novelty, the *whole* existing order must be, if ever so slightly, altered; and so the relations, proportions, values of each work of art toward the whole are readjusted; and this is conformity between the old and the new.[1]

The academic critics, through their failure to realize that several new works of art have arrived in the last twenty or thirty years (the poetry of Eliot himself, for

[1] *The Sacred Wood* (1920), pp. 44–5. Eliot may perhaps be accused of using unnecessarily mystical terms. The essential point is that, by virtue of being a member of a particular social order, the modern reader of poetry necessarily has mental habits and prepossessions different from those of readers of the past. A mental adjustment is therefore necessary in his case if he is to undergo the *demi-métamorphose* into a contemporary of Shakespeare's, for example. As the metamorphosis cannot be complete, the twentieth-century reader's reactions to Shakespeare must be different from the nineteenth-century reader's. In other words the poet-reader relationship 'Shakespeare' has *changed*. In so far as a man fails to read the best poems of his own day he is an *incomplete* member of his own society—in the terminology of ancient Athens, an ἰδιώτης.

example, or that of Auden, whom I am inclined to think the greatest English poet since Keats), have not appreciated that the existing monuments have been modified pretty considerably. In discussing Shakespeare or Spenser or Donne from their Edwardian standpoints they are talking about something that is no longer there. Hence—in spite of the occasional critical shrewdness, the learning gracefully worn, the brilliant literary detective-work—the feeling of enormous futility that their books generate, A. C. Bradley is out of date now, but he can still be read on Shakespeare because the Shakespeare he discusses did once really exist. Dover Wilson's Shakespeare is not even a ghost.

III

But the concept of poetry as a society at its point of maximum consciousness is too general to be used as a critical tool. We need to know, in addition, (i) what constitutes a society (what are its spatial and temporal boundaries?) and (ii) what the social elements are that get into poetry (is poetry a reflection or a distillation of social life—if the latter what is the process's formula?).

The two problems are closely related and can be best approached via the spoken language, of which, as we have seen, poetry represents a specialized form. A society, whatever else it is, is the sum of the individuals speaking the same language. Its boundaries are determined therefore by the speakers' consciousness of differences between one side and the other of a fence created by (i) national allegiances, (ii) regional differentiations, (iii) class distinctions, and (iv) the lapses of time.

In modern times a society, in the sense of a linguistic unit, rarely overflows the political boundaries of the nation-state. The borderline cases in the history of

English poetry are the Scotsmen, the Anglo-Welsh and the Anglo-Irish. Before 1603 few if any natives of Scotland aspired to be members of an English social group, but in the seventeenth century a certain number of Scottish aristocrats were assimilated into the English ruling class, and in the eighteenth and nineteenth centuries large numbers of middle-class Scots became to all intents and purposes Englishmen. Drummond, Thomson, Scott and Stevenson are obviously on the English side of the fence, whereas Dunbar, Ramsay and Burns obviously aren't. The social attachments of the Welshman and the Anglo-Irish are perhaps less clear-cut, because the English that they speak is essentially our English, though modified by Celtic influences. On the whole an Irishman's brogue and a Welshman's accent are not felt as social barriers, since the semantic content of their speech is more or less identical with our own (another instance of the primacy of sense over sound).[1]

The existence of clearly differentiated regional and class dialects in England is evidence of the coexistence of a number of separate social groups within the nation-state. But the paucity and inferiority of the poetry that

[1] The important difference between the native English writer and the *métèque* (the writer with a non-English linguistic, racial or political background) is the latter's lack of respect for the finer points of English idiom and grammar. This allows the Anglo-Irishman (like George Moore) or the Anglo-Scot (like Stevenson) to attempt effects of style, sometimes successfully, that the English writer would feel to be a perverse defiance of the genius of the language. In the field of eighteenth-century poetry there are the cases of James Thomson (of *The Seasons*) and 'Ossian' Macpherson. More recently there have been Yeats, the Anglo-Irishman, and Eliot, the Anglo-American. Although there can be no doubt that Yeats's and Eliot's lack of linguistic inhibition has extended the range of modern English poetry, the influences of the native poets Hopkins, Hardy and Owen, will probably prove to have been healthier in the long run. In second-rate writers on the linguistic fringe—Anglo-Jews like Guedalla, Anglo-Scots like Compton Mackenzie, Anglo-Welshmen like Emlyn Williams —there is a particular temptation to bogus slickness. On the other hand, the disregard of the organic structure of the language often enables the *métèque* to achieve a peculiar lucidity in prose.

most of them have left behind, at any rate since the fifteenth century, suggests that there can have been little vitality in their social life. At any one period, indeed, there would seem, on the evidence of the poetry, to have been only one social group in England that was functioning healthily. This was generally, but not always, what is vaguely called the ruling class. The ruling class's speech set the standards of 'correctness' of the moment, to which careerists and parasites born outside its ranks tended to conform. Linguistic correctness being the outward and visible sign of social conformity, its essential criterion is not spelling or pronunciation but meaning (social intention). Quantitatively, therefore, a society, in the sense in which the word can be used to define English poetry, is the sum of the individuals whose semantic speech-habits conform to those of a dominant group. Qualitatively, however, a society *is* the dominant group within the nation-state, since this group's characteristics are the shibboleths which determine the admission of others to its ranks.

A society's effective life can be measured in economic and political terms, but the history of the language provides a more sensitive index to the births and deaths of the dominant groups. It is generally agreed, for example, that the 1650's are a social watershed in English history. They mark, among other things, the end of the inflationary period, the degradation of the monarchy, the abolition of feudal tenures, the end of centralized government, colonial expansion and the struggle against Dutch maritime supremacy, the beginning of religious and racial tolerance, the foundation of what was to be the Royal Society, and a trend to a scientific agriculture. Taken singly, however, each of these changes wears something of an accidental look. There was no *special* reason why any one of these things had to happen in the 1650's. But where politics and economics offer only tentative approximations, the linguistic evidence is conclusive. Indeed, the revolutionary character of the 1650's might almost be demonstrated from the history of one word—the word *romantic*. Until 1650 no need seems to have been felt for an adjective for the common word 'romance.' But between 1650 and 1659 the word *romantic* is used by no less than seven writers—T. Bayly (1650), J. Bourne (1650), S. Sheppard (1651), J. Evelyn (1654), W. Lower (1656), the anonymous translator of Pierre de Marmet (1658) and H. More (1659).[1] On most of these occasions the word would seem to have been an independent creation. No less than four other attempts were also made during the 1650's to create an adjective for the word 'romance': *romance* (as adjective, 1653), *romancial* (1653), *romancy* (1654), *romancicall* (1656).[2] None of these forms were in use as adjectives before 1650. In the light of this evidence it is clear that in the 1650's a general need suddenly made itself felt for a special word to distinguish the kind of fiction retailed in Sidney's *Arcadia*, with its deplorable tendency (as Sprat put it when using the word in 1667) 'to frame more perfect images of things, than the things themselves will bear.'[3] The nature of the need does not concern us for the moment.[4] What is significant is the revolution in the climate of opinion to which all this

[1] See F. Baldensperger, *Harvard Studies and Notes in Philology and Literature*, vol. xix (1937), pp. 13 ff., and W. L. Ustick, *Times Literary Supplement* (21 Dec. 1933).

[2] See L. P. Smith, 'Four Romantic Words' (in *Words and Idioms* (1925)). The adjective 'romancy' was used by three writers in the 1650's—Edmund Gayton (1654), Anthony Wood (1659), and (probably) John Aubrey (*Natural History of Wiltshire*, begun 1656).

[3] *The History of the Royal Society* (1667), p. 331.

[4] The intellectual climate of opinion includes (i) Hobbes's attack on metaphor, (ii) the Royal Society's campaign for one word for one thing, (iii) the Cartesian interest in the nature of truth.

word-creation bears witness. Most words come into a language gradually, over a long period of years. That thirteen writers should have been feeling their way independently to what is essentially the same new word within the short period 1651-9 is evidence of an exceptional and violent disturbance of the linguistic *status quo*. A new English language was, in fact, in process of creation, and this language, as we can now see, was the mouthpiece of the 'squirearchy,' the new dominant group that achieved its maximum consciousness, its ideal self-projection, in the poetry of Dryden, Swift and Pope.

What, however, is it in the social order that is projected in the poetry? It is time to come down to the brass tacks. Two recent comments on the poetry of Andrew Marvell will provide a convenient test-case. Obviously the American professor who thinks that 'The Nymph Complaining for the Death of her Fawn' may represent 'an Anglican's grief for the stricken Church' is talking through his Yankee hat.[1] Obviously the Marxist who equates Marvell's 'Mower' impartially with 'the power of Love,' 'the scythe of Death or Fate,' 'the revolutionary armies,' 'the productive classes as against the drones,' and 'a pre-commercial simplicity,' is also seeing things that aren't really all of them there.[2] But it is easier to feel that this sort of thing is wrong than to be able to say specifically why it is wrong. The fundamental error, it seems to me, lies in identifying a social order with the concrete particulars, human or institutional, that make up its cogs and shafts, instead of with its prime mover, the basic human incentive that is ultimately responsible for setting

[1] Douglas Bush, *English Literature in the Earlier Seventeenth Century* (1945), p. 161. It is only fair to add that this is an isolated lunacy. The book is a sensible, if somewhat superficial, guide-book to the period.

[2] Christopher Hill, 'Society and Andrew Marvell,' *The Modern Quarterly* (Autumn 1946), p. 18. In spite of some rather wild identifications this is a most interesting article.

in motion the particular manifestations, political, econo-
mic, religious and literary.[1] The social order that finds its
expression in Marvell's lyrics cannot be defined in terms of
social cogs like the Anglican Church and the New Model
Army. To do so is to confuse effects with their causes.
Even the political and economic systems of the English
Renaissance are not the essential features of its social order.
The fundamental question is a 'Why.' Why was the
English ruling class the agent of such systems? The
formula that we need must be one that defines the human
motives that controlled the social behaviour of this
dominant group.

What was the motivating force *par excellence* of the
English Renaissance? I believe the one-word answer to
this question is 'self-interest.' The self-interest, however,
of the new ruling class of the 'King's Servants,' who had
displaced the feudal aristocracy of the Middle Ages, was
neither narrow nor calculated. The sheep-farming that
created deserted villages and the usury that financed
piracy and the slave-trade were accompanied by more
reputable titillations of the ego—among them military
and athletic prowess, the art of dress, the patronage of
culture, the ability to write a love-poem, the ambition of
universal learning, and the delights of introspection.
Unlike nineteenth-century individualism the individualism of the Renaissance was not specialized or one-sided.

[1] It is the failure to realize this that vitiates L. C. Knights's *Drama and Society
in the Age of Jonson* (1937), the most ambitious attempt since Buckle and Taine
to relate English literature to the social background. Knights provides an
admirable summary of English economic history, 1550-1650, and follows this
with two excellent critical essays on Ben Jonson and some rather more per-
functory ones on Dekker, Heywood, Middleton and Massinger. The idea is
that the economic analysis will illuminate the literary criticism. In fact, however, the two halves of the book do not coalesce, and the reader lays it down
with a feeling that the claims made in the Introduction have not been justified.
Knights handicapped himself unnecessarily by excluding the political and
religious influences.

H

According to the theory of the handbooks of 'courtesy,' like Castiglione's *Il Libro del Cortegiano* and Peacham's *The Compleat Gentleman*, success in the competition for the Prince's favour went to the accomplished individual, the man who had brought to perfection all the different sides of his personality. And during the reigns of the Tudors at any rate the theory had a certain basis in fact. The careers of Leicester, Sidney, Ralegh and Essex were, up to a point, an exemplification of it. Even more important, however, than the many-sidedness of Renaissance individualism is its mysticism. The *étalage du moi* was not a deliberate exploitation of the anti-social instincts, but a spontaneous response to a universe that had suddenly become increasingly unpredictable. The destruction of the feudal and ecclesiastical hierarchies of the Middle Ages had knocked the bottom out of the 'chain of being' explanation of the world and its associated doctrines.[1] On the political plane, instead of the hierarchical series of villein : manorial lord : feudal magnate : king, or family : tithing : hundred : county : kingdom,

> There was naught but a naked people under a naked crown.

And Protestantism was also busy removing the theological intermediaries—Pope, saints and angels—between God and the individual worshipper. In the end, indeed, there were only four certainties left—God, the Prince, the head of the family and the ego. In every other province of human life *anything* might be true. Hence the omnivorous

[1] E. M. W. Tillyard (*The Elizabethan World Picture* [1943]) and Hardin Craig (*The Enchanted Glass* (1936)) stress the persistence of the theory. It survived in the sense in which the Christianity of *Hymns Ancient and Modern* survives to-day—as popular mythology, part of the fabric of thinking. Its fantastic correspondences (flames, blood, gold, mint, crocodiles and swans were some of the things that were 'solary,' i.e. attracting to oneself the virtue of the sun) were a gift to the poets, but only the cranks took them seriously.

curiosity and credulity of the Elizabethans. Hence too the new fear of witchcraft and the growth of interest in alchemy and astrology. The wildcat speculations and the financial extravagance, the travellers' tales and the sensational news-sheets, the eccentric religious sects and the 'Heath Robinson' inventions were only different aspects of the same exuberant irrationality. It was a world in a state of nature in which everything was possible, if only four things were certain.

It was this world-picture that was displaced in the 1650's by the man-made world of the scientists and of 'common sense,' in which probability was the guide of life and there were no certainties outside mathematics. Here is the background against which Marvell's lyrics must be read. They were written in the late 1640's and early 1650's by a man whose heart and head were divided. Marvell's heart was with the old world of mystical individualism which he associated with the unconscious life of young growing things (flowers, fawns, children, and grass, especially grass) and with their custodians, the mowers and gardeners. His enemies were those who interfere with nature—the lovers who cut their names on trees, the architects who 'square and hew' the green trees of the forest, the troopers who shoot the nymph's fawn. It is all summarized in 'The Mower, Against Gardens':

> Luxurious man, to bring his vice in use,
> > Did after him the world seduce,
> And from the fields the flowers and plants allure,
> > Where Nature was most plain and pure.

So much for the heart. Marvell's head was on the other side. Politically he was a Parliamentarian, intellectually he was a rationalist, temperamentally he was a satirist.

And the head refused to allow the heart to take itself too seriously. The mower's case against gardens is so over-stated that it is clear it is largely only a pretext to describe their charm. Marvell's irony enabled him to have it both ways. He retained the mystical individualism of the Renaissance while recognizing its inadequacy, and as a consequence a tension is generated in his poetry compar-able to that in the later poems of Yeats, who also had a foot in two cultural camps.

There may well be details in the preceding analysis that can be questioned, but it is at this level of abstraction at any rate that the social significance of Marvell's poems, and indeed of all poems, must be determined. The prin-ciple is inherent in the nature of poetry. The subject-matter of poetry is not 'things,' but conflicting moods and attitudes, *human nature in its social relations*. Even important 'things,' like an economic or political system, cannot be the subject-matter of poetry except as the objects of human emotions and reflections. The inner meaning of a poem is the synthesis of conflicting attitudes and not the conflict of institutions. To interpret a poem as an allegory of incidents on the political scene, like the Puritan attack on the Anglican Church, or on the economic scene, like the struggle between capitalism and pre-com-mercial morality, is really to condemn it as poetry and reduce it to *roman à clef*. All that the poet can do *qua* poet is to dramatize the basic human attitudes that have been institutionalized as Anglicanism or Puritanism or what-ever it is. This is what Marvell has done in 'A Dialogue between the Resolved Soul and Created Pleasure,' a poem with far more strictly social significance than 'The Nymph complaining for the Death of her Fawn' or the 'Mower' poems. In this poem Marvell introduces a 'Soul' which rejects *seriatim* the temptations dangled before it by 'Pleasure.' The temptations begin with the pleasures of the senses (taste, touch, smell, sight and sound in that order) and conclude with the lusts for feminine beauty, gold, power and knowledge. The poem is clearly intended to symbolize Marvell's rejection of the Renaissance world (it was to satisfy precisely these lusts that Faustus had sold his soul to Lucifer), and it is reasonable to describe it as an exposition of an intellectual Puritanism. But this is a very different thing from the disguised history of the Civil War that the writers I have referred to wish to ascribe to him.

My conclusion, therefore, is that the social content of poetry must not be identified with the concrete particulars of everyday life. There is no reason why teapots, Proportional Representation and the Crystal Palace should not be introduced into a poem, but again there is no reason why they should be. The imprint of the social order must be looked for at a higher level of abstraction, and to the casual reader it may easily not be visible at all. It will normally be concerned with the basic incentives, the human prime mover, that a particular society offers its members. In English Renaissance poetry its centre of interest seems to lie in variations round the theme of a mystical individualism.

CHAPTER FOUR

SCHOOLS OF POETRY

I

EXCEPT by implication little or nothing has been said in the preceding pages about the literary tradition. Of the four *essential* elements of poetry, the removal of any one of which from a poem is literally impossible without the poem ceasing to exist, distinguished in Chapter Two—viz., the poet, the reader, a common language and a common literary tradition—it is the one that usually receives disproportionate attention. There are books and articles galore on the history of the English sonnet, the evolution of blank verse, Elizabethan tragedy, Restoration comedy, the poetry of natural description, poetic diction, satirical and mock-heroic poetry, *et hoc genus omne*. They make dreary reading because it is all so unreal and external—the form without the content, and the form treated not as meaning but as a sort of envelope. The history of the sonnet, for example, is reduced almost entirely to a matter of rhyme-schemes (*abbaabbacdecde* fighting it out with *ababcdcdefefgg*). To all such Dryasdusts I commend the dilemma with which, according to Robert Bridges, Professor J. J. Sylvester posed a poor translator of Horace: 'If he thought the original was like that, what can he have seen in it to make him think that it was worth translating?' If the important thing about Milton's sonnets is the rhyme-schemes—their discussion occupies two-thirds of the commentary devoted to the sonnets in the best recent edition of Milton's shorter poems[1]—why do you expect us to read them?

The futility of the literary historians derives from the vicious circle of their assumption that literature can only be explained in terms of itself. If you exclude all unliterary factors from the comparison, virtually the only thing that the sonnets of Surrey and the sonnets of Shakespeare will have in common is the rhyme-schemes and the Petrarchan conceits. As Fluellen learnedly concluded in another sixteenth-century comparison, there is salmons in both.

The literary historian, who draws an indelible line between poetry and life, is faced with the problem of explaining how a literary tradition begins.[2] The standard solution, in the textbooks of English literature, is 'foreign influence.' Even W. P. Ker, who was much more than a writer of textbooks, was apparently satisfied with this easy answer:

> In the larger fashions of poetry, the fashions of thought and imagination, and diction and ornament—not merely the fashions of verse—there is seldom any great change without some foreign influence, sometimes France, sometimes Italy, while at the back there are always the ancients, the poets of Greece and Rome; and at any age in English poetry there is always the possibility of new study of the ancients and new inferences to be drawn from them.[3]

And, according to J. M. Robertson,[4] 'The dramatic efflorescence of the last fifteen or twenty years of Elizabeth's reign was one of the results of a rapid fertilization

---

[1] *Shorter Poems of John Milton*, ed. B.A. Wright (1938).
[2] Even Walter Bagehot, who certainly didn't live in an Ivory Tower, has to ascribe the cause of a change of literary style to 'accident.' See *Physics and Politics*, chaps. i and iii.
[3] *Form and Style in Poetry* (1929), p. 194.
[4] *Elizabethan Literature* (1914), pp. 242-3.

of the English intelligence by a variety of forms of foreign culture'; and the decline of the drama in the seventeenth century was because 'culture did not pour in as before.'

Such pronouncements skate on very thin ice. To those who say that a *genre* is transmitted from one literature to another by a kind of process of infection the obvious rejoinder is: (i) How did the process ever start? (English allegory derives from the French, and the French get it from the late Latin poets, who derive from Virgil, who derives from Homer, who derives from . . . ?). (ii) Why is a country more susceptible to a particular infection at one time than another? No purely literary answer to the two questions is possible. As Brunetière found, *l'évolution des genres* is ultimately only explicable in social terms. It would be premature, however, to attempt such an explanation of the evolution of English poetry before the literary pattern has been defined.

There is, in my opinion, no good history of English poetry. This is not because our literary historians are particularly incompetent; they are not (indeed, the intelligence diverted into 'research' in the 1900's and 1920's that might then have reorganized British industry provides a nice social problem), but because, strictly speaking, there is no such thing as 'English poetry.' The *corpus poetarum anglorum*—*all* the English poems of *all* the English poets, from Cædmon to Dylan Thomas—cannot be treated historically, since the only unity it possesses is accidental and superficial. A history is only possible if there is an organic relationship between the component parts, and there is no such relationship between Old English poetry and that of the present day, or indeed between any two schools of English poetry, except where one school immediately preceded or succeeded another. Such surveys as there are generally consist of a series of isolated and detachable chapters, each of which is devoted to a separate 'period,' 'movement,' or 'school.' G. H. Mair's excellent little manual *English Literature: Modern* in the 'Home University Library' can be taken as typical. It consists of chapters on 'The Renaissance,' 'Elizabethan Poetry and Prose,' 'The Seventeenth Century,' 'The Age of Good Sense,' 'Dr. Johnson and His Time,' 'The Romantic Revival,' 'The Victorian Age' and 'The Present Age.' The particular labels used by Mair may not always strike one as happy (the *differentia* is sometimes political, a reign; sometimes chronological, a century; sometimes cultural, a dominant trend; and once it is attached to a particular writer, Johnson), but his general formula is obviously sound. The only concrete realities, about which historical propositions can be made, are the English poems (or novels or plays, etc.) of a *limited* period. English poetry in its entirety, like the English town or the English character, is too wide a field for profitable historical treatment.

The existence of schools of English poetry was recognized by the Elizabethan critics. Puttenham, for example, distinguished between the 'new company of courtly makers' (Wyatt, Surrey, Vaux, etc.), who 'sprong up' towards the end of Henry VIII's reign, and 'an other crew of Courtly makers' (Sackville, Sidney, Ralegh, etc.), who 'sprong up' in Elizabeth's reign. And an explicit recognition of the connection between schools of poetry, the language and the social order is to be found in Sir Kenelm Digby's note 'Concerning Spencer':

It is true that the vicissitudes of things (change being a necessary and inseparable condition of all sublunary creatures) and the inundations of barbarous nations, may overgrow and overrun the vulgar practise of the perfectest languages, as we see of the forementioned Greeke and Latine, yet the use of those toungues will flourish among learned men as long as those excellent authours remaine in the world. Which maketh me consider that noe fate nor length of time will bury Spencers workes and memory, nor indeed alter that language that out of his schoole we now use untill some generall innovation happen that may shake as well the foundations of our nation as of our speech: from which hard law of stepmother nature what Empire or Kingdome hath ever yet bin free?[1]

But there has been little or no serious attempt made to analyse the implications of such pronouncements, or even as far as I know to collect them, though they have, of course, become increasingly frequent since Puttenham's and Digby's time.

At least three major schools of poetry are now recognized to have intervened between the early sixteenth century and our own time. A recent textbook defines them as follows: (i) The Renaissance ('from Sir Thomas More to Milton, of course including both'); (ii) the Eighteenth Century ('The term "eighteenth century" is used here according to the usual convention to denote a period of our literature with a more or less uniform character of its own. Thus it includes Dryden, who was born in 1631, if not Waller, who was born in 1606, while it excludes Wordsworth, who was born in 1770'); (iii) the Nineteenth Century ('For the historian of literature the nineteenth century may be taken as beginning with the publication of *Lyrical Ballads* in 1798 and con-

---

[1] *The Poets and their Critics*, ed. H. S. Davies (1943), pp. 37–8. Davies dates Digby's note, which has only recently been printed, *c.* 1638, but it cannot be later than 1637 as Jonson is referred to as still alive. It was 'wrote at Mr. May His Desire,' and Thomas May had dedicated his *Tragedie of Cleopatra* to Digby as early as 1626. See E. W. Bligh, *Sir Kenelm Digby and his Venetia* (1932), p. 278.

tinuing well into the twentieth century').[1] A somewhat similar division was made by Peacock as early as 1820 in his *Four Ages of Poetry*. According to Peacock, the English age of gold was that of Shakespeare, with Milton standing between the ages of gold and silver, the latter ('beginning with Dryden, coming to perfection with Pope, and ending with Goldsmith, Collins and Gray') being succeeded by the age of brass of Wordsworth, Coleridge and Southey. A more accurate statement of the respective *termini a quibus* and *ad quos* would perhaps be:

(i) *Renaissance poetry*: Wyatt (1503?–42) to Traherne (1636?–74). Wyatt's earliest sonnets were written about 1528, and the last genuinely Renaissance poem of any merit is perhaps Congreve's 'On Mrs. Arabella Hunt Singing' (*c.* 1692).

(ii) *Augustan poetry*: Waller (1606–87) to Crabbe (1754–1832) or Gifford (1756–1826). Waller's 'Of the danger His Majesty escaped' was written *c.* 1624, though it was not until 1635, according to Clarendon, that he acquired any reputation as a poet; Gifford's last satire was published in 1800, and Crabbe's *Tales of the Hall* in 1819 (though several of the tales had been written by 1814).

(iii) *Romantic poetry*: Chatterton (1752–70) to Rupert Brooke (1887–1915). Chatterton's Rowley poems date from *c.* 1768; the only surviving Romantic poet of any distinction is de la Mare (b. 1873), whose last collection of poems came out in 1945.

In the foregoing summary the *termini a quibus* are probably more reliable than the *termini ad quos*. The peculiar importance ascribed by their successors to the experiments of Wyatt and Surrey, Waller and Denham, and Chatterton

---

[1] J. A. K. Thomson, *The Classical Background of English Literature* (1948), pp. 166, 199.

is well known. These men were recognized by their followers as the founders of new schools of poetry. The last poets of a decadent tradition, on the other hand, tend not to be noticed by their contemporaries, unless they survive as the figures of fun of a new school. Somebody might investigate this question of the Aunt Sallies of criticism. The Augustans' principal butts among their immediate predecessors appear to have been Quarles (*Emblems*, 1635), Benlowes (*Theophila*, 1652) and Flecknoe (*Miscellanea*, 1653) who were born in 1592, *c.* 1603 and *c.* 1620 respectively. The Romantics seem to have assigned a somewhat similar rôle to Erasmus Darwin (*The Loves of the Plants*, 1789), who was born in 1731. And in our own days Alfred Noyes (*The Torchbearers*, 1922–30) has served as the special scapegoat of Romanticism. Noyes was born in 1880. It will be noticed that the birth dates and the *floruits* of the 'butts' are somewhat earlier than the dates suggested above for the *termini ad quos*. The latter are therefore probably the *outside* temporal limits of the three schools.

Perhaps the most interesting point that emerges from this summary is that the three schools of poetry each had an effective life of about the same length. There were intervals of 133 years, 148 years and 135 years between the dates of birth of Wyatt and Traherne, Waller and Crabbe, and Chatterton and Brooke respectively. Between the writing of the first and last work in each school the intervals, taking the schools in chronological order, were 164 years, 193 years and 178 years.

The school preceding Renaissance poetry—the school of Chaucer, as it is sometimes called, from its greatest though not its most representative poet—also followed the same general pattern. After a hiatus in the early fourteenth century (when literary output was 'small in quantity' and 'negative and disappointing' in quality[1]) there was a sudden flowering of English poetry about 1350—the approximate date of 'Wynnere and Wastere' (Langland's model in *Piers Plowman*), 'Sir Gawayne and the Grene Knight,' 'The Tale of Gamelyn,' and the earliest miracle plays and 'Robin Hood' ballads. The Chaucerian school petered out in Skelton, whose last poem (*Why come ye not to court*) was written in 1522. This gives it a duration of 172 years. There may have been a still earlier school, beginning in the late twelfth century with Layamon and Orm—when 'the break with the past is so sharp' that it 'would be chosen with more justice than Chaucer's time as the starting-point for a study of modern literature'[2]—and ending in the early fourteenth century, but too little verse of the period survives to make it possible to clinch the conjecture. W. P. Ker has described this poetry as 'generally directed towards the ideal of French poetry, a struggle to realize in English what had been already achieved in French, to make English literature polite.'[3] It might be called the Anglo-French school. Finally there is clearly a school of modern poetry. Its beginnings can perhaps be ascribed to a group of poets who were born in the 1840's—Hopkins, Hardy, Bridges and Doughty—and its end does not seem to be in sight yet. The more important later names seem to be those of Yeats, Edward Thomas, T. S. Eliot, Wilfred Owen, Robert Graves, W. H. Auden, and Dylan Thomas. Its earlier phases overlapped the tail-end of the Romantic school, just as the early Augustans overlapped the later Renaissance poets, and the early Romantics overlapped the last Augustans.

[1] K. Sisam, *Fourteenth-century Verse and Prose* (1921), p. xvi.
[2] *Ibid.*, p. x.
[3] *English Literature Medieval*, Home University Library, p. 102.

As a working hypothesis, we can perhaps say that a poetic school spans five generations, each of about thirty-five years.[1] The five stages might be labelled (i) the Experimental Initiators (Wyatt, Waller, Chatterton, Hopkins), (ii) the Protagonists of a New Style (Spenser, Dryden, Wordsworth, Eliot), (iii) the Assured Masters (Donne, Swift, Keats, Auden), (iv) the Polished Craftsmen (Herrick, Pope, Tennyson), (v) the Decadents, that is, men reduced to 'stunts' to get new effects out of the exhausted tradition (Cowley, Collins, Swinburne). I am not suggesting that each school conforms exactly to this pattern, but that the general trends are towards something like it. And there are naturally plenty of borderline cases. Milton *ought*, judging by the date of his birth and his place in the Renaissance tradition, to have been either a Polished Craftsman or a Decadent. In fact he is both and a good deal more. Dryden is both the Protagonist of a New Style and an Assured Master. Marvell and Cowley begin as Renaissance Decadents and end as the Experimental Initiators of Augustan poetry. And other qualifications will no doubt suggest themselves.

In each school the poetry of its third generation, the stage I have called that of the Assured Masters, may be expected to constitute its classic expression. Here is the golden moment of equipoise between the forces of development and the forces of decay. I am inclined to believe that the foregoing is the only sense in which the word *classic* can now be usefully employed in literary criticism. I find some confirmation of this belief in T. S. Eliot's essay *What is a Classic?* (1945). For Eliot the test of a classic age is maturity:

[1] No special virtue is claimed for the subdivision by generations. The curve of a poetic school's rise and fall should be thought of as an arc which can be marked off in any number of equally spaced divisions. I use the five generations because they provide a simple and familiar formula.

The age which precedes a classic age, may exhibit both eccentricity and monotony; monotony because the resources of the language have not yet been explored, and eccentricity because there is yet no generally accepted standard—if, indeed, that can be called eccentric when there is no centre. Its writing may be at the same time pedantic and licentious. The age following a classic age, may also exhibit eccentricity and monotony: monotony because the resources of the language have, for the time at least, been exhausted, and eccentricity because originality comes to be more valued than correctness. But the age in which we find a common style, will be an age when society has achieved a moment of order and stability, of equilibrium and harmony; as the age which manifests the greatest extremes of individual style will be an age of development or an age of decay.[1]

It is true, I think, that the Protagonists of a New Style tend to exhibit both eccentricity and monotony. The diction of Spenser, of the early Dryden (e.g. *Annus Mirabilis*) and of the Wordsworth of *Lyrical Ballads* can certainly be called eccentric, and their poems are sometimes in danger of becoming monotonous. It is also true that the Polished Craftsmen and the Decadents are frequently either monotonous or eccentric. Herrick, Collins and Swinburne exemplify both defects. But Eliot's conclusion, which is that neither Shakespeare nor Marlowe nor even Pope (who came nearest to it) can be called classics, does not seem to be justified. These poets may not be mature in the sense in which Virgil is mature —that is a matter of opinion (Eliot's essay was originally an address delivered before the Virgil Society)—but their writing surely exhibits as much maturity as the particular

[1] pp. 13–14.

poetic tradition that they inherited was capable of. After all, if the test is to be maturity, a ripe blackberry can be as mature as a ripe peach, though it may be less luscious.

The classic moment will naturally be the central point in the cycle of a poetic school's evolution. Applying this criterion to the terminal dates of the Renaissance and Augustan schools, I get 1570 and 1680 as the dates of birth of their potentially classic poets, and 1610 and 1720 as the theoretical dates of their most classic poems. These dates fit the facts reasonably well. Shakespeare was born in 1564 and Donne in 1576, while *The Tempest* was probably written in 1611, and Donne's 'Twicknam Garden' and 'A Valediction: forbidding mourning,' two of the best of his *Songs and Sonets*, and *An Anatomie of the World* and its sequel, all date from this period. The only poet I know of who was born in 1680 is William Oldis-worth, a very minor poet indeed who edited *The Examiner* for some years, but Addison was born in 1672 and Pope in 1688. And the last two volumes of Pope's *Iliad* came out in 1720, a year which represents a half-way point between his early poems like *The Rape of the Lock* and the later satires. The Romantic school is less accommodating, the classic year coming out according to our formula as 1837 and the birth-date of the classic poet as 1820. Both of these dates are clearly too late; Matthew Arnold, who was born in 1822, can hardly qualify as an Assured Master. However, this exception may only prove the general rule. Most English poets have achieved their master-pieces when middle-aged, when between forty and fifty years old, but the Romantics generally wrote their best poems when they were about thirty or even younger (no doubt because the subconscious mind becomes more sluggish after sexual maturity has been reached). This suggests that the standard poetic generation of thirty-five years, on which these calculations have been made, may need to be amended in the case of the Romantic school.

Finally, it is interesting to find that the application of the standard formula (thirty-five years to each of the five poetic stages) to the modern school of poetry suggests that *our* classic year is 1950 or thereabouts.

II

Parallel with the six consecutive poetic schools—Anglo-French, Chaucerian, Renaissance, Augustan, Romantic and Modern—our hypothesis requires six distinguishable social orders whose basic incentives will provide a poetic content in the central line of evolution of each school. In terms of the source of the ultimate social influence a tabulation that commends itself to me is:

1. The Period of Lawyers' Feudalism
                    (Henry II–Edward III).
2. The Local Democracy of the Yeomanry
                    (Edward III–Henry VII).
3. The Centralized Absolutism of the Prince's Servants
                    (Henry VII–Cromwell).
4. The Oligarchy of the Landed Interests
                    (Charles II–George III).
5. The Plutocracy of Business
                    (George III–George V).
6. The Managerial State   (George V– ?).

The second item on this list may seem an anomaly. Clearly the yeomen of the fifteenth century were not in any sense the ruling class of the period, even in local government. The feudal aristocracy however, who were the real ruling class, had by then become a purely repressive and disintegrating force, and the social initiative in local affairs was almost invariably taken by the church-wardens, the juries of the manorial courts, the religious

I

and charitable guilds, and similar middle-class bodies. The yeomanry and their urban counterparts were undoubtedly the centre of *effective* social influence, so far as the period had one at all.[1]

Each dominant group has marked the consolidation of its power by a dramatic 'demonstration' against its immediate predecessors, which has made it perfectly clear who the new masters are. Episodes that exemplify this are the Peasants' Revolt, the Tudor Enclosures, the Expulsion of James II, the Reform Bill, and the General Election of 1945 (with the nationalizations consequent on it). Such episodes are evidence that a new class is firmly in the saddle (the Peasants' Revolt of 1381, though repressed, achieved its moral effect), and they are therefore *consequent* upon its accession to power. A period of some forty years separates most of these episodes from what I should regard as the real social watersheds, viz. the Black Death, the Fall of Wolsey (with its consequences—Protestantism, the suppression of the monasteries, and the creation of a new landed gentry), the execution of Charles I, the French Revolution and the 1906 Election. It will be seen that the dates—1348–9, 1530, 1649, 1789, 1906—coincide, with only minor discrepancies, with the dates of the Experimental Initiators of the various schools of poetry. But both series of revolutions, political and

[1] 'In the political struggle of the Wars of the Roses the "great connections" found their doom. As a result of that struggle the new men, who in the preceding two or three generations had succeeded to the commanding position in rural economy, were also able to succeed to local power and political influence' (M. M. Postan, 'Some Social Consequences of the Hundred Years' War,' *Economic History Review*, vol. xii (1942), p. 12). In other words, the *social* dominance locally of the 'new men' in the later fourteenth and fifteenth centuries, preceded their *political* dominance in the sixteenth century. Postan includes among the 'new men' (1) local men of the humblest origin, the 'kulaks' of the English countryside, 'who had been assembling land piece by piece for many years,' (2) 'reeves, manorial officials or other officers of noble households,' (3) 'merchants, clerks, or returned captains . . . the *nouveaux riches* of the war.'

literary, must be regarded as the reflection of more
fundamental changes in the effective social incentives. It
remains to define, in the most summary terms, what
those changes were.

In terms of social trends the change from the Lawyers'
Feudalism of the thirteenth century to the Yeoman
Democracy of the fifteenth century, which was accel-
erated by the Black Death and the resulting shortage of
manpower, was one from centralization to local autonomy
and from a hierarchical class-division to egalitarianism.[1]
The new motive force was still custom, but a native
custom, the democratic tradition of the Saxon agricultural communities on which a Continental feudalism
had been superimposed.

The sixteenth-century incentives have already been
discussed, but the urban origins of its mystical individualism deserve emphasis. The contrast between the get-
rich-slow economics of the Golden Age of the English
Peasantry (Thorold Rogers's term for the fifteenth
century) and the get-rich-quick mentality of Henry
VIII's courtiers, who were largely recruited from the
ranks of the earlier city merchants,[2] is the key to the two

[1] The economic recession of the fifteenth century—see M. M. Postan,
Economic History Review, vol. ix (1939), pp. 160–7—acted as an unseen Robin
Hood, making the rich poorer and the poor richer. Its effects were most
noticeable in the country, but egalitarian tendencies were also to be felt in the
towns. 'The view of medieval town-economy as one of restriction and
egalitarian monopoly, held and propagated by nineteenth-century historians,
largely derives from the municipal and guild documents of the late fourteenth
and fifteenth centuries; and what is sometimes regarded as evidence of a
typical medieval regulation is in fact nothing else than instances of fifteenth-
century departure from the freer and more speculative conditions of the earlier
centuries' (*ibid.*).

[2] Although the lesser Tudor gentry were mainly the sons and grandsons of the
fifteenth-century yeomen, the new aristocracy was almost completely non-
agricultural. According to J. H. Round, the Spencers of Althorp were the
only noble family that 'owed their riches and their rise neither to the favour of
a court nor to the spoils of monasteries, nor to a fortune made in trade, but to
successful farming' (*Studies in Peerage and Family History* (1901), p. 281).

periods, with inflation exerting an influence similar to that of the Black Death though in the opposite direction. (It encouraged the capitalist entrepreneur and depressed the peasantry and the craft-guilds.)

The eighteenth century represents a reversal of these trends with a decentralized régime, internal *laissez-faire*, and a dominant and prosperous countryside. Its prosperity apparently derived from the technological progress that was the fruit of a co-operative rationalism, which had displaced the mystical individualism of the Elizabethans. The system collapsed *economically* when the balance of wealth passed from the landed interests to the urban capitalists who had been the junior partners in the 1689 Settlement, and *morally* with the emergence of a half-starved overworked proletariat as a result of the rapid growth in the population.

In the nineteenth century the co-operative rationalism of the squirearchy, typified in the early membership of the Royal Society, ceases to be the dominant philosophy, and with the predatory capitalism of 'each for himself and the devil take the hindmost' there is a reversion to an urban mystical individualism. But this is a specialized individualism, suppressing important parts of the personality and over-encouraging others. The unpredictable rhythm of slumps and booms is paralleled by a pervasive irrationality in the ruling 'upper middle class' (who had retained the landed aristocracy as their political executives, but kept all the essential power in their own hands).

To-day the ruling specialists, thrown up from all classes but increasingly from the working class, are primarily rationalists. Their incentive to promotion is to an exceptional degree the *intellectual* interest of the higher posts. The success of our civilization will probably depend as much as anything on the degree to which the technicians and the Civil Service can be humanized. The condition of modern poetry, uncertain in tone and somewhat irresponsible but intelligent and emotionally mature, is not unreassuring.

If we exclude the Anglo-French school of poetry and the Lawyers Feudalism with which it runs parallel—on neither of which am I competent to express any opinion—the dominant incentives of the remaining social orders, in which the *contents* of the consecutive schools of poetry tend to centre, can be summarized, in the baldest terms, as follows:

1. Local Democracy of the Yeomanry: traditional egalitarianism based on country life. (School of Chaucer.)

2. Centralized Absolutism of the Prince's Servants: mystical individualism of complete personality based on London. (Renaissance School.)

3. Oligarchy of Landed Interests: co-operative rationalism (non-specialized) based on country life but revolving round London. (Augustan School.)

4. Plutocracy of Business: mystical individualism (specialized) based on manufacturing towns. (Romantic School.)

5. Managerial State: co-operative rationalism (specialized) without local basis. (Modern School.)

The summary, over-simplified though it necessarily is, has the merit of bringing out some of the long-term rhythms of English social life, notably the ways in which an individualist cycle follows one in which the emphasis had been on the claims of society, and an urban cycle follows one based on country life. The sequence of rural collectivism and urban individualism may perhaps explain the affinities between Chaucer and Dryden (which Dryden himself recognized) and between Shakespeare and Keats (on which Middleton Murry has expatiated), and more generally between (i) the Renaissance and the nineteenth century, and (ii) the later seventeenth century and our own day.

III

In the definition of poetry in Chapter Two four stages were distinguished in the process of reading a poem: (i) the translation of the printed letters into words, (ii) the combination of the words into phrases and short sentences (units of meaning), (iii) the synthesis of conflicting or contrasted phrases (the creation of the poetic unit), and (iv) the further synthesis of the separate poetic statements into the complex unity that represents the total meaning of the poem. It was then suggested that the modern reader who aspires to understand a poem of the past will need to know a good deal about the intellectual habits of its original readers at each of these stages. So far this chapter and its predecessor have been mainly concerned with the fourth and final stage of the process. But the second and third stages are also important. Unless we know not only the precise meaning the words bore to their original readers but also the kind of associations they attached to them we are in constant danger of going slightly wrong and assigning a meaning to the poem that it never had. I have discussed this problem at length in an earlier essay[1] and shall say no more about it here, confining myself to the third stage—that of poetic sentence-patterns or the 'figures of speech.'

The form of poetic statement that is most characteristic of English poetry of the Renaissance is undoubtedly the metaphor. C. S. Lewis has said that 'a riot of images tumbling over one another to greet every single idea was

[1] *English Poetry and the English Language* (1934).

for the Elizabethans the essential faculty of the poet.'[1]
M. Praz has described the seventeenth century as 'that
century in which the tendency to images reached its
climax.'[2] And other testimonies to the same effect could
no doubt be assembled. But why was the Renaissance
the metaphoric period *par excellence*? C. S. Lewis has
suggested that the origins of the habit 'lie in Medieval
Latin literature of the rhetorical type,'[3] but there is no
need to look as far afield as this. The suggestion, indeed,
is typical of the straits into which the purely literary
critic is driven when faced with the problem of poetic
change. Elizabethan imagery is not confined to the poets;
it is found everywhere—in business letters and in Acts of
Parliament, in sermons and in school books. Its sources
lie, I believe, in the mystical individualism that I have
suggested characterizes Renaissance society. John Hoskins,
writing about 1599, has a definition of metaphor which is
also a characteristic example of the metaphoric outlook:

> A METAPHOR, or TRANSLATION, is the friendly and neigh-
> bourly borrowing of one word to express a thing with more
> light and better note. . . . The rule of a metaphor is that it
> be not too bold nor too far-fetched. And though all
> metaphors go beyond the signification of things, yet are
> they requisite to match the compassing sweetness of men's
> minds, that are not content to fix themselves upon one
> thing but they must wander into the confines; like the eye,
> that cannot choose but view the whole knot when it
> beholds but one flower in a garden of purpose; or like an
> archer that, knowing his bow will overcast or carry too
> short, takes an aim on this side or beyond his mark.[4]

[1] *Rehabilitations and Other Essays* (1939), p. 170.
[2] *Studies in Seventeenth Century Imagery* (1939), p. 12.
[3] *Rehabilitations and Other Essays* (1939), p. 180.
[4] *Directions for Speech and Style*, ed. H. H. Hudson (1935), p. 8. There is a
useful discussion of this passage in Rosemond Tuve's *Elizabethan and Meta-*

Hoskins's similes bring vividly before us the greedy eye of the Renaissance Englishman, to whom all sensual experience was equally welcome, and the adventurous hit-or-miss philosophy of his practical life. In the unpredictable universe *anything* might turn out to be the image or double of anything else. The metaphors are the complement of the mysticism.

A metaphor is a synthetic statement (two heterogeneous meanings fused into a new complex unity), and is therefore, according to our definition, a miniature poem. To some critics, indeed, metaphor is the basis of *all* poetry. But this is to go too far. The metaphor is not the only basic synthetic statement, just as Renaissance poetry is not the only kind of poetry. The other English poetic schools have their own basic forms of synthetic statement, their favourite 'figures of speech,' which are the reflection of their own social orders, and the reader who aspires to understand the whole range of English poetry will need to familiarize himself with all of them.

If the original metaphor, the brand-new coinage of the individual poet, is the basis of Renaissance poetry, the popular simile or proverbial comparison would seem to underlie the poetry of the Yeoman Democracy of the later fourteenth and the fifteenth centuries. Langland is always saying that something is not worth a rush, a mite, a pea, a grain or even, once, a pie-crust. And Chaucer adds to this list *inter alia* a straw, a leak, a fly, a gnat, a butterfly, a haw, a bean, a toad, a hen and an old shoe. Similar catalogues could be constructed of the similes of quantity, colour, temperature, noise, ignorance, beauty, etc.

physical Imagery (1947), p. 124. Miss Tuve's book is much the most detailed and intelligent discussion of Renaissance imagery that I know, though the native English trends opposed to Continental poetic theory are unduly minimized. And the influence of the social background is not discussed at all.

Such comparisons, which normally derive from popular usage and are never the copyright of the individual poet, add enormously to the vividness and liveliness of the poems not only of Chaucer and Langland but also of Gower, the miracle plays (especially the Towneley series), 'Sir Gawayne and the Grene Knight,' the best ballads and carols, Skelton's doggerel of genius, and indeed all the genuine poetry of the period. The content of these similes is in sharp contrast with that of the metaphors of the Renaissance. For the latter, as Johnson said, the whole of nature and art were ransacked. On the whole, at any rate in the Polished Craftsman and Decadent phases of the school, the more fantastic and far-fetched their metaphors the better the Renaissance poet and his readers were pleased. Chaucer's similes, on the other hand, apart from a diminishing number derived from the French tradition of the *Roman de la Rose*, are familiar and parochial, smelling of the village green and the village ale-house rather than of the arts of poetry and the bestiaries. And some of his most characteristic effects are obtained by going one better than the popular idiom. The Monk, for example, is described in the General Prologue as regarding monastic asceticism as out of date:

> He yaf nat of that text a pulled hen,
> That seith that hunters ben nat hooly men,
> Ne that a monk, whan he is recchelees,[1]
> Is likned til a fissh that is waterlees,—
> This is to seyn, a monk out of his cloystre.
> But thilke text heeld he nat worth an oystre.

In this passage the similes of the plucked hen and the fish out of water are, of course, popular idioms, but the

[1] 'Neglectful of duty and discipline' (Robinson).

grotesque oyster is Chaucer's own importation.[1] And how *right* it is!

The Augustans make little use of metaphor. One of the difficulties, indeed, that stand in the way of our appreciation of Dryden and Pope is their frequent insensitiveness to the metaphors latent in popular speech. The following passage from the 'Elegy to the Memory of an Unfortunate Lady' is spoiled for me by the mixed metaphors, though Pope and his contemporary readers probably never noticed anything wrong:

> Ambition first sprung from your blest abodes;
> The glorious fault of Angels and of Gods:
> Thence to their Images on earth it flows,
> And in the breasts of Kings and Heroes glows!

Here 'sprung' and 'flows' suggest that ambition is being compared to a stream, but it is difficult to visualize this stream flowing through the air into the images and impossible to understand why it 'glows' when it gets there. The metaphoric confusion embarrasses the modern reader. To Pope, however, it is clear that the verbs were almost abstract and had lost most of their sensuous associations. The whole trend indeed of Augustan diction was to 'the Mathematical plainness' that the Royal Society tried to exact from its members, and neither metaphor nor simile is the basic synthetic statement of its poetry. Their place is taken by *paradox*, the simultaneous advancement of two contradictory propositions both of which turn out to be true, *irony*, the apparent contradiction between what is said and what is meant, *oxymoron*, 'the rhetorical term for the combination of words, generally epithet and subject, of opposed and contradictory meanings,'[2] and similar devices.

[1] He had found the rhyme in Jean de Meun's *Testament*.
[2] P. Vivian, *A Dictionary of Literary Terms*.

In pious times, e'r Priest-craft did begin,
Before *Polygamy* was made a Sin . . .

Meerly for Safety after Fame they thirst;
For all Men would be cowards if they durst . . .

Or plung'd in Lakes of bitter *Washes* lie,
Or wedg'd whole Ages in a *Bodkin's* Eye . . .

How vain the ardour of the Crowd,
How low, how little are the Proud,
How indigent the Great!

It is in such passages as these that the sceptical rationalism
of the Augustans achieves memorability. The quality
that they valued most in poetry was Surprise. In spite of
the tameness of his own verse Addison was fully aware
of the importance of a semantic gap between the two
elements in a synthesis. In the essay on true, false and
'mixed' wit in *The Spectator*[1] he adopts Locke's definition
('the Assemblage of Ideas') with the qualification 'That
every Resemblance of Ideas is not that which we call Wit,
unless it be such an one that gives *Delight* and *Surprise* to
the Reader: These two Properties seem essential to Wit,
more particularly the last of them. In order therefore
that the Resemblance in the Ideas be Wit, it is necessary
that the Ideas should not lie too near one another in the
Nature of things; for where the Likeness is obvious, it
gives no Surprise.' And Johnson's definition of the
Sublime ('the first effect is sudden astonishment, and the
second rational admiration'[2]) in effect limits sublimity to
the paradox. The Romantic Sublime—of which Burke
was the first prophet[3]—was provocative, on the contrary,
of *irrational* admiration.

[1] *The Spectator* (11 May 1711).   [2] Life of Cowley.
[3] *A Philosophical Inquiry into the Origin of our Ideas of the Sublime and Beautiful*
(1756).

With the mystical individualism of nineteenth-century plutocracy the metaphor comes back as the basic poetic form of statement in the form of symbolism:

> There are no lines with more melancholy beauty than these by Burns:
>
>> The white moon is setting behind the white wave,
>> And Time is setting with me, O!
>
> and these lines are perfectly symbolical. Take from them the whiteness of the moon and of the wave, whose relation to the setting of Time is too subtle for the intellect, and you take from them their beauty. But, when all are together, moon and wave and whiteness and setting Time and the last melancholy cry, they evoke an emotion which cannot be evoked by any other arrangement of colours and sounds and forms. We may call this metaphorical writing, but it is better to call it symbolical writing, because metaphors are not profound enough to be moving, when they are not symbols, and when they are symbols they are the most perfect of all, because the most subtle, outside of pure sound, and through them one can the best find out what symbols are.[1]

The Romantic symbol differs from the Renaissance metaphor in two important respects: (i) its function is not to compare one thing with another, but to provide the objective correlatives to subjective experience; (ii) unlike a metaphor it can be used more than once by the same poet though, unlike the popular similes of the Chaucerians, it is not generally transferable from one poet to

[1] W. B. Yeats, 'The Symbolism of Poetry' (*Essays* (1924), pp. 191–2). The lines from Burns are misquoted. What Burns wrote ('Open the Door to me, oh') was:

> The wan moon is setting ayont the white wave,
> And time is setting with me, oh!

another. Wordsworth's 'rocks, and stones, and trees' are peculiar to Wordsworth. Coleridge's symbolic effects of light are peculiar to him. And Blake's symbolism is so much his own that a key is needed to it as much as to his mythology.

The typical symbols of the Romantics are from wild nature. Of the forty-three animals introduced or alluded to in *Prometheus Unbound* only four are domestic (horse, dog, sheep, goat). There are no cattle, pigs, cats, rats, mice, or poultry of any description in the poem. The 'infinitude of truth' that Wordsworth demanded in poetry[1] preferred the untethered and far-ranging species as its symbols. Birds were particularly suitable. Romantic poetry without its skylarks, nightingales, cuckoos and albatrosses would be unthinkable.[2] And water in its various forms—brooks, rivers, seas, mists, clouds and sunsets—had similar attractions. The operative condition was the absence of human association. The ex-page of Rydal Mount told Canon Rawnsley that Wordsworth hadn't been interested in agriculture: 'farming, nor beast, nor sheep, nor fields wasn't in his way, he asked no questions about flocks or herds.' On the other hand, 'He was a man as noticed a deal stones and trees, very particular about trees, or a rock wi' ony character in it.'[3] Fundamentally it is a townsman's interest in the country. The country for the Romantics is not a place where men and women wrest a difficult and precarious living from the soil. It is primarily simply a place to escape to out of the towns. To one who has been long in city pent— Keats adopted the Miltonic line to open an early sonnet

[1] 'Celebrated Epitaphs Considered.'
[2] 'In a note on *Calvary* he [Yeats] explains that certain birds, "especially such lonely birds as the heron, hawk, eagle, and swan, are the natural symbols of subjectivity"' (Louis MacNeice, *The Poetry of W. B. Yeats* (1941), p. 147).
[3] *Trans. Wordsworth Soc.* No. 6 (1882), pp. 189, 191.

describing a day in the country[1]—the attraction of the country is its unlikeness to the town. The emphasis is on its wildness, its solitariness, its freedom from human contamination. The inferiority of the man-made town to the God-made country parallels the inferiority of conscious mind, the product of the social environment, to uninhibited instinct.

If the nature-symbol, the synthetic link between the conscious and the subconscious mind, is the basic unit of Romantic poetry, what is it that takes its place in post-Romantic poetry? It is perhaps too soon to be sure, but I am inclined to think that modern poetry also bases itself upon the symbol, though our symbolism is not restricted to wild nature and makes no pretension to the mystical significances of Romanticism. As compared with Shelley's Cloud Eliot's Waste Land gives an impression of calculated exploitation. The cloud exists for Shelley in its own right, and he is merely the recorder of its exuberances. Eliot's Hanged Man, Tereus, Tiresias, Phlebas the Phœnician and the Fisher King have a far less substantial existence. Their value to him is as shorthand transcriptions of certain facets of human experience. Essentially they are simply *extensions of his vocabulary*, with no more independent reality than the quotations from Shakespeare, Marvell, Dante, etc., which appear side by side with them. Our situation in fact is the obverse of the Renaissance predicament. Then every myth had potential poetic significance because they were all equally credible. In the unpredictable universe one religion was as likely to be true as another. To-day every variety of religious experience is potentially significant not because

---

[1] The features of the rustic scene itemized by Keats in this sonnet sufficiently indicate the limitations of his interest in the country. They are the blue sky, the grass, a nightingale and the sunset clouds!

it is considered objectively true now but because it has once been thought true. It is a scrap more *evidence* how the human mind works. 'All a poet can do to-day,' Owen wrote in the fragmentary Preface that has become the testament of modern poetry, 'is warn. That is why the true Poets must be truthful.' The warnings must have a *factual* basis. They are necessary because of the human proneness to illusion that Romanticism had encouraged with disastrous social consequences. The crucial poetic influence of anthropology and psycho-analysis to-day derives from their assumptions rather than their conclusions, and particularly from their central assumption that the subconscious mind, racial and indivi-dual, is capable of rational study. Modern poetry might be described as a rationalization of Romanticism. The exploits of the subliminal self, which could do no wrong in Romantic eyes, are viewed by us in the sardonic light of a socially conscious science. Our symbols are often identical with theirs, but the synthesis is not between the subconscious mind and the non-human physical world but between the two parts of the mind, the conscious-ness and the subconsciousness. We are struggling towards the recovery of an integrated personality. Modern poetry is the record of that struggle; its warnings are of the dangers of a relapse.

.   .   .   .   .

The preceding discussion has inevitably been dogmatic and over-simplified. To attempt one-page summaries of England's literary and social evolution is to invite dissent on one count or another. They are presented as at any rate better than nothing. Here is a wood without trees. If the map of the wood is a bit crude, as I am afraid it is, part of the responsibility for its inadequacy must lie with those catalogues of trees without a wood in which my colleagues in the world of scholarship have specialized. The subject demands a *combination* of induction and deduction. The specialist investigations must build up into conclusions of general applicability and the wide-ranging generalizations must break down into a technique for dealing with concrete particulars. Until they do, however, there is a clear case for the amateur's home-made makeshift.

So far this book has been an attempt to work out a number of critical formulas. In the earlier chapters it was possible to illustrate such a formula as the Principle of the Semantic Gap by an analysis of familiar poems or passages of English poetry. But the formulas proposed in this chapter have not lent themselves to incidental illustration in the same way. Part Two of the book is intended to remedy this deficiency. Some examples will be found there of the way in which a poetic school can be divided into five phases or generations, but the formula that the discussion of most of the poems revolves round is the suggested identification of the successive poetic schools with the changes in dominant social incentives in this country since the fourteenth century.

Part Two

APPLICATIONS OF THE DEFINITION

CHAPTER FIVE

THE YEOMAN DEMOCRACY AND CHAUCER'S 'MILLER'S TALE'

It was only in 1340, until recently the accepted date of Chaucer's birth,[1] that Presentment of Englishry ceased to be law. The repeal of this piece of racial discrimination relieved the hundred or township, in a case of suspected murder, of the *onus* of proving that the victim was an Englishman, in order to escape the heavy communal fine levied for the murder of a Norman. But, though the conquerors and the conquered had at last merged into one nation, it was not yet certain what language this new England would speak. The upper classes still spoke French. Higden, whose *Polychronicon* dates from this period, noted that the gentleman's child spoke French 'in the cradle,' and that the snobbery of the yeomanry was making them learn French too. French was the language of the Court, of Parliament, and of the various law courts. And in the grammar schools Latin was invariably taught in French and not in English.

But the predominance of French was not to last. In 1356 it became illegal to plead cases in the London Sheriff's Courts in any language except English. In 1362 English superseded French as the spoken language of the King's law courts. In 1363 the Chancellor opened Parliament in an English speech, and, though Edward III may not have known much English, Henry IV claimed

---

[1] The date now favoured by the experts is *c.* 1343-4.

the throne before Parliament 'in Englyssh tonge.'[1]
Trevisa, Higden's translator, writing in 1385, reported
that by then the use of French had been entirely given up
in the grammar schools, and that 'gentil men habbeth
now moche yleft for to teche here childern Frensch.'
And William Nassyngton was able to claim about 1375,

> lerid and lewid, old and young
> *All* understanden English tongue.

Trevisa considered that the dividing line was the 'furste
moreyn,' i.e. the Black Death of 1348-9. It is probable
enough *a priori* that the acceleration of economic processes brought about by the Black Death[2] would be
accompanied by equivalent social changes. But the
rapidity and extent of the linguistic revolution has not
been appreciated. It all happened in thirty years. It is as
though since 1920 Cockney had suddenly displaced the
King's English as the Received Standard, and we were
now all trying to talk and write like the East End. The
social implications of such a change can be imagined. In
the fourteenth century the victory of English meant a
discrediting of the whole of Norman-French culture—
among other things, of feudalism, of the international
church, of courtly love and of poetic rhetoric—and a
partial return to the older, simpler culture based essentially
on the co-operative open-fields agriculture. A new *class*
was suddenly taking the social initiative. (The Peasants'
Revolt of 1381 has been described by a modern economist

[1] See G. G. Coulton, *Chaucer and his England* (4th ed., 1927), pp. 3-4.
[2] 'If there had been no pestilence on the scale of the Black Death, the disinte-
gration of the manor as the result of the working of purely natural forces—
the gradual permeation of a money economy; the demand of the lord for a
more flexible instrument than the inelastic and cumbrous labour dues; the
accumulation of capital in the hands of the servile tenants; the growth of
urban markets—must assuredly have been an infinitely slower process'
(E. Lipson, *The Economic History of England*, vol. i (8th ed., 1945), p. 102).

as 'the first great struggle between capital and labour; and the first notable occasion on which the latent feeling of class antagonism was openly manifested.'[1]) Inevitably a new literature came into being as the point of maximum consciousness of this new social order, the 'yeoman minstrelsy,' as Sir Edmund Chambers has called it, of the the Robin Hood ballads, the group of narrative poems on the King and Subject theme and similar writings,[2] to which the miracle plays and most of the writings in the alliterative metre can perhaps be added.

Nobody has noticed how interested Chaucer was in this contemporary class-struggle. As a boy he had served as a page in the household of Prince Lionel and his earliest poems are redolent of the French culture of the court. But as he approached middle age his poetry becomes noticeably more English and more popular. The gradual change of allegiance can be measured by the decrease in the proportion of rhetorical figures in his poetry and the increase in the number of proverbs and popular idioms.[3] By the 1390's, when he was writing the *Canterbury Tales*, though he is never a partisan, his fundamental sympathies seem to be mainly with the new yeoman democracy of the countryside. It is noteworthy that the only mystical figures in the General Prologue are the Ploughman—who is presumably related to Langland's Piers Plowman—and his brother the Country Parson. But Chaucer is less comfortable with these symbols of the *ideals* of the yeomanry than with such concrete exemplars of the class as the Franklin and the Wife of Bath, and their humbler allies the Miller and the Reeve.

[1] Lipson, *op. cit.*, p. 121.
[2] A good specimen is *Gamelyn* (c. 1350) which there is reason to believe Chaucer had intended to retell as a tale for the Squire's Yeoman.
[3] See J. M. Manly, *Chaucer and the Rhetoricians*, British Academy (1926), and B. J. Whiting, *Chaucer's Use of Proverbs* (Harvard, 1934).

By their side the embodiments of 'gentilesse'—the Knight, the Squire, the Clerk and the Prioress—seem unreal and ineffective, while *their* poor relations the 'gentil Maunciple' and the 'gentil Pardoner' are as unedifying as they are secretly unhappy.

The 'Miller's Tale' is almost the best thing Chaucer ever wrote, but except for a passage in Aldous Huxley's brilliant but neglected essay[1] it has received little critical attention. And its heroine Alison, who is described as fit 'for any good yeman to wedde,' can be regarded as the embodiment of the yeoman's philosophy of life, much as Shakespeare's Cleopatra embodies the Renaissance idea, Millamant the Restoration's, and Becky Sharp the nineteenth century's. The Tale follows the 'Knight's Tale' and the comic competition of Nicholas and Absolon for the carpenter's wife is obviously intended to provide a worldly contrast to the tragic rivalry of 'gentil' Palamon and Arcite, 'of chivalrie the flowr,' for the angelic Emelye ('as an aungel hevenysshly she soong'). This social contrast is underlined in the preliminary 'wordes bitwene the Hoost and the Millere,' from which we learn that, when all the pilgrims had pronounced the 'Knight's Tale' 'a noble storie,'

> And namely the gentil everichon,

the Host, who has invited the Monk, another 'gentil,' to contribute a tale, is interrupted by the drunken Miller, who announces

> I have a noble tale for the nones,
> With which I wol now quite the Knyghtes tale.

The Miller, in other words, is going to give *his* (English) idea of nobility.

[1] *On the Margin* (1923), pp. 203–29. A somewhat fuller discussion will be found in E. M. W. Tillyard's *Poetry: Direct and Oblique* (1934).

Characteristically Chaucer carefully dissociates himself in advance from this 'cherles tale.' He assures 'every gentil wight' that he is a mere reporter who has to record all that occurred on the pilgrimage, and recommends the prudish to turn over the page to another tale, where he will find plenty

> Of storial thyng that toucheth gentillesse,
> And eek moralitee and hoolynesse . . .

With this gesture to respectability—which can hardly have been meant very seriously[1]—Chaucer proceeds to his merry tale.

One's first impression is of an earthy physical solidity. This bedroom farce is firmly anchored to the real world. The contrast with the rarefied sentimentality of the 'Knight's Tale' is immediately enforced by the repetition of a line that Arcite had just used in his dying speech, as he moralized on the transitoriness of a man's life, now the happy lover, now in the cold grave,

> Allone, withouten any compaignye.

In the 'Miller's Tale' the line is applied to Nicholas, the Oxford post-graduate student, sitting in his 'digs' and planning the seduction of his landlady! There are no emotional overtones in yeoman minstrelsy and there is no vagueness. We know exactly what the parish clerk, Absolon, looked like, *and* Nicholas, *and* the carpenter and his wife, and what clothes they wore. We know their respective ages and their social status. The carpenter owed his downfall to his social presumption:

[1] The curious figure that Chaucer cuts in his own poems presents a nice critical problem. In the *Canterbury Tales* it is pretty clear that we must not take him too seriously. His apology at the conclusion of the General Prologue for not having introduced the Pilgrims in their order of social precedence is,

> My wit is short, ye may wel understande!

Men sholde wedden after hire estaat.

But, because he had money, old John, the simple carpenter of Oseney Abbey, had succeeded in making the young and beautiful Alison his wife. In doing this he had offended not only against the law of 'kind' (nature), which requires the young to marry the young, but also against the social values of the marriage-market. In getting Alison to marry him he had been guilty of matrimonial sharp practice, because her beauty and vitality ought to have earned her a mate higher up the social scale:

> She was a prymerole, a piggesnye,
> For any lord to leggen in his bedde.
> Or yet for any good yeman to wedde.

Alison's *proper* place in the social hierarchy would have been to be either a lord's mistress or a yeoman's wife. The carpenter, therefore, receives no sympathy at the end of the Tale when he breaks his arm and is made at once a cuckold and the laughing-stock of Oxford. Consistently with this his wife, who has been unfaithful to him and has also connived in the practical joke against him, escapes scot-free. It is significant that of the four protagonists she is the only one who emerges from the episode unscathed and without a stain on her character. Alison is a feminine type that recurs in Chaucer. She is related both to Criseyde and to May in the 'Merchant's Tale,' and it is not impossible that she might grow up to be a Wife of Bath. Compared to the talkative males, it is true, she has little to say. Her longest speech only runs to six lines and she is usually content with a few emphatic remarks—though the last word is generally hers. But Alison is a good deal more than a young woman who knows what she wants. The long description that introduces her to the reader might be compared to Enobarbus's picture of Cleopatra on the Cydnus. Here is a whole culture, a way of life, concentrated in a single representative figure. The passage is worth examining in detail.

Although she lives in Oxford Alison is a village girl ('of towne'[1]) and her looks and costume are described in a series of the similes from country life that were characteristic both of yeoman poetry and of the proverbs of the time. The portrait begins as a study in black and white. Under the white cap Alison's eyebrows are as black as a sloe, and her white smock is embroidered with coal-black silk. Her apron is as white as morning milk. And a lovely simile clinches the contrasting colours:

> She was ful more blisful on to see
> Than is the newe pere-jonette tree.

(The pear flowers before the leaves show, and the effect in spring, when the tree is 'newe,' is of white blossoms against black boughs.) But the description is not only a symphony in colours. Alison is also as slim as a weasel, as soft as wool, and the gayest creature in the world. She sings too like a swallow sitting on the barn, and is as gamesome as a kid or a calf. Her breath is as sweet as mead, or as apples stored in hay or heather. And she is as skittish as a colt. Altogether there are seventeen similes in the thirty-four lines, most of them from the animal or vegetable kingdom. The *animals* are all domestic and reassuring—except one. The description begins,

> Fair was the yonge wyf, and therwithal
> As any wezele hir body gent and smal.

[1] This interpretation is confirmed by the marginal note in some MSS.: 'Unde Ovidius: Ictibus agrestis.' Chaucer's source, *not* Ovid, has not yet been identified.

This simile of the weasel follows a couplet in which we were told that the carpenter, by marrying a young wife, had 'fallen in the snare.' Alison is the weasel, the carpenter apparently is the rabbit! The implication provides an ironical comment on the passage a few lines before:

> Jalous he was, and heeld hire narwe in cage,
> For she was wylde and young and he was old,
> And demed hymself been lik a cokewold.

How right the carpenter was! In the end it is not the young wife but he that is in the cage. And Alison retains a suggestion of something wild, aloof and slightly sinister, a hint of a fertility spirit, through the rough and tumble of the tale.

In Alison Chaucer's synthetic genius has succeeded in fusing two contradictory elements, the human and the animal. The breath of a nature red in tooth and claw blows through her, but on the whole she is the attentive wife, the compassionate lover and the ingenious practical joker. And this dual nature is communicated to the reader by the piling up of similes from the world of domestic animals (who are related both to wild nature and to man). When Nicholas seemed to be attempting to rape her,

> She sproong as a colt dooth in the trave,
> And with hir heed she wryed faste away,
> And seyde, 'I wol nat kisse thee, by my fey!'

Like this young colt Alison was full of spirit, but she was potentially tameable, as Nicholas soon found. She symbolizes in her gaiety and good nature the Merry England of a yeoman democracy that had set its face against the theoretical asceticism of the Continental church, on the one hand, and the practical brutality of Continental feudalism, on the other. Its ideals were not particularly high but they were *attainable*, and the evidence of court rolls, field orders and guild records is that, in spite of the Wars of the Roses and the French wars, they were in fact attained more often in the fifteenth century than in other and more splendid periods.

CHAPTER SIX

SIR THOMAS WYATT AND THE RENAISSANCE

To the lower classes of the sixteenth century, looking back into the past, the England of the fifteenth century seemed above all a 'merry world.'[1] Shakespeare's John Holland who complains in *Henry VI*, Part 2, that it 'was never merrie worlde in England, since Gentlemen came up' is using the identical phrase and argument that some Oxfordshire anti-enclosure rioters were actually to employ in 1596.[2] The new ruling class of 'Gentlemen' were predominantly the sons and grandsons of the city merchants of the fifteenth century, and the capitalist agriculture that they forced on the countryside meant the end of the old rural democracy and its yeoman minstrelsy. Instead of the simple, almost anonymous 'merry tales,' with their frank animalism, poetry passes into the keeping of Renaissance courtiers, learned and passionate, who

> poor Petrarch's long-deceasèd woes
> With new-born sighs and denizen'd wit do sing.

Sir Thomas Wyatt, courtier and diplomatist and the grandson (through his mother) of a fifteenth-century

---

[1] Although the primary sense of *merry* in this phrase, as in 'merry England,' was *pleasant*, it seems clear that two other contemporary senses of the word are also implied, viz. *fine* (of climate) and *joyous* (as in modern English).

[2] The ringleaders promised 'a merry world shortly . . . and asked if there were not 100 good men who would rise and knock down the gentlemen and rich men who made corn so dear and who took the commons' (Cal. State Papers Dom. Eliz. (1595–7), p. 316). The phrase recurs again and again in the pamphlets and broadside ballads.

nouveau riche, was the originator of this new poetry. So successful was he that his friend Surrey believed that Wyatt had actually 'reft Chaucer the glory of his wit.' And Leland, the antiquary, was certainly justified in claiming, in his fluent Latin elegy, that Wyatt had initiated a whole school of court poets:

> Nobilitas dedicit te praeceptore Britanna
> Carmina per varios scribere posse modos.

The courtiers Wyatt, Surrey, Sidney, Ralegh, Donne, Carew and Suckling represent the central line in English Renaissance poetry—from which even Spenser, Marlowe and Milton are only magnificent offshoots—and its social basis deserves a more detailed examination than it has hitherto obtained. Here it will only be possible to make a few of the principal points.

The following sonnet appears to be one of the earliest of Wyatt's poems:

> Whoso list to hunt, I know where is an hind,
>> But as for me—helas, I may no more,
>> The vain travail hath wearied me so sore,
>> I am of them that farthest cometh behind.
> Yet may I, by no means, my wearied mind
>> Draw from the deer; but as she fleeth afore
>> Fainting I follow. I leave off therefore,
>> Since in a net I seek to hold the wind.
> Who list her hunt, I put him out of doubt,
>> As well as I, may spend his time in vain.
>> And graven with diamonds in letters plain
> There is written, her fair neck round about:
>> *Noli me tangere*, for Caesar's I am,
>> And wild for to hold, though I seem tame.

Wyatt's hind is Anne Boleyn, who was almost certainly his mistress before she was appropriated by Henry VIII.

It is true J. M. Berdan[1] and others have argued that the poem cannot be autobiographical, as it is based on a sonnet of Petrarch's. But a comparison of the two poems shows that Wyatt has merely *adapted* Petrarch—as he also adapted Petrarch's rhyme-scheme—for his own purposes.[2] Petrarch does not *hunt* his beautiful white deer, and the deer is not Cæsar's *property* but has been liberated by him. In Wyatt the hunting metaphor is the key to the poem. It is precisely Anne's elusiveness that is so aggravating. Wyatt's egotism—he refers to himself ('I,' 'me' or 'my') no less than twelve times, whereas Petrarch has only four similar references—had been deeply wounded, and is only partly assuaged by the arrogant casualness of the 'and' in line 11 ('I advise you not to waste your time on this elusive creature—and *incidentally* she is the King's property'), and by the hint to Henry in the last line that even he might have trouble with Anne (as, indeed, he did). The poem is intensely personal and yet attains a certain cool objectivity—largely, I think, by the help of the hunting metaphors.

A related poem is the famous 'They flee from me, that sometime did me seek':

[1] *Early Tudor Poetry* (1920), p. 483.

[2] Una candida cerva sopra l'erba
           Verde m'apparve, con due corne d'oro,
           Fra due rivere, all' ombra d'un alloro.
           Levando'l sole, a la stazione acerba.
      Era sua vista si dolce superba,
           Ch'io lasciai per seguirla ogni lavoro;
           Come l'avaro che'n cercar tesoro
           Con diletto l'affanno disacerba.
   'Nessun mi tocchi,' al bel collo dintorno
           Scritto avea di diamanti et di topazi;
           'Libera farmi al mio Cesare parve.'
      Et era'l sol gia volto el mezzogiorno;
           Gli occhi miei stanchi di mirar, non sazi
           Quand'io caddi l'acqua, et ella sparve.
                          (*In vita Laurae*, No. clvii.)

They flee from me, that sometime did me seek,
With naked foot stalking in my chamber:
I have seen them gentle, tame, and meek,
That now are wild and do not remember
That some time they put themself in danger
To take bread at my hand; and now they range
Busily seeking with a continual change.

Thankèd be Fortune, it hath been otherwise
Twenty times better; but once, in special,
In thin array, after a pleasant guise,
When her loose gown from her shoulders did fall,
And she me caught in her arms long and small,
Therewithal sweetly did me kiss,
And softly said, 'Dear heart, how like you this?'

It was no dream; I lay broad waking:
But all is turnèd thorough my gentleness
Into a strange fashion of forsaking;
And I have leave to go of her goodness;
And she also to use new-fangleness.
But since that I so kindèly am servèd,
How like you this, what hath she now deservèd?[1]

The editor of *Tottel's Miscellany* (1557), where Wyatt's
poem was first printed, prefixed an elaborate title to
it, 'The lover sheweth how he is forsaken of such as
he sometime enjoyed.' It is not by any means certain,
however, that Wyatt's poem is concerned with more
than one mistress. The 'they' and 'them' of the first
verse are at least partly metaphorical—deer perhaps, as
in the sonnet. The vagueness is clearly intentional, and
it throws the detailed picture of the second verse into

[1] In the last line, where Wyatt's autograph MS. has 'I would fain know
what she hath deserved,' I have followed Tottel's brilliant emendation (which
may derive from Wyatt himself).

greater relief. The third verse returns to the implications of the original metaphor. It appears that Wyatt and the lady are both of them alternately hunters and hunted. (i) When Wyatt was a potential source of *danger* the lady was *gentle* and *tame*, but with his new *gentleness* she has become *wild* and is *forsaking* him. (ii) Previously she had come *stalking* him and *caught* him, but now she has begun to *range*. And Wyatt's problem, since she is treating him *so kindly*, i.e. according to the law of kind, is what to do about it? In another poem he had written

> it is of kind
> That often change doth please a woman's mind.

His lady, he reflects, is only a wild thing after all, obeying her natural instinct to *continual change*; and to suggest that she may deserve a punishment is to invoke a moral law that would be beyond her comprehension. Wyatt is really more sorry for himself than irritated with this illogical inconsistent woman.

This analysis should have made it clear what a sophisticated poem 'They flee from me' is. A comparison of it, and the sonnet, with the 'Miller's Tale,' will bring out the essential difference between Chaucer's similes and Wyatt's metaphors. In Alison Chaucer effected a synthesis between his own humanism and the primitive nature-mysticism of the countryside. The world of man and the world of growing things, vegetable and animal, come to terms in agriculture—which is basically a *partnership* between the farmer and his fields and livestock. Alison, like the domestic animals and vegetables with which she is compared, is a link therefore between the two worlds. She represents a happy balance of the physical and the spiritual, neither denying her animal instincts nor dominated by them, a human being, affectionate and intelligent, but with no pretensions to being an angel like Emelye—or Dante's Beatrice and Petrarch's Laura. Like Criseyde she might have said,

> What, par dieux! I am not religious.

Nor did the yeoman democracy she typifies take kindly to the 'religious' (nuns, monks and friars). The one topic on which the yeoman minstrels—and their allies in Church and court, like Langland and Gower—are unanimous is the detestability of the medieval Church. It is usually said that only ecclesiastical corruption was attacked, and that is no doubt generally true. But the extraordinary vigour and venom of the satire suggest a profounder opposition. At bottom the yeoman democracy was still largely pagan, still maintaining the old fertility rituals with maypole and Whitsun ales, harvest and New Year festivals, moon-worship, sacred wells, and even in places the Saxon deities themselves. The Italian *pagani* had been the countrymen, and Christian asceticism, which was born in the towns of the Roman Empire, has always had an uphill fight in agricultural communities. It is significant that the Lollards made their converts in the small towns of East Anglia, the Chilterns and Somerset, and not in the villages. It is perhaps equally significant that when Chaucer tries to write like a 'religious'—in the Tale of Melibee, and the Tales of the Man of Law, the Second Nun and the Parson—he becomes a bore.

Wyatt and his mistresses belong to a different world. The synthesis that Wyatt achieves by his metaphors is between sexual love and the chase, and its implications are worth pursuing. Note first of all that the lover *qua* hunter is primarily a seducer. Love is a sport which reaches its consummation in the capture or killing of the lady. It

L

is natural, therefore, for the deer to fly from the hunter-lover, and their occasional tameness, the rare moments when they seek him out and take bread from his hand, is not traceable to anything he has done but is a kind of miracle, for which 'Fortune' is to be thanked. The seducer, therefore, is not a calculating seducer *à la* Stendhal. His successes and failures just *happen*, without his being able to understand why or to repeat them.[1]

Here we are in the unpredictable universe of the Renaissance with its typical central figure of the Fortune Hunter. The fortune might be economic (the 4,700 per cent interest that Drake paid the investors in the *Golden Hind*), or political (the Prince's favour—an even chancier 'risk'), or religious (the lotteries of 'grace' and predestination), or sexual. But the motives and attitudes are essentially the same. Opposed to the unpredictable universe is the mystical individualist, the Renaissance man who believed in himself and in his luck, not really on rational grounds (in spite of the propaganda for education and 'courtesy') but simply *because he was himself*. The fascination of the ego sounds through the whole of the poetry of the period from the sensualists like Marlowe to the mystics like George Herbert.

Note too that in this world each man kills the thing he loves. The chase ends in the *battue*. With the seduction completed the love-affair is over. The relationship between the mystical individualist and the unpredictable universe is one, not of co-operation (as in Alison and the yeoman democracy), but of hostility. Society is a chaos of competing individuals, each for himself, with the Devil (the God of Bad Luck) taking the hindmost. And

---

[1] The word *happy* acquires its modern sense in the sixteenth century. To the Renaissance *happiness*, the favour of fortune, was the supreme felicity. The earlier meaning of *happy* is taken over during the sixteenth century by *lucky*.

social order can only be imposed by force from above. The young Edward VI summed it all up in a schoolboy essay:

> This is the true ordering of the state of a well-fashioned commonwealth, that every part do obey one head, one governor, one law, and all parts of the body obey the head, agree among themselves, and one not to eat another up through greediness.[1]

Edward's metaphor was, of course, as much a commonplace as his argument. Indeed, as in the case of Wyatt's metaphor of the chase, the metaphor *is* the argument. Renaissance thinking is based on analogy rather than analysis, and the primary object of the analogy is not to convince but to startle or excite. The metaphors appeal to a pre-social, pre-logical level in the mind. As Eliot has put it, in a striking phrase, 'Their words [the words of Shakespeare, Donne, Webster, Tourneur, and sometimes Middleton] have a network of tentacular roots reaching down to the deepest terrors and desires.' The shimmer of the subconscious plays over the surface even of Wyatt's verse:

> It was no dream; I lay broad waking.

In the act of denying the dream he has made the poem more dreamlike. The mysterious vagueness of the setting and the actors—but a vagueness punctuated by brilliantly vivid details like 'naked foot,' 'bread at my hand,' and the whispered 'Dear heart, how like you this?'—takes the poem out of any social reality. The hunter-lover is not really going to shoot the hind-mistress. Anne Boleyn is safe. And so when a comparison is made between Wyatt's 'her arms long and small' and old January in

---

[1] *Literary Remains*, ed. J. G. Nichols (1857), vol. ii, p. 482.

Chaucer's 'Merchant's Tale,' licking his lips as he mentally undresses May ('Hir myddel smal, hire armes longe and sklendre'), it must be realized that the comparison is not *in pari materia*. Wyatt, it is true, finds it difficult to see the hind's point of view (only Shakespeare and Donne manage to do this), but he is not a vulgar sensualist like January so much as a man *imprisoned in the world of the senses*. His own phenomenal world is the only reality that he can recognize, and he lapses finally into a stoical subjectivism:

> Then seek no more out of thyself to find
> The thing that thou hast sought so long before,
> For thou shalt feel it sitting in thy mind.[1]

The 'thing' still sits in his brilliant, disturbing but unsatisfying poems, as it once sat in the minds of the subtle and brutal courtiers of Henry VIII.

[1] 'Of the mean and sure estate.'

CHAPTER SEVEN

THE MONEY-LENDER'S SON: 'L'ALLEGRO' AND 'IL PENSEROSO'

To understand Wyatt's poems it is only necessary to know something of the mental climate that they reflect. The man himself is so representative that his own career throws relatively little light on the poetry. The best commentary on it is not the gossip about Wyatt's relations with Anne Boleyn but a general history of the English Renaissance. Milton's case is different. Milton, like Spenser, is an offshoot from the central trunk of English Renaissance poetry. Sidney's disparagement of the Poetry of Art sums up the critical case against both of them:

> Undoubtedly (at least to my opinion undoubtedly) I have found in divers smal learned Courtiers, a more sound stile, than in some professors of learning, of which I can gesse no other cause, but that the Courtier following that which by practice he findeth fittest to nature, therein (though he know it not) doth according to art, though not by art: where the other using art to shew art and not hide art (as in these cases he shuld do) flieth from nature, indeed abuseth art.[1]

Unlike the professional poet, the courtier had the advantage of inheriting both a living tradition and an intimate audience. 'Skill of a Sonet' was a recognized

[1] *The Defence of Poesie*, ed. A. Feuillerat, *Works of Sidney*, vol. iii (1923), p. 43.

pathway at court not only to the mistress's favour but also to the Prince's, and the circulation of poems in MS. kept the courtier-poet in constant touch with a discriminating and stimulating poetry-reading public. A momentary glimpse of that public at the end of the sixteenth century is provided by John Hoskins, a good minor court poet:

> It is true that we study according to the predominancy of courtly inclinations: whilst mathematics were in requests, all our similitudes came from lines, circles, and angles; whilst moral philosophy is now a while spoken of, it is rudeness not to be sententious. And for my part I'll make one. I have used and outworn six several styles since I was first Fellow of New College, and am yet able to bear the fashion of the writing company.[1]

There in all its sophistication you have the *milieu* of the young Donne[2]—'who leaving *Oxford*, lived at the *Innes of Court*, not dissolute, but very neat; a great visiter of Ladies, a great frequenter of Playes, a great writer of conceited Verses.'[3] Somehow or other Shakespeare also insinuated himself into it ('witnes,' as Meres said in another context, 'his sugred Sonnets among his private friends,' to say nothing of *Love's Labour's Lost*). But Spenser, the journeyman tailor's son, in spite of his connection with Sidney and Ralegh, always remained on the outside of this privileged community. His accent is never quite that of the initiate, in spite of the *roman à clef* passages of court

---

[1] *Directions for Speech and Style*, ed. H. H. Hudson (1935), p. 39. Hoskins became a Fellow of New College in 1586. He was writing *c.* 1599.

[2] It is tempting to connect the simile of the compasses in 'A Valediction: forbidding mourning' with the period 'whilst mathematics were in requests.' Walton dates it 1611, but Walton is often wrong (see R. E. Bennett's edition of Donne [1942]).

[3] Sir Richard Baker, *A Chronicle of the Kings of England* (1643), p. 156. Baker had known Donne personally.

history in the poems. And, though there are a few
Elizabethan MSS. of his minor poems (but not of *The
Faerie Queene*), they are hardly ever of any textual significance. It seems certain that Spenser preferred to present
himself to his readers in the form of the printed book. This
may have made for legibility, but it interposed a barrier,
a social interval, between the poet and his original readers
that a court poet escaped. It meant, in particular, that
Spenser never quite knew whom he was writing for—he
could not foresee precisely who the purchasers of his first
editions would be—nor how much he could take for
granted in the exposition, for example, of his allegories.
Compared with even the minor court poets Spenser's
impact on the reader is blurred and lacking in intimacy
and directness.[1]

Milton told Dryden, it will be remembered, that
Spenser was 'his original.' And it was as the modern
Spenser that Humphrey Moseley, the publisher, intro-
duced the author of the 1645 volume to the 'Gentle
Reader':

> Let the event guide itself which way it will, I shall deserve
> of the age, by bringing into the Light as true a Birth, as the
> Muses have brought forth since our famous *Spenser* wrote;
> whose poems in these English ones are as rarely imitated,
> as sweetly excell'd.

The money-lender's son, like the tailor's son, was something of a social anomaly. Outside the family circle there
was no ready-made London audience to which he could
attach himself. The court was out of reach and was soon
to prove itself religiously and politically obnoxious, and
the commissions that his father's friend Lawes obtained

[1] The moral ambiguity can perhaps be also ascribed to Spenser's uncertainty
as to his audience. (If the *Bower of Bliss* was destroyed by his Puritan readers,
its charms had been created by the Renaissance elements in his audience.)

for him with the Egerton family apparently led to nothing. In the end, partly perhaps through the pamphlets and partly through the connections he had made as Latin Secretary, a public was to welcome *Paradise Lost*. Between 1,300 and 1,500 copies were sold in the first year and a half after publication. But Milton's relationship with these Puritan intellectuals, some of whom we meet in the later sonnets,[1] is not likely to have been creative. The 'fit audience' that he hopes his Muse will secure is one that she must 'find.' It is not there already. The only reading public that Milton was *conscious* of at this stage apparently was those 'vulgar Readers' whose love of rhyme is curtly censured in the note on 'The Verse' prefixed to the later issues of the first edition of *Paradise Lost*.

But there was one period in his poetic career when Milton was free from this sense of literary isolation. At Cambridge, both as an undergraduate and a B.A., he had felt the stimulating influence of an *audience*, with poet and reader acting and reacting upon each other. There are even traces of an interchange of MSS. with the poets of other colleges. Milton of Christ's has

So bucksom, blith and debonair. ('L'Allegro.')

And Randolph of Trinity has

To make one blithe, buxom and debonair. (*Aristippus*, 1630.)

---

[1] The composition of *Paradise Lost* began in the 1650's. At this period, according to Edward Phillips, 'he was frequently visited by persons of quality, particularly my Lady Ranalagh, whose son for some time he instructed; all learned foreigners of note, who could not pass out of the city, without giving a visit to a person so eminent; and lastly, by particular friends that had a high esteem for him, viz., Mr. Andrew Marvel, young Lawrence (the son of him that was president of Oliver's council), to whom there is a sonnet among the rest, in his printed *Poems*; Mr. Marchamont Needham, the writer of *Politicus*; but above all, Mr. Cyriack Skinner whom he honored with two sonnets' (J. H. Hanford, *A Milton Handbook*, 4th ed. (1946), p. 52).

Obviously one of them was plagiarizing the other, and as obviously it doesn't really matter who was the plagiarist and who was the victim.

'An Epitaph on the Marchioness of *Winchester*,' one of the last of Milton's Cambridge compositions, is his only poem to have been included in any of those MS. collections of the period which were the normal form of circulation for court poetry. It is subscribed there 'Jo Milton of Chr: Coll. Cambr.' In the 1645 volume it is grouped with four other occasional poems ('Song on May Morning,' 'On Shakespear,' and the two epitaphs on Hobson), all written in the same or the previous year (1630-1), to all of which the same signature might have been appended. It 'places' their author. He is that well-known University Wit, Milton of Christ's. A number of the Latin poems of this period are also occasional. There is one on the death of the Vice-Chancellor of the University, another on the Bishop of Ely's death, and a third, which is lighter in tone, on the death of the University Beadle. All of these poems can be called *functional*. Milton wrote them either in response to a specific commission or because he felt that the 'meed of some melodious tear' was expected of him by his academic audience. 'Lycidas' therefore is only the last of a series. And the fact gives the poem a special interest. It is the academic terminus, a valediction. The audience that 'Lycidas' implies is in the past. King is dead and their Cambridge contemporaries, the men who got the Fellowship Milton might have had, have sold their souls in pursuit of worldly success:

> What recks it them? What need they? They are sped;
> And when they list, their lean and flashy songs
> Grate on their scrannel Pipes of wretched straw.

Verity thought these lines 'reflect on the lack not only of moral worth in the sermons preached, but also of literary grace and polish.' A more natural interpretation would be to apply them to the *poetry* of the clergy of the period—reverend gentlemen like Herrick, Corbet, Cartwright, Mayne and Strode whose love-poems were not always strictly decorous. The early pamphlets are full of denunciations of the 'libidinous and ignorant Poetasters' of the time, and Milton was always more interested in poetry than in sermons. It is not impossible, indeed, that there is a specific reference in this passage to John Cleveland, the metaphysical poet, who had been Milton's contemporary at Christ's and had secured a Fellowship at St. John's in 1634, a step that must have involved his taking orders, though Cleveland, a seventeenth-century Charles Churchill, can obviously have had no real sense of ecclesiastical vocation. Cleveland incidentally was another of the contributors to the *Justa Edouardo King*.

In 1637 (when 'Lycidas' was being written) a social chasm, the foretaste of the Civil War, yawned between Milton and men like Cleveland. And yet ten years earlier, when they had been undergraduates together, their social-literary assumptions and background may easily have been almost identical. Milton's early poetic history is one of a surrender to Cambridge, and the Renaissance world that the University stood for, followed by a profound moral revulsion from it. In this psychological drama the key-poems are, I believe, 'L'Allegro' and 'Il Penseroso' though their significance has been misunderstood hitherto because they have been misdated.

Tillyard has recently demonstrated how 'academic' the two poems are.[1] The system of disputations—with one

---

[1] E. M. W. Tillyard, *The Miltonic Setting* (1938). A useful essay, but Tillyard has failed to convince me either that the day-versus-night theme is important

student maintaining in a formal Latin speech and another opposing with equal formality some familiar philosophical proposition set them by the University authorities—naturally encouraged a *pro* and *con* structure. And the elaborate mythological preludes are entirely in the style of contemporary Cambridge disputations, if we may judge by Milton's own university exercises (the so-called 'Prolusions'). According to Tillyard the poems were written in the summer of 1631 (Milton's last Long Vacation). A more probable date is the late summer or autumn of 1629.[1] They are almost certainly the pastoral poems referred to in the final couplet of 'Elegia Sexta' (a letter in Latin verse to his friend Diodati written either at the very end of 1629 or the beginning of 1630):

> Te quoque pressa manent patriis meditata cicutis,
> Tu mihi, cui recitem, judicis instar eris.

('For you other strains too are waiting, strains oft

---

or that the opening of 'L'Allegro' is burlesque. The strict parallelism between the two poems would have required, in the latter case, a burlesque opening to 'Il Penseroso'—which we do not get. Cleanth Brooks has an ingenious chapter on the light symbolism of the poems in *The Well Wrought Urn* (1947), which would be more persuasive if he had taken into account (i) Milton's own weak eyesight, (ii) the Latin-Italian literary tradition of a sunshine that is always uncomfortably hot and bright.

[1] Some incidental confirmation of the earlier date is provided by the verbal forms and spellings. The form 'ycleap'd' ('L'Allegro' 12) is paralleled by 'ychain'd' ('Nativity Ode' 155) and 'Star-ypointing' ('On Shakespear' 4). Milton never used y- forms after 1630. The spellings 'Wher' ('L'Allegro' 60, 79), 'Streit' ('L'Allegro' 68), 'lincked' ('L'Allegro' 140) and 'Cipres' ('Il Penseroso' 35) in the 1645 text are unique in Milton and differ considerably from the *Comus* spellings. The volume claimed to have been 'Printed by his true Copies,' and these forms look more like author's spellings than printer's spellings. The order of the poems in the 1645 volume is generally believed to have been roughly chronological. Milton seems to have divided the poems into three groups: (i) religious verse ('Nativity Ode'—'At a Solemn Musick'); (ii) occasional pieces (Winchester Epitaph—Hobson epitaphs); (iii) Renaissance pieces ('L'Allegro'—*Comus*). Note that in the third group 'L'Allegro' and 'Il Penseroso' *precede* the Sonnets—the earliest of which are generally dated 1630 (Milton bought his copy of Della Casa's sonnets in December 1629).

practised, strains struck out from my native country's reeds: you shall serve as the critic to whom I shall recite them.'[1])

Unless the reference is to some English pastorals now lost,[2] Milton *must* be alluding to 'L'Allegro' and 'Il Penseroso,' perhaps in an unrevised form, which had apparently been written since he had last seen Diodati.[3]

This dating of the poems gets over the difficulty of the 'Anglo-Catholic' conclusion of 'Il Penseroso.' In 1631 Milton had almost certainly already made up his mind not to go into the Church, as it had been his original intention to do. The decision reflects a growing Puritan antipathy to the High Church trends represented by Laud and Andrewes. In 1631 stained glass-windows, organs and anthems would have been 'impossible,' except as the objects of satire or denunciation. In 1629, however, Milton was still a humanist and an æsthete, and these poems are catalogues of rival 'pleasures' and 'delights,' not of competing duties and contradictory obligations. There is even an occasional suggestion of comedy. For example, the cock, who

> Stoutly struts his Dames before,

or the Breughel interior of the 'up-land Hamlet,' beginning

[1] This is the Columbia Edition translation (vol. I, pt. i, p. 215). The translation in the Oxford Milton is on the same general lines. Masson took the reference to be to the 'Nativity Ode' which Milton had just been describing, but the use of the word *cicuta* (invariably used in Latin poetry, in a literary context, to describe pastoral poetry) makes this impossible. I am indebted to Professor Eduard Fraenkel for assistance with this passage.

[2] This is most unlikely. Milton even preserved his schoolboy translations of Psalms 114 and 136 as well as the fragment 'The Passion' which he had abandoned 'nothing satisfi'd with what was begun.'

[3] We can be certain that Milton had seen Diodati in July 1629, when the latter obtained an M.A. degree at Cambridge. Diodati had got his Oxford M.A. in 1628.

> She was pincht, and pull'd she sed,

or that delightfully casual apology for mythological incest,

> His daughter she (in *Saturns* raign,
> Such mixture was not held a stain).

The conflict between reason and passion that dominated the later Milton has not yet made its appearance. Instead we have a fusion of two elements that lay nearer the surface of his mind. They are (i) the world of classical mythology, and (ii) the English countryside.

Leavis has pointed out how the verse comes to life in *Paradise Lost* whenever there is an 'evocation of that serene, clear, ideally remote classical world so potent upon Milton's sensibility.'[1] This is true and important. But in *Paradise Lost*, *Paradise Regained* and *Samson Agonistes* the references to classical mythology are normally accompanied by a reminder that it is not *true*. In many passages the reader is specifically warned that these things are 'fables' or 'fabled,' and the words 'feign'd,' 'erring,' 'mystic,' 'dreams,' a mere 'name' accompany many of Milton's other allusions to classical legends. These notice-boards, as they might be called ('Warning. This way to beauty. Go back for truth'), are an indication of the arrival of Eliot's 'dissociation of sensibility.' Sprat's *History of the Royal-Society of London*, which was published in the same year as *Paradise Lost*, had contained a tart dismissal of the 'Wit of the Fables and Religions of the Antient World':

> The Wit of the Fables and Religions of the Antient World is well-nigh consum'd. They have already serv'd the *Poets* long enough; and it is now high time to dismiss

---

[1] F. R. Leavis, *Revaluation* (1936), p. 45.

them; especially seeing they have this peculiar *imperfection*, that they were only *Fictions*, at first: whereas *Truth* is never so well express'd or amplify'd, as by those Ornaments which are *Tru* and *Real* in themselves.[1]

But all this was still a long way off in the 1620's. Questions of truth, and even of goodness, had not arisen yet, as Milton read and re-read 'the smooth Elegiack Poets, whereof the Schooles are not scarce. Whom both for the pleesing sound of their numerous writing, which in imitation I found most easie; and most agreeable to natures part in me, and for their matter which what it is, there be few who know not, I was so allur'd to read, that no recreation came to me better welcome.'[2]

The schoolboy's intoxication with classical mythology is one element, then, in 'L'Allegro' and 'Il Penseroso.' The poems' peculiar distinction derives from their blend with the English landscape and English social life. Eliot has complained that the imagery is 'all general,' quoting:

> While the Plowman neer at hand,
> Whistles ore the Furrow'd Land,
> And the Milkmaid singeth blithe,
> And the Mower whets his sithe,
> And every Shepherd tells his tale
> Under the Hawthorn in the dale.

On which Eliot comments: 'It is not a particular plough-man, milkmaid, and shepherd that Milton sees (as Wordsworth might see them); the sensuous effect of these verses is entirely on the ear, and is joined to the concepts of ploughman, milkmaid, and shepherd.'[3] But this is to

[1] p. 414.
[2] *Apology for Smectymnuus* (1642). Columbia Edition, vol. III, pt. i, p. 302.
[3] 'A Note on the Verse of John Milton,' *Essays and Studies*, English Association (1936).

miss the point. In this passage Milton is providing a list of morning *sounds*—exactly comparable, as it happens, with the two catalogues of evening sounds in Wordsworth's *An Evening Walk*—and, if there are no details about the ploughman, etc., that is because the Cheerful Man is only concerned with them as *noise-producers*. How carefully the young Milton could use his eyes is demonstrated by the lines immediately following those quoted by Eliot:

> Streit mine eye hath caught new pleasures
> Whilst the Lantskip round it measures,
> Russet Lawns, and Fallows Gray,
> Where the nibling flocks do stray.

The second couplet is a masterpiece of concentrated observation. The sheep have broken through the temporary fence round the parish's fallow field, no doubt because the common pastures are 'Russet,' the short-rooted grass having 'burned,' as farmers say, in the hot dry weather. 'Russet' is decidedly not the epithet one would have expected for 'Lawns' (the later Milton would have preferred 'green' or perhaps 'verdurous')—nor is 'Gray' what one would have expected for 'Fallows.' Milton must have had his eye on a real field. Most fallows after the summer ploughing are brown, but this field, perhaps because the subsoil was chalk, was grey. Milton is quite as specific about it as Wordsworth could have been.[1]

---

[1] Milton is a much better farmer than one might have expected. The 'Taint-worm' described in 'Lycidas' as killing 'the weanling herds that graze' is obviously the intestinal worm that the modern farmer calls 'husk,' which is normally only fatal, as Milton correctly says, to newly weaned calves when they start grazing   Milton's grandfather and uncle farmed at Stanton St. John near Oxford, and Milton must have stayed at the farm when he was wooing Mary Powell, whose father was the squire of the neighbouring village of Forest Hill. No doubt there had been earlier visits too. Stanton St. John may be the 'up-land Hamlet' of 'L'Allegro.'

Various attempts have been made to identify the scenes described in the two poems as at Horton in Buckinghamshire or in the Cambridge and Oxford districts. The significant thing is that such attempts can quite plausibly be made. Milton's landscapes at this stage are the real thing; they have not come out of books, like those in 'Lycidas.' The obvious parallel with 'L'Allegro' and 'Il Penseroso' is 'The Scholar Gipsy' and 'Thyrsis.' Arnold gives the place-names and Milton doesn't, but the poetic formula, an unselfconscious blend of classical pastoral and English landscape, is the same. It is effective because it is detailed and actualized. We believe in the neat-handed Phyllis and the savoury dinner she has prepared for Corydon and Thyrsis because we can *see* that smoking cottage 'betwixt two aged Okes.'

The day-boy of St. Paul's had already acquired the taste for classical mythology, but this vivid, loving, humorous faculty of exact observation was the gift of Cambridge. Cambridge provided Milton with his first glimpse of the real adult world. With the hot-house atmosphere of Bread Street left behind—unlike the Ruskins, the Miltons *père* and *mère* did not follow their prodigy to the University—Milton was at last able to stand on his own feet. The Cambridge letters of 1628 to his Left-wing friend Alexander Gill—who was to find himself in hot water the next year for drinking the health of Buckingham's murderer—are one of the few pieces of first-hand evidence we have of the kind of person Milton was at this time. Their tone, humorous and self-assured, is exactly that of 'L'Allegro' and 'Il Penseroso.' A Fellow of the College has asked him to provide his (the Fellow's) verses for the next graduation ceremony, 'being himself already long past the age for trifles of that sort!' And he ends another letter with a nice mock-solemnity: 'Vale Vir Erudite' ('Farewell, Learned Sir').

But Cambridge society, though it provided the stimulus to the cool, cultured objectivity of the two poems, was too limited and fragmentary to be able to satisfy Milton for long. The five elegiac couplets that are appended to 'Elegia Septima' are the formal retractation:

> Haec ego mente olim læva, studioque supino
> Nequitiæ posui vana trophæa meæ.

'Sex has been exorcized. The reading of Plato has quenched its fires.' This is the gist of what is not the least remarkable of Milton's autobiographical excursions. In striking contrast to the modesty and impersonality of 'L'Allegro' and 'Il Penseroso' here we have the ego enthroned in all its formidable arrogance. Unfortunately the lines are undated, but they can hardly be earlier than 1635. ('Elegia Septima' was written in 1628, and *olim* presumably implies an interval of at least seven years.) They are perhaps the most repellent product of that social vacuum to which Milton consigned himself in the reaction against Cambridge, but they are not alone. They had been preceded many years before by the last of the Latin elegies. The 'Elegia Sexta' (1629), in addition to the allusion to his new English pastorals, provides a kind of parallel to 'L'Allegro' and 'Il Penseroso' in the portraits it paints of the typical elegiac poet, who sings of love and wine, and the typical epic poet, who tackles higher themes and must lead a more ascetic life. The elegiac poet is Diodati and perhaps the Milton of the last few years; the epic poet represents the new rôle in which Milton has now cast himself:

> Let him live a simple, frugal life, after the fashion of the teacher who came from Samos [Pythagoras], let herbs offer him food that works no harm, let pellucid water stand near

M

him, in a tiny cup of beechen wood, and let him drink only sober draughts from a pure spring. On such a poet are imposed, too, a youth free of crime, pure and chaste, and a character unyielding. . . . In this way, story says, wise Tiresias lived, after the light had been swept away from him, and Ogygian Linus, and Calchas, exiled from his hearth, a hearth doomed to destruction, and aged Orpheus, in the lonely grots.[1]

Here is 'The Hairy Gown and Mossy Cell' and the 'Prophetic strain' of 'Il Penseroso's' conclusion. But it is all a degree more solemn. The flavour of irony with which the twenty-year old poet had looked forward to spending his 'weary age' botanizing and astronomizing in a hermitage is no longer there.

By 1631, the date of the Seventh Prolusion, the prophetic solemnity has deepened and we are not far off the morbidities and contradictions of *Arcades* and *Comus*. The poet, it seems, must be a polymath. If he is also strictly chaste, the whole world of nature and universal history will be intelligible to him. One such man can reform a whole state! Milton even specifies the number of years it will take to acquire polymathy. Provided one starts young enough and works every day it should be possible to complete the cycle of the sciences 'within the age of Alexander the Great.'[2] Alexander died when he was thirty-three. Milton, who had fulfilled the other conditions by then, celebrated his thirty-third year by writing his first pamphlet—which nobody read. He celebrated his thirty-fourth year by taking to himself a wife—who promptly left him. The difficult years that followed were spent in unlearning the half-baked Christian Platonism of which 'Il Penseroso' provides the first glimpse. Though

[1] Columbia Edition translation, vol. i (1931), pp. 211–13.
[2] ibid., vol. xii (1936), p. 279.

he was never to recapture the cool realism of 'L'Allegro,' *Paradise Lost* attained its own massive objectivity. It has been compared to Joyce's *Ulysses*. Accepting the parallel one might equate *Comus* with the *Portrait of the Artist* and 'L'Allegro' and 'Il Penseroso' with *Dubliners*. The crystal perfection with which both Joyce and Milton began was short-lived precisely because it had no effective social basis. The accident of birth had deposited the Anglo-Irishman and the money-lender's son a little to the side of the central literary current of their times. The reservations that, with all their greatness, their writings continue to excite, are primarily attributable to this social accident.

Milton was unlucky in another way. By the time he reached Cambridge the classic moment in English Renaissance poetry had already passed. If he had not been the son of a money-lender he would still have been faced with the problems set by a literary tradition that was already past its prime. As it was he did not escape altogether from the limitations of the Polished Craftsman. His poetical contemporaries, the men who were more or less his own age, were men like Habington, Randolph, Davenant, Fanshawe, Waller, Suckling and Cartwright. In spite of the grace and charm of their verse—Davenant in particular deserves to be more read than he is—they are all distinctly minor poets, metaphysical *epigoni*. With the exception of Waller (who became the first Augustan) their essential achievement is limited to elegant variations in the tradition of courtly wit. The compliment that Suckling paid Davenant applies to the whole group:

> Since the great lord of it [wit],
> Donne, parted hence, no man has ever writ
> So near him, in's own way.

Milton was a good deal more than a sedulous ape, and he had no use for Donne, but his imitations, which are not always distinguishable from plagiarism, sometimes compromise the purity of the poet-reader relationship. Our admiration for the learning distracts our attention from the argument. 'L'Allegro' and 'Il Penseroso' are perhaps less liable to this criticism than *Comus*, 'Lycidas,' and *Paradise Lost*, in which the style often seems to have a life of its own that is independent of the poems' overt intentions. A further difference is that in 'L'Allegro' and 'Il Penseroso' the objects of imitation are English. No contemporary reader would have failed to recognize the allusion to Marlowe's 'Passionate Shepherd' and Ralegh's reply in

> These delights, if thou canst give,
> Mirth with thee, I mean to live.

and

> These pleasures *Melancholy* give,
> And I with thee will choose to live.

And the general influence of Spenser—especially in the catalogue of horrors at the opening of 'L'Allegro'—and such Spenserians as Sylvester, Browne and Wither (a favourite of Milton's headmaster Gill)—is equally clear. But if the poems are in a sense literary exercises they are exercises of genius. At the age of twenty Milton had already all but exhausted the possibilities of the English pastoral. Those who have attempted it since—Pope, Gray, Cowper, Wordsworth (in *An Evening Walk*), Arnold and Blunden—have added little or nothing to the strains this astonishing young man 'struck out on his native country's reeds.'

CHAPTER EIGHT

A WORD FOR WALLER

WALLER is the Augustan Wyatt. 'Unless he had written,'
Dryden owned, 'none of us could write.'[1] In the memorial
volume that Rymer, the critic and historian, edited in
1688 Sir Thomas Higgons compared Waller's contribution to the English language with Petrarch's to Italian:

> The *English* he hath to Perfection brought;
> And we to speak are by his Measures taught.
> Those very *Words*, which are in Fashion now,
> He brought in Credit half an Age ago.
> Thus *Petrarch* mended the *Italian* Tongue:
> And now they speak the Language which he sung.[2]

And Atterbury paid a similar tribute in 1690:

> He undoubtedly stands first in the List of Refiners, and
> for ought I know, last too; for I question whether in
> *Charles* the Second's Reign, *English* did not come to its full
> perfection; and whether it has not had its *Augustan Age*, as
> well as the Latin . . . In the mean time, 'tis a surprizing
> Reflection, that between what *Spencer* wrote last, and
> *Waller* first, there should not be much above twenty years
> distance; and yet the one's Language, like the Money of
> that time, is as currant now as ever; whilst the other's words

---

[1] Preface to Walsh's *Dialogue concerning Women* (1691).
[2] *Poems to the Memory of that Incomparable Poet Edmund Waller Esquire by
Several Hands* (1688), p. 3. Leland had compared Wyatt with Dante and
Petrarch in the same way.

are like old coyns, one must go to an Antiquary to understand their true meaning and value.[1]

Nor was it only on historical grounds that Waller was
admired. Hume considered him the English Horace.[2]
Chesterfield recommended him to his son for spare-time
reading with Horace, Boileau and La Bruyère.[3] And he is
frequently quoted by the two most dazzling creations of
Restoration comedy—Etherege's Dorimant[4] and Congreve's Millamant.[5]

But to-day Waller's name is mud. The following is a
typical pronouncement:

> No poetical reputation of the seventeenth century has
> been so completely and irreparably eclipsed as that of
> Edmund Waller. . . . Whereas Cowley and Cleveland can
> still give pleasure, Waller's name calls up scarcely more than
> two lyrics of attenuated cavalier grace, 'On a Girdle' and

---

[1] *The Second Part of Mr. Waller's Poems* (1690), Preface. This passage
appears to be the first in which the term 'Augustan' is applied to the English
language. The political analogy had been drawn by Waller himself in 'A
Panegyric to my Lord Protector' (*c.* 1654):

> As the vexed world, to find repose, at last
> Itself into Augustus' arms did cast;
> So England now does with like toil oppressed,
> Her weary head upon your bosom rest.

In *Astræa Redux* (1660), ll, 320–3, Dryden transferred the compliment to
Charles II. The first use of 'Augustan' in connection with English literature is
apparently in John Oldmixon's *Reflections on Dr. Swift's Letter* (1712). Oldmixon considered Charles II's reign 'the Augustan Age of English Poetry.'

Atterbury's difficulties with Spenser were shared by many of his contemporaries. In 1687 'a Person of Quality' brought out a modernization of the
first book of *The Faerie Queene* in heroic couplets as *Spencer Redivivus*. It
begins:

> A Worthy Knight was Riding on the Plain,
> In Armour Clad, which richly did Contain
> The Gallant Marks of many Batels fought,
> Tho' he before no Martial Habit sought.

[2] 'Of the Rise of Arts and Sciences,' *Essays Moral and Political* (1741).
[3] Letter of 5 Feb. 1750.
[4] *The Man of Mode* (1676), I, i (*bis*); II, ii; III, iii (*bis*); V, i; V, ii.
[5] *The Way of the World* (1700), IV, i (*bis*).

'Go lovely Rose,' and a dim memory of much compli-
mentary and occasional verse. . . . Any public or private
occasion could release a stream of his lucid rhetoric. . . .
For us he remains a fluent trifler, the rhymer of a court
gazette.[1]

The gap between the eulogies of the seventeenth and
eighteenth centuries and the modern assessment is clearly
a wide one. It can only be bridged, I believe, by the
application of the critical principles laid down earlier in
this book. In particular we need to know what the
audience was that Waller originally addressed and what
that audience expected from poetry.

Goldsmith included two poems by Waller in his
Beauties of English Poesy (1767). They were not, however,
'On a Girdle' and 'Go lovely Rose,' but 'On the Death
of the Lord Protector' and 'The Story of Phœbus and
Daphne Applied.' And Goldsmith, in his critical notes,
makes no mention of Waller's cavalier grace. What he
says is: 'A modern reader will chiefly be struck with the
strength of thinking.' The fact is there are two Wallers
—a minor Renaissance poet and a major Augustan poet.
To concentrate on the former and overlook the latter is as
uncritical as it would be to identify Yeats with 'The Lake
Isle of Innisfree' and then complain of his attenuated
Romanticism.

Miss C. V. Wedgwood has recently accused the cavalier
poets of belonging 'to the *arrière*, not to the *avant garde*':

Their whole trend of thought reached back into a re-
ceding past, away from the cold and probing realism, both
in thought and politics, which was gradually submerging
the older world. They were in fact anti-political, just as the

[1] Douglas Bush, *English Literature in the Earlier Seventeenth Century* (1945),
p. 166.

King's view was anti-political—an attempt to do without politics, not an attempt to reform them.[1]

Waller at any rate escapes this indictment. He was an extremely able Member of Parliament, and after the Restoration, as Father of the House, exercised a useful restraining influence on royalist extremists. And Waller's best poem, 'A Panegyric to my Lord Protector' (*c.* 1654) is specifically political, one of the finest political poems in English. It might be described as a seventeenth-century equivalent of W. H. Auden's 'Spain,' or of the 'Prologue' to his *Look, Stranger!* Although the phrasing is not as brilliant as in Marvell's famous 'Horatian Ode' (1650), it is in some ways a better poem because it makes better sense. The political advice that Marvell gave Cromwell was much of it extremely inept—the recommendation to invade France and Italy, for example, or to exterminate the Scots. Waller's prescriptions, in these two matters, were the eminently sensible ones of a balance of power policy in Europe and a union with Scotland. And the analysis of England's economic position is equally shrewd. Unfortunately the poem is too long to quote. Here instead is 'The Story of Phœbus and Daphne Applied,' which Goldsmith admired and which Elijah Fenton (Pope's collaborator in the translation of the *Odyssey*) considered 'one of the most beautiful Poems in our own, or any other modern language':[2]

> Thyrsis, a youth of the inspirèd train,
> Fair Sacharissa loved, but loved in vain.
> Like Phœbus sung the no less amorous boy,
> Like Daphne she, as lovely and as coy.

[1] 'Poets and Politics in Baroque England,' *Penguin New Writing*, No. 21 (1944), pp. 129-30.
[2] 'Observations on some of Mr. Waller's Poems,' p. xl (appended to Fenton's edition of Waller, 1729).

With numbers he the flying nymph pursues,
With numbers such as Phœbus self might use.
Such is the chase when Love and Fancy leads,
O'er craggy mountains and through flowery meads
Invoked to testify the lover's care
Or form some image of his cruel fair.
Urged with his fury, like a wounded deer,
O'er these he fled; and now approaching near,
Had reached the nymph with his harmonious lay,
Whom all his charms could not incline to stay.
Yet what he sung in his immortal strain,
Though unsuccessful, was not sung in vain.
All but the nymph that should redress his wrong,
Attend his passion, and approve his song.
Like Phœbus thus, acquiring unsought praise,
He catched at love, and filled his arm with bays.

The poem's success is primarily due to the series of *surprises* that the working out of the Waller-Sacharissa and Phœbus-Daphne parallel provides. The impersonality of the poem is in striking contrast to Renaissance egotism. Although in comparing himself to Phœbus Waller might be thought to run the risk of being caught blowing his own trumpet, in fact he is so detached from the whole situation that the danger does not arise. His love for Sacharissa and her rejection of it have been abstracted out of their human context and are here simply disembodied concepts that the mind can play with in the dry light of reason. Even metaphor, the fundamental Renaissance device, is adapted to non-Renaissance uses. Half-way through the poem, indeed, the metaphoric level suddenly changes. The mountains and meads begin, as it were, in quotation marks; they are simply the conventional similes of the conventional love-poet. But at

'Urged with his fury' the imagery turns into real places that the poet is imagined to be actually traversing, and he is finally said to be 'like a wounded deer.' There are therefore three metaphoric levels altogether: (i) the conventional similes, (ii) Waller imagined on the mountains, (iii) Waller on the mountains compared to a deer. Though this confusion is, I think, attractive, the metaphoric sophistication it implies is an indication how far Waller is outside the Renaissance tradition. Such acrobatics would have been impossible for a poet like Donne, a fantastic, who thought in metaphors. Waller is *playing* with metaphor here in the interests of paradox.

It is tempting to compare the poem with Marvell's 'Garden.' It is even possible that Marvell's

> Apollo hunted Daphne so
> Only that she might laurel grow

derives directly from Waller's poem. But the basic attitudes to life are very different. Marvell's green thought in a green shade is sheer solipsism, even if it is tinged with irony. Waller, on the other hand, is well aware of the worldly value of a crown of bays. He is the man of sense for whom a success in one direction compensates a disappointment in another. Here there are no heart-breaks. The synthesis of man the individual and man the social unit is complete.

Waller's reputation as a poet has suffered because of his political changes of front. To Gosse he is 'the easy turncoat,' the author of 'smooth emasculated lyrics.'[1] And H. J. Massingham, after a cascade of inaccurate abuse, sums it all up in the statement that 'his literary product is no less contemptible than his public career.'[2]

---

[1] *Seventeenth Century Studies* (1914), pp. 221, 227.
[2] *A Treasury of Seventeenth Century English Verse* (1920), p. 373.

It is true that Waller was an ardent Royalist in the Civil War, that he made his peace with Cromwell, who was his cousin, in 1651, and that at the Restoration he gave Charles II an effusive poetic welcome. But in all this he was only doing what the rest of his class were doing, if rather more noisily. The younger squires were not believers in the Divine Right of Kings or of anybody else. Intellectually they were rationalists (Waller, Denham and Dryden were among the earliest members of the Royal Society), and their economic roots were not at court but in the land. Their principal political requirement was a government that would enable them to develop their country estates without interference. Waller's objection to the abolition of episcopacy was not religious but economic:

> I look upon episcopacy as a counterscarp or outwork, which, if it is taken by this assault of the people . . . we may in the next place have as hard a task to defend our property as we have lately had to recover it from the prerogative. If, by multiplying hands and petitions, they prevail for an equality in things ecclesiastical, the next demand may perhaps be *Lex Agraria*, the like equality in things temporal.[1]

And this was essentially the point of view taken by Cromwell and Ireton in the Army's Leveller debates. Ireton's objection to universal suffrage was: 'If you admitt any man that hath a breath and being . . . we destroy propertie. . . . Noe person that hath nott a locall and permanent interest in the Kingdome should have an equal dependance in Elections.'[2]

To Waller and to Ireton property *is* land. 'Real' estate, as it came to be called at this period[3] in contradis-

---

[1] Cit. M. Dobb, *Studies in the Development of Capitalism* (1946), p. 174.
[2] *Clarke Papers*, vol. ii, p. 314.   [3] See O.E.D. s.v. 'real' and 'estate.'

tinction to the intangible estates of the merchants, provided the only rational basis of society. 'Law,' as Swift put it, 'in a free Country: is, or ought to be the Determination of the Majority of those who have Property in Land.'[1] The conclusion reflected fairly enough the distribution of wealth at the time. According to Gregory King's estimate, the capital value of the country's land and buildings in 1688 was £234 millions, whereas the liquid capital, including livestock, only amounted to £86 millions. As long as the balance of property retained this ratio, as Harrington, the political theorist of the squirearchy, had shown, the ruling class was necessarily made up of the landowners, of whom the King was only one. The balance only swung away from land about 1800, when a new ruling class of urban capitalists emerges.

The agricultural roots are important if Augustan poetry is to be read and understood. When the King of Brobdingnag had completed his cross-examination of Gulliver on European institutions he 'gave it for his opinion, that whoever could make two ears of corn or two blades of grass to grow upon a spot of ground where only one grew before, would deserve better of mankind, and do more essential service to his country than the whole race of politicians put together.'[2] There are two points to be noted in this famous pronouncement. The first is the *animus* against 'politicians,' who represent the central government—an artificial creation often at cross-purposes with the 'natural' autocracy of the Justices of the Peace. The second is the emphasis on agricultural improvement—a movement generally associated with the second half of the eighteenth century, the period of the Parliamentary Enclosures and Arthur Young's Board of Agriculture, but in fact already active, as the Royal

---

[1] *Thoughts on Various Subjects.* [2] *A Voyage to Brobdingnag,* ch. vii.

Society's inquiries had shown, at the Restoration. The two points are complementary and they must both be borne in mind when reading the poems of the great Augustans—Dryden, Pope, Gray, Goldsmith and Cowper, as well as Swift—and the plays of Gay and Fielding.

Agricultural improvement meant the so-called 'Norfolk' or 'four-course' system, which by diversifying corn crops with roots and one-year leys provided winter fodder for more livestock while raising cereal yields at the same time. But the introduction of the system normally involved (i) costs of enclosure beyond the average farmer's purse, and (ii) a squeezing out of the smallholders. In the process the three-tier rural hierarchy emerged of landlords, tenant farmers and agricultural labourers. Lilliput, it will be remembered, had a similar class-structure. The rural elements in Augustan society were therefore anti-egalitarian and were consequently in uneasy partnership with its urban rationalism, which presupposed a measure of social equality. As against the 'private sense' of the Renaissance (alias 'enthusiasm' or 'inspiration'), the Augustans had set up 'common sense,' i.e. the rational faculty that is common to all human beings, except lunatics and babies, and that distinguishes us from animals. It was in the name of this common sense that they justified the rule of landed property. The new science was also the product of common sense. And their ethical Christianity was a common-sense religion. But this community of sense was not allowed to become a community of votes, education or income. Theoretically men were all equal, but in most of the practical affairs of life a rigid social stratification determined their relations with their fellows.

This central contradiction is the ultimate explanation of the pretentiousness and the emptiness of much Augustan poetry. With no mystical or traditional basis of authority on the one hand, and no rational basis on the other, except in the single field of agricultural improvement, the ruling class could only justify its privileges in the eyes of the nation by being an *aristocracy*, living in the best houses, eating the best food, reading the best books and patronizing the best poets. Hence their 'ritual of conspicuous waste'—Palladian mansions that were too large to live in, Pindaric odes that were too dull to read. None of the Augustan poets entirely resolves the contradiction, and there is therefore no Augustan poem that can quite be called great, but the better poets succeed in mitigating it. Waller's 'Panegyric to my Lord Protector,' Dryden's 'Secular Masque,' Rochester's 'Satyr against Mankind,' Pope's portrait of Lord Timon (in the fourth 'Moral Essay'), and Gray's brilliant 'On Lord Holland's Seat near Margate' go some way at any rate to salving the period's social conscience.

CHAPTER NINE

SWIFT'S 'DESCRIPTION OF THE MORNING'

IT is time Swift's status as a poet was reconsidered. Although his verse is uneven and often slipshod, at his best he seems to me one of the great English poets. I prefer him to Pope. Pope is a superb *talker* in verse, endlessly vivacious and amusing, but it is difficult to take him or his opinions very seriously. His pet theory of the Ruling Passion can only be described as half-baked. Swift, on the other hand, though he restricted himself to light verse, is fundamentally one of the world's most serious poets. Even his jokes have metaphysical implications. But to understand Swift he must be read in the social context of his own time.

The 'Description of the Morning' was originally published in the ninth *Tatler* (20 April 1709), where it was preceded by a note by Steele, who explains that its realism is an attempt to avoid the usual neo-classic conventionalities (such as Dryden's description of night in *The Indian Emperor* which Rymer had recently extolled as the *ne plus ultra* of poetry[1]):

> Now hardly here and there an hackney coach
> Appearing, showed the ruddy morn's approach.
> Now Betty from her master's bed had flown,
> And softly stole to discompose her own;
> The slipshod 'prentice from his master's door
> Had pared the dirt, and sprinkled round the floor.

[1] In the preface to his translation of Rapin's *Reflections on Aristotle's Treatise of Poesie* (1674).

Now Moll had whirled her mop with dexterous airs,
Prepared to scrub the entry and the stairs.
The youth with broomy stumps began to trace
The kennel-edge,[1] where wheels had worn the place.
The small-coal-man was heard with cadence deep,
Till drowned in shriller notes of chimney-sweep.
Duns at his lordship's gate began to meet;
And brick-dust Moll had screamed through half the street.
The turnkey now his flock returning sees,
Duly let out a-nights to steal for fees:
The watchful bailiffs take their silent stands,
And school-boys lag with satchels in their hands.

The opening couplets are a straightforward parody of
the heroic style. It is possible Swift had in mind a recent
address to London in Congreve's *Pindarique Ode . . . On
the Victorious Progress of Her Majesty's Arms* (1706):

> Rise, Fair *Augusta*, lift thy Head,
> With Golden Tow'rs thy Front adorn;
> Come forth, as comes from *Tithon's* Bed
> With cheerful Ray the ruddy Morn.

But the parody is almost immediately abandoned for a
catalogue of the activities of a Saturday morning (the
traditional 'scrubbing day'[2]) in the West End of London.
The clue to the poem's peculiar flavour—the quality that
Coleridge distinguished in Swift as *Anima Rabelaisii
habitans in sicco*[3]—is the juxtaposition of what is morally
neutral (the street cries, the charwoman, the boy searching
the gutter), or at most venial behaviour (the careless
apprentice, the loitering schoolboy), with real social

---

[1] The 'kennel' is the gutter in the middle of the street. The boy was hoping
to find old nails.

[2] See Gay's *Trivia* (1716), vol. ii, pp. 421-4.

[3] *Table Talk*, 15 June 1830.

evils (the sexual immorality and financial irresponsibility of the upper class, the appalling prison system). The implication is: 'This is life. Here you have a corner of London at the beginning of the daily round. You recognize the accuracy of the picture, don't you? A, B and C, men and women with immortal souls, are each carrying out in an almost instinctive way his or her particular function, side by side and yet completely independent of each other. But some of these functions, which we all take for granted, are criminal, aren't they? What sort of a society is this in which you, gentle reader, are so deeply compromised?'

A paradox emerges. Like the Yahoos, these Londoners are human beings and yet they are *not* human beings. The dissociated individual, mechanically pursuing his own professional function, irrespective of its social consequences, and oblivious of the activities of his neighbours, possesses none of the qualities that constitute real humanity. In the terminology of *The Battle of the Books*, he is a spider and not a bee.

The social order that Swift is attempting to discredit in this poem is the *laissez-faire* individualism of urban capitalism, and the moral that he is enforcing is the Christian one that we are members of one another. 'Only connect.' But behind the ethical humanism, giving it depth and force, is something more primitive—the countryman's sense of fact. It is this conviction of actuality that makes the poem refreshing instead of depressing. Bad though the state of the towns may be there is no need to despair, Swift implies, as long as it is possible to face the facts of the situation. The amoral urban automata, once seen in their true light, *must* become objects of contempt. There is also an implicit contrast between the uncreative activities of London—

N

even the coalman and the charwoman, whose professions might be thought useful, are only engaged in moving carbon from one place to another—and the rural partnership of man with nature. 'The difference is, that, instead of dirt and poison, we have rather chosen to fill our hives with honey and wax, thus furnishing mankind with the two noblest of things, which are sweetness and light.' The tonic quality of Swift's poem derives from the *sanity* of the underlying philosophy of life. Because he was insane when he died the nineteenth century dismissed everything that he wrote with which they did not agree as mad. To-day it is the Victorian division of labour and the Victorian piling up of *things* that seem mad. Swift's special distinction is that he exposed *laissez-faire* capitalism, and all that it stands for, while it was still no bigger than a cloud the size of a man's hand.

To some extent Swift's satiric effectiveness derives from the attitude he adopts towards his readers. This is different from either Dryden's or Pope's, or indeed any of his contemporaries. As James Sutherland has recently pointed out in a useful pioneer survey of the poet's audience in the eighteenth century, the reading public Swift was addressing was not *primarily* that of the upper classes of society:

It was his practice, we are told, to have two of his menservants brought in to listen to his poems being read, 'which, if they did not comprehend, he would alter and amend, until they understood it perfectly well, and then would say, *This will do: for I write to the vulgar, more than to the learned.*'[1] How well he succeeded may be seen on almost any page of his poetical works, where the idiomatic and familiar style carries his meaning easily and forcibly to the

[1] *Works* (1762), vol. i, 'To the Reader.'

least learned reader. But here, as in some other matters,
Swift was not wholly at one with his age.[1]

Sutherland appears to impute *eccentricity* to Swift. In
reality, in my opinion, he was not at one with his age
only because he transcended it. The poems were, of
course, read by the aristocracy. The parody in the
opening lines of the 'Description of the Morning' would
only have been intelligible to the polite world. But
Swift's uniqueness in his century lay in his ability to
appeal to several social levels in one and the same work.
It is this that sets him by Chaucer and Shakespeare.

Unlike Pope Swift's principal object as a satirist is not
to get the reader 'on his side' against his enemies. The
futility of such satire is the subject of his recurrent scorn.
'Satire is a sort of glass, wherein beholders do generally
discover everybody's face but their own; which is the
chief reason for that kind reception it meets in the world,
and that so very few are offended with it.'[2] Swift's
technique, on the contrary, is to insinuate himself into the
enemy ranks disguised as a friend, and once he is there to
spread all the alarm and despondency he can. 'I never
wonder,' he wrote in *Thoughts on Various Subjects*, 'to
see men wicked, but I often wonder to see them not
ashamed.' It was above all a sense of shame that he tried
to inculcate in the capitalists of the middle class. In *A
Modest Proposal for Preventing the Children of Ireland from
being a Burden to their Parents or Country* (1729), perhaps
the greatest of the prose ironies, the real object of Swift's
attack is not, as is often asserted, the Irish policy of the
Whig Government. The satire goes much deeper. It is

[1] *A Preface to Eighteenth Century Poetry* (1948), p. 48.
[2] *The Battle of the Books*, 'The Preface of the Author.' F. R. Leavis has a
brilliant exposition of Swift's satiric methods in *Determinations* (1934), pp. 79–
108.

an exposure of a whole social philosophy, of which the English economic discrimination against Ireland was only one instance. As in the 'Description of the Morning,' which can be considered an early experiment in the *genre* perfected in *A Modest Proposal*, it is again competitive capitalism that Swift is trying to discredit, but the mode of insinuation is more carefully chosen. The satire in the 'Description' had camouflaged itself behind the parody of a recognized literary form. As such, however, it cannot have been likely to have attracted the attention of the City merchants, who were Philistines almost to a man. The trap had the wrong kind of bait. *A Modest Proposal*, on the other hand, talks the actual language of Cheapside and Threadneedle Street. It is to all appearances another essay in the 'political arithmetic' that was so popular in the City of London during the later seventeenth and early eighteenth centuries. The tone of voice, the method of argument, the statistical approach are exactly the kind of thing that the business world of the time had been accustomed to meet in the pamphlets of Sir William Petty, Charles Davenant and Daniel Defoe. Here was their old friend the Economic Man! The opening paragraphs have lulled any suspicions that Swift's authorship might have aroused, and the reader, who finds the Economic Man disposing of his surplus children to the butcher, is brought suddenly face to face with the contradiction between his own week-day and Sunday religions. It is the Augustan paradox, the familiar formula of the poetry of the squirearchy, but here it operates on a grander scale, charged with a higher intensity, than any of Swift's contemporaries were able to command.

CHAPTER TEN

GRAY'S *ELEGY* RECONSIDERED

THE most popular poem in the English language has received curiously little critical attention. Thus in H. S. Davies's useful and representative anthology of criticism *The Poets and their Critics* (1943) Gray's unsatisfactory *Odes* obtain more than twice the space allotted to the *Elegy*. Matthew Arnold thought the *Elegy* had received 'a too unreserved and unbounded praise,' but he seems to have made no attempt to elaborate this *obiter dictum*. Indeed, in the whole of his thirty-page essay on Gray the poem is only referred to this once. Cleanth Brooks has recently devoted a chapter to the *Elegy* in the collection of 'studies in the structure of poetry' that he has called *The Well Wrought Urn* (1947), and this is the most elaborate critical discussion that Gray's poem has received since the anonymous *A Criticism on the Elegy written in a Country Church Yard* (1783).[1] (The treatment in Roger Martin's *Essai sur Thomas Gray* (1934), though detailed, I found unrewarding.) But Brooks, if always interesting,

[1] Generally attributed to John Young, who was Professor of Greek at Glasgow from 1774 to 1820, and claimed in later life to be the book's 'editor.' The internal evidence suggests to me an Englishman with an Oxford education:

(i) The author was a friend of Bowyer the printer (p. 8), of Calvert Blake (p. 38), and of Dr. Curzon of Brasenose College (p. 53)—all Englishmen.

(ii) His knowledge of English poetry is impressive, especially of Thomson, Collins, Pope and Milton, but he shows little detailed familiarity with the classics.

(iii) He is a bigoted Tory and objects strongly to Gray's Whig views of Cromwell.

Though unfair to Gray the book makes decidedly interesting reading. The book's authorship is discussed by a number of correspondents in *Notes and Queries* (1857 and 1858).

is somewhat less persuasive in this essay than on most occasions. Too often he seems to be forcing a meaning on Gray's words that isn't really there,[1] and the poetic 'structure' that he uncovers doesn't amount to very much. The dramatis personæ of the poem, apparently, are (i) the *storied urn* of the abbey church, (ii) the *shapeless sculpture* of the village churchyard and (iii) the final 'Epitaph,' and there is a suggestion that the opposition between the first two is reconciled in the third. But the details are left discreetly vague.

The inadequacy of Brooks's account—which I do not wish to over-stress (the essay is much the best thing that I have met with on the *Elegy*)—is traceable, I believe, to his exclusion of the social and historical factors. It is dangerous to abstract any poem from its historical setting. In the case of a poem already two hundred years old and the product of a society so different from our own as that of the mid-eighteenth century the procedure is peculiarly imprudent.

The most important *fact* about Gray's poem is that it was composed in two instalments. The first seventy-two lines (i.e. up to 'Far from the madding crowd's ignoble strife') were written at Stoke Poges in the summer or

---

[1] The identification of the numerous personifications with 'the allegoric figures, beloved by the eighteenth century, which clutter a great abbey church such as that at Bath or at Westminster' (p. 100) is most unconvincing. Nor can I detect 'brilliant irony' in the phrase *animated bust*. According to Brooks 'An "animated" bust would presumably be one into which the breath of life had been breathed—a speaking likeness endowed by the chisel of the sculptor with the soul itself. But the most "animated" bust (*anima*—breath, soul) cannot call the fleeting *anima* of the dead man back to its "mansion." And the mansion receives its qualification in the next line: it is no more than silent dust" (p. 102). This will never do. All that Gray means by *animated* surely is a good bust, a bust fulfilling the function of a bust, viz., of being an accurate portrait. Brooks's interpretation, taken literally, would mean that the dead man's soul had migrated from his body to the sepulchral bust. *Quod est absurdum.* It is only fair to add that many of Brooks's incidental comments are shrewd and relevant. They do not, however, *add up* to anything very substantial.

autumn of 1742.[1] In the Eton MS. (an early draft in Gray's autograph) they are followed by sixteen lines which were later cancelled (though some of the phrases were utilized in the final version). 'And here,' says Mason, Gray's literary executor and biographer, 'the Poem was originally intended to conclude.'[2] To avoid confusion I shall refer to this first draft, which constitutes a complete, self-contained poem of great beauty, as the *Stanzas*. (The Eton MS. is headed 'Stanza's Wrote in a Country Church-Yard,' and Dryden's *Heroick Stanzas* on Cromwell's death, also in decasyllabic quatrains rhyming *abab*, may well have been Gray's metrical model.) The poem as we know it, here referred to as the *Elegy*, consists of the *Stanzas*, *minus* their last sixteen lines and *plus* fifty-six new lines. The new lines were completed in June 1750, though it is not known exactly when Gray began work on them. They may have been the 'few Autumnal verses' that Gray wrote to a friend (in September 1746) then made up, with the reading of Aristotle, his 'entertainments during the fall of the leaf.'

The first critical point that must be made in any discussion of the poem is the inferiority of the last fifty-six lines.[3] Apart from the fragments salved from the rejected conclusion of the *Stanzas*, the only lines that can possibly be called great poetry are in the two verses beginning 'For who to dumb Forgetfulness a prey.' Their precise relevance, however, at this point is not

[1] See H. W. Garrod's important 'Note on the Composition of Gray's Elegy,' pp. 111–16 of *Essays on the Eighteenth Century Presented to David Nichol Smith* (1945).

[2] *The Poems of Mr. Thomas Gray* (1775), p. 107.

[3] In Landor's *Imaginary Conversation* between Johnson and Tooke (*Works* (1876), vol. iv, p. 192), Tooke says: 'Expunge from his Elegy the second and third stanza, together with all those which follow the words "Even in our ashes live their wonted fires," and you will leave a poem with scarcely a blemish: a poem which will always have more readers than any others in any language.'

clear. The preceding verse had described the misspelled inscriptions and their texts,

> That teach the rustic moralist to die.

Presumably this means that the more philosophically minded villagers, wandering round the churchyard, read the texts on the gravestones and by doing so learned to resign themselves to the inevitability of death. Between this perambulation and the ensuing death-bed scene there is a logical gap that makes me suspect that the two verses have been transferred from some other poem or fragment. The remaining verses (with the exception of the 'Epitaph') can only be described as *thin*. Their diluted humorous elegance compares unfavourably with the concentrated force of the *Stanzas*. And the pervasive 'literariness' is scarcely distinguishable from plagiarism.[1] Gray's notes point out two distant parallels in Petrarch, but omit all reference to Drummond's 'Far from the madding worldling's hoarse discords,' and the 'hoary-headed Swain's' debt to the description of Jaques in *As You Like It*

> he lay along
> Under an oak whose antique root peeps out
> Upon the brook that brawls along this road,

and the echoes of 'L'Allegro,' 'Il Penseroso' and 'Lycidas.' The final 'Epitaph'—that 'tin-kettle of an epitaph tied to its tail,' as Landor is said to have called it[2]—is less empty and elegant, but it is clumsily written and the account that it provides of the dead man differs in several respects from that given by the Swain. (To the latter he was a

[1] Gray wrote to Bedingfield, 27 Aug. 1756: ' . . . do not wonder therefore if some Magazine or Review call me Plagiary: I could shew them a hundred more instances, wch they never will discover themselves.'

[2] I have not been able to trace the source of this quotation.

sort of Scholar Gipsy, eccentric and unsociable, whereas the 'Epitaph' applauds his social virtues, his sympathy with the unfortunate and his devotion to his friend.)

If the last fifty-six lines are so inferior to the first seventy-two, why were they written? Why was Gray not satisfied with the brilliant *Stanzas* of 1742? I believe the sixteen cancelled lines, which rounded off the original poem, provide the explanation. They run as follows:

> The thoughtless World to Majesty may bow
> Exalt the brave, & idolize Success
> But more to Innocence their Safety owe
> Than Power & Genius e'er conspired to bless
>
> And thou, who mindful of the unhonour'd Dead
> Dost in these Notes their artless Tale relate
> By Night & lonely Contemplation led
> To linger in the gloomy Walks of Fate
>
> Hark how the sacred Calm, that broods around
> Bids ev'ry fierce tumultuous Passion cease
> In still small Accents whisp'ring from the Ground
> A grateful Earnest of eternal Peace
>
> No more with Reason & thyself at Strife
> Give anxious Cares & endless Wishes room
> But thro' the cool sequester'd Vale of Life
> Pursue the silent Tenour of thy Doom.

Although there are one or two obscurities that a later revision would have smoothed out—'their Safety' is not quite *le mot juste*—there can be no doubt about the literary quality of these lines. They are superb. But they are also extremely personal. They remind me of the still greater Sapphics that Cowper wrote after his attempted suicide in 1763 ('Hatred and vengeance, my eternal portion').

Gray, too, is thinking aloud. He is trying to cheer himself up in the face of a bitter disappointment. The
'anxious Cares & endless Wishes' are not poetical ornaments but his own private demons, the 'fierce tumultuous
Passion' of a young man who has found 'Reason' an
insufficient support in a suddenly hostile world. It will
be remembered that the *Stanzas* probably date from the
late summer of 1742. In May 1741 Gray had quarrelled—
irrevocably, as it then seemed—with Horace Walpole.
His father had died the following November, leaving
only a fraction of the substantial fortune that he had had a
short time before, though it was not until some six months
later that Gray finally learned that he was to all intents
and purposes a pauper. And in June 1742 Richard
West, apart from Walpole his only intimate friend, died
suddenly from consumption. These facts provide the
sombre autobiographical background against which the
poem must be read.

They also provide a clue to the inner conflict in Gray's
poem. The opposition between the natural, almost
animal life of the village (the 'lowing Herd' and the
'Plowman' merge into each other) and the futile artificial
life of the 'Proud' is the Gray of 1742 arraigning the
Gray of 1741. This picture of the heartless insincerity of
high life—the hypocritical funeral anthem (l. 40), the
flattery of the expensive epitaph (l. 44), the lying and
brazenness (ll. 69–70), the poetical eulogizing of the
proud and luxurious (ll. 71–2)—is a reflection of his own
recent dependence on Walpole, the Prime Minister's son.
And the revulsion from his earlier fashionable self is
accompanied by a realistic recognition of what his poverty
will now entail. *His* heart is pregnant with celestial fire,
but chill penury will soon repress *his* noble rage and
freeze the current of *his* genius. And there is no attempt

to blink the consequences. The tenor of his doom must in future be 'silent'—as indeed it was. Between 1742 and 1747—with the possible exception of the 'Autumnal verses' of 1746 already mentioned—Gray wrote no poems at all.

With so much of himself and his own private affairs in the *Stanzas* it was natural for Gray to refuse to allow their publication. They were shown to Walpole not long after their reconciliation at the end of 1745, and it is possible that their transmutation into the *Elegy* is attributable to Walpole's enthusiasm and encouragement. Essentially the addition of the final fifty-two lines was an attempt to *depersonalize* the poem. Unfortunately they only succeed in this at the expense of the poetry. The central figure is no longer Thomas Gray, the middle-class youth who had been admitted for a few golden years into the inner ranks of the aristocracy. His place is taken by a conventional literary figure, the Melancholy Man, who could not possibly be identified with anybody, and it is only in the 'Epitaph'—and then somewhat obscurely—that the real living Gray returns:

> A Youth to Fortune and to Fame unknown,
> Fair Science frowned not on his humble birth,
> And Melancholy marked him for her own.

Gray was a reserved, sensitive man, and it is easy to believe that the publication of the *Stanzas* might have had distressing consequences. At least one of his contemporaries was shocked even by the *Elegy*: 'Delicacy and taste recoil at the publication of internal griefs. They profane the hallowedness of secret sadness; and suppose selected and decorated expression compatible with the prostration of the soul.'[1] On the other hand Gray was

---

[1] *A Criticism on the Elegy written in a Country Church Yard* (1783), p. 11.

right in thinking that the poem would be of public interest to the England of his time. He had not written it entirely as an act of private catharsis. The poem was a protest, a *cri de cœur*, not only against his own personal misfortunes but also at the social order that had made them possible.

Like Pope's *Elegy to the Memory of an Unfortunate Lady* —the poem that seems to have been Gray's principal model—Gray's poem is partly an indictment of the ruling aristocracy. The condemnation of 'Pride' (l. 71) and 'ye Proud' (l. 37), which is also found in the *Ode on the Spring* and the *Hymn to Adversity* (both written in the same summer of 1742), is indeed a recurring theme in Pope's verse. The word *pride* occurs twenty-three times in the *Essay on Man* alone. The trouble with Timon, the incarnation of aristocratic pride in the *Epistle to Burlington*, was his uselessness, and Gray points the same contrast between the 'useful toil' of the villagers and the 'pomp of pow'r.' With Gray's

> Oft did the harvest to their sickle yield,
> Their furrow oft the stubborn glebe has broke,

one can compare Pope's lines foretelling the disappearance of Timon's pretentious villa and purely ornamental gardens:

> Another age shall see the golden Ear
> Embrown the Slope, and nod on the Parterre,
> Deep Harvests bury all his pride has plann'd,
> And laughing Ceres re-assume the land.

Of course, neither Pope nor Gray was a revolutionary. They had no wish to overthrow the squirearchy. Their satire was aimed essentially at shaming the arrogant oligarchy into a recognition of the original egalitarian basis of the régime. They would, no doubt, have been perfectly satisfied with a return to the less rigidly stratified class-system of the Restoration, when a statistician like John Graunt, a shopkeeper's son like themselves, was proposed for the Royal Society by no less a person than the King.[1]

If the 'proud' have this dual significance for Gray, as both public and private symbols, so have the 'rude Forefathers of the hamlet.' Their home is not Stoke Poges, or indeed any real recognizable place. Whatever Gray was doing he was not writing with his eye on a phenomenal object. The descriptive inaccuracies therefore do not matter. It is true that cattle do not normally 'low' or 'wind' their way at sunset, and that 'drowsy tinklings lull the distant folds' is a confusion of two sheep-farming systems (if the sheep are folded there is no need for a bell-wether). It is also true that owls do not really 'mope' or 'complain,' and that elms are not particularly 'rugged.' But literal accuracy would have been inappropriate in a description of a symbolic village, whose essential function was simply to be the opposite of 'polite Company.'[2] Its inhabitants are 'rude,' 'lowly,' 'busy,' 'jocund,' 'sturdy,' 'useful,' 'homely,' and 'obscure,' primarily as a foil to 'Ambition,' 'Grandeur,' 'pow'r,' and their attendants 'Honour,' 'Flatt'ry,' 'Knowledge' and 'Luxury.' The idyll of the village is opposed to the satire of 'the Town,' not because Gray was under any

---

[1] See Sprat's *History of the Royal Society* (1667), p. 67. Sprat also contrasts (p. 407) the snobbery of the previous generation with the country gentlemen of his own time: 'The cours of their *Ancestors lives* was grave and reserv'd ... now they are engag'd in freer modes of *Education*: now the vast distance between them and other orders of men is no more observ'd ...'

[2] cp. Voltaire's comment on Congreve's comedies: 'The Language is every-where that of Men of Honour, but their Actions are those of Knaves; a proof that he was perfectly well acquainted with human Nature, and frequented what we call polite Company' (*Letters concerning the English Nation* (1733), p. 188).

pastoral illusions, but to give picturesque emphasis to his argument. Indeed, in the central section of the poem he has explicitly recognized that human nature does not change much whatever the environment may be. The village Hampdens, Miltons and Cromwells—'Cato,' 'Tully,' and 'Cæsar' in the *Stanzas*—have the same virtues and vices as their national counterparts; it is only their *range* that is circumscribed.

The country hamlet is not the only recurrent symbol in the poem. More interesting, because it is probably unconscious, is an apparent identification of the 'thoughtless World' with noise and of the 'Innocence' of the village with silence. Thus the initial landscape is characterized by 'a solemn stillness,' which the occasional natural sounds only emphasize, and the *Stanzas* conclude in a 'sacred Calm' punctuated by 'still small Accents.' Opposed to it are the 'pealing anthem' of the proud man's funeral, the loud flattery of 'Honor's voice,' the lyre 'wak'd to ecstasy' by a Milton who is *not* mute, and the 'list'ning senates' intent on a Cromwell's oratory. In the light of this symbolism Gray's final decision in the *Stanzas* to 'Pursue the silent Tenour' of his doom takes on a further meaning. The fine Alcaics written at the Grande Chartreuse in August 1741 on his journey home after the quarrel with Walpole had already recorded his regret that his lot forbade him to enjoy the monks' sacred rule of silence:

> invidendis sedibus et frui
> Fortuna sacra lege silentii
> Vetat volentem.

In this concept of a Sacred Silence, positive and rational, both the public and the private conflicts of the *Elegy* find their solution. It is not the silence of death, though it resembles death (hence the appropriateness of the church-yard setting), but of 'eternal Peace.' The Christian humility that is to provide the solvent of his personal difficulties is paralleled by the Christian charity that is the implied prescription for the social ills of Augustan England.

The presence of symbolism, though Gray's differs from Romantic symbolism both in the mode of action and in the choice of symbols (Gray shows little interest in wild nature), is a reminder that the *Elegy* came some twenty-five years after the classic moment of the Augustan tradition. The Polished Craftsman was feeling his way towards a variation of the Augustan formula. The personal note in the four cancelled verses was also new. They should be compared with the parallel passage in the *Elegy to the Memory of an Unfortunate Lady* (which was written about 1717):

> Poets themselves must fall, like those they sung;
> Deaf the prais'd ear, and mute the tuneful tongue.
> Ev'n he, whose soul now melts in mournful lays,
> Shall shortly want the gen'rous tear he pays;
> Then from his closing eyes thy form shall part,
> And the last pang shall tear thee from his heart.
> Life's idle business at one gasp be o'er,
> The Muse forgot, and thou belov'd no more!

Here Pope is merely striking a series of rhetorical attitudes. As I. A. Richards has said in commenting on this poem, 'the poet's eye is very plainly on himself and on his reader rather than on the imaginary object.'[1] In Gray, on the other hand, the imaginary object is himself. Here, as occasionally in Shenstone, Cowper and Frances Greville[2]—all contemporaries of Gray's—is authentically

[1] *Practical Criticism* (1929), p. 356.
[2] 'A Prayer for Indifference' is the one great poem written by an English-woman in the eighteenth century. Its first appearance in print was in the

introspective poetry. Quantitatively, though, the personal element does not bulk large in Gray's verse. The autobiographical conclusion of 'The Progress of Poesy' is so inconspicuous that many readers have failed to realize that it is Gray who is 'Beneath the Good how far—but far above the Great.' And perhaps the most important thing about the cancelled stanzas in the *Elegy* is that they *were* cancelled. In spite of the occasional deviations Gray is primarily an Augustan poet. Unlike Collins (who is most successful when he is least Augustan—and was absurdly over-rated by the Romantics in consequence),[1] Gray writes best when he keeps to the central literary tradition of Dryden and Pope. It is significant that there are no paradoxes in the last fifty-two lines of the *Elegy*, whereas the first seventy-two lines are full of them, or of related figures.[2] The central section on the village Hampdens, Miltons and Cromwells—in my own opinion the best passage in the poem—is a continuous *expanded paradox*. The concept of a 'village-Hampden' *appears* to be a contradiction in terms. (How can you be a national hero *and* unknown outside your own village?) Its resolution, carrying with it the implication that the smaller

---

Annual Register for 1762, pp. 202–3, though it was probably written some years before. The text in the *Oxford Book of Eighteenth Century Verse* is inferior to that in I. A. Williams's *Shorter Poems of the Eighteenth Century*.

[1] C. S. Lewis, one of our latter-day Romantics, has recently attributed to *How Sleep the Brave* a 'depth and ambiguity of real experience' not to be found in Donne! (See *Seventeenth Century Studies presented to Sir Herbert Grierson*, (1938), p. 80.) This 'Ode, Written in the beginning of the year 1746' is merely a deft medley of Collins's own poem on the death of Colonel Ross (killed at Fontenoy, 11 May 1745) and a passage from Pope's *Unfortunate Lady*. Saintsbury thought it 'faultless' (*C.H.E.L.*, vol. x, p. 144), but the repetition of *their* and *there* eight times in twelve lines is clumsy, and 'Choirs unseen' would have been better than 'Forms unseen' in l. 8.

[2] e.g., 'short and simple annals' (l. 23), 'The paths of glory lead but to the grave' (l. 36), the 'gem of purest ray' in 'The dark unfathom'd caves' (ll. 53–4), etc. The zeugmas of 'leave the world to darkness and to me' (l. 4) and 'By Night and lonely contemplation led' (l. 7 of the cancelled stanzas) are a kind of paradox.

unit is at least as favourable a soil for the display of moral grandeur, shows Gray equally in the central social tradition of his time. The *Elegy*, in addition to all the other things that it is, was a tract for the times. It was a plea for decentralization, recalling the over-urbanized ruling class to its roots in a rural society based upon the benevolent despotism of the manor-house.[1]

[1] The change from Cato to Hampden and from Cæsar to Cromwell clinched the argument. The historical Hampden and Cromwell had in fact owed their later success to the training they had acquired in the 'village.'

O

CHAPTER ELEVEN

THE QUICKEST WAY OUT OF MANCHESTER: FOUR ROMANTIC ODES

I

DRINK was only one of the ways of getting out of the Manchesters of the nineteenth century. The worship of the Gin-Juggernath that Cruickshank portrayed in 1834 in an effective print was confined to all intents and purposes to the working classes. But the middle classes, especially the self-styled 'upper middle class'—which soon after 1800 had become in effect the English ruling class, only retaining the aristocracy as its administrative agents[1]—were able to escape from social realities quite as effectively via Romantic poetry, the historical novel and the Anglo-Catholic religion. The motives for escape were, of course, not the same. The Ancoats millhands, the Yorkshire miners and the agricultural chain-gangs of East Anglia drank their gin as an alleviation of sheer physical misery. The Victorian *bourgeois gentilhommes*, on the other hand, *physically* were extremely well off. Food was cheap, servants were plentiful, wives did their duty and property was relatively secure. Their troubles were psychological—a sense of guilt, a consciousness of sin.

---

[1] Matthew Arnold ('My Countrymen,' *Cornhill Magazine* [Feb. 1866]) quotes Sir Robert Lowe as saying that England was happy in having her middle part strong and her extremes weak, and adds, 'though we are administered by one of our weak extremes, the aristocracy, these managers administer us, as a weak extreme naturally must, with a nervous attention to the wishes of the strong middle part, whose agents they are.' Arnold's whole essay is a brilliant piece of sociological analysis. It is reprinted in the 'Everyman' edition of *On the Study of Celtic Literature*.

> Each with never-ceasing labour,
> Whilst he thinks he cheats his neighbour,
> Cheating his own heart of quiet.[1]

The upper middle class had inherited from their humble seventeenth-century ancestors, along with the energy and the 'horse sense,' a Christian conscience. 'Thou shalt love thy neighbour as thyself' was a command impossible to obey under the economic conditions of the nineteenth century. A cut-throat competitiveness is the logical essence of *laissez-faire* capitalism. But the Puritan conscience didn't like it. The left hand refused to acknowledge what the right hand was doing, and a division of labour began to operate in the individual *psyche*. The Understanding, in Coleridge's terminology, remained in the counting-house, the calculable world of cause and effect; the Reason plunged into the mysterious sea of the subconscious mind, the world of 'imagination.' Nevertheless this process of psychic specialization tended to remain incomplete. Expelled by the economic pitchfork human nature had a way of reasserting itself in its old integrated totality. And it is essentially this conflict, between the personality integrated in a social environment and the anti-social 'split man' (Dr. Jekyll and Mr. Hyde), that is mirrored in Romantic poetry. In so far as the poetry was in the central tradition of Romanticism the Split Man was its hero and Society was its villain. But in so far as the poetry was *poetry* (by the standards set by the Greek and Latin classics, which the Romantics accepted as fully as the Augustans) the issue of the conflict had to appear to hang in the balance. The hero (the ideal) must not win too easily; the villain (social reality) must be given a chance. And so by a curious paradox to be a good

[1] Shelley, *Peter Bell the Third*, pt. 3, stanza xi.

Romantic poet you had to know the case against Romanticism. You had to be a rationalist as well as an irrationalist, a functioning member of society as well as a social revolutionary or a social escapist. There were therefore two dangers to which the Romantic poet as such was exposed. On the one hand, he could be too Romantic—in which case his poetry would degenerate into verse because there was no genuine basic conflict. This is what seems to have happened in Wordsworth's later work as well as in much of Shelley's poetry. On the other hand, he could be too anti-Romantic—in which case he would find it difficult to write any poetry at all. (It was a fundamental thesis of the theoretic argument in Chapter Four that, within broad limits, only one *kind* of poetry can be written successfully at one time.) And this, I suggest, is why Coleridge's later writings are almost all in prose. If Keats had lived to be thirty-five, it is possible, I think, that he too would have abandoned poetry.

It is proposed to attempt to substantiate these propositions by a detailed examination of Wordsworth's 'Intimations of Immortality from Recollections of Early Childhood' (begun March 1802), Coleridge's 'Dejection: An Ode' (April 1802), Shelley's 'Ode to the West Wind' (October or November 1819), and Keats's 'Ode on a Grecian Urn' (early summer 1819).

II

The peculiar importance that Wordsworth attached to his 'Ode,' as it was originally called (the polysyllabic subtitle was not added until 1815), is shown by its position in the editions of his poems issued in his lifetime. In *Poems in Two Volumes* (1807), where the poem made its first appearance, it comes at the very end of the second volume with a special half-title (it is the only poem to be so distinguished), the verso of which reads *Paulo majora canamus*. It retains the same honourable segregation—*finis coronat opus*, as it were—in the collected *Poems* of 1815 as well as in the later editions of Wordsworth's poetical works. And this splendid isolation is generally maintained in modern editions.

On the whole, the critics have accepted the poem at Wordsworth's implied valuation, though with some reservations. A. C. Bradley, for example, an expert Wordsworthian, has pronounced the Ode '[his] greatest product, but not his best piece of work.'[1] There is certainly some verbal imprecision. A number of the phrases are tautological,[2] and it is clumsy to say 'there hath past away a *glory* from the earth' (l. 18) immediately after calling the sunshine 'a *glorious* birth' (l. 16).[3] Moreover there are rather too many quotations and accidental literary reminiscences. Daniel's 'humourous stage' (l. 104) and Gray's 'meanest floweret' (l. 203) were hardly worth the carriage. And it is decidedly disconcerting to be reminded of the Ghost in *Hamlet* in

> High instincts before which our mortal Nature
> Did tremble like a guilty Thing surprised;[4]

as it is to learn that 'Our noisy years' (l. 155) comes straight out of an anonymous 'Address to Silence' that Dorothy Wordsworth had copied out of the Sherborne *Weekly Entertainer; Or, Agreeable and Instructive Repository*.

---

[1] *Oxford Lectures on Poetry* (1909), p. 117.
[2] e.g., beautiful and fair' (l. 15), 'young lambs' (l. 20), 'A mourning or a funeral' (l. 95).
[3] There is a similar contradiction between the Youth who is 'Nature's Priest' (l. 73), i.e., the antenatal glory's, and the Earth's yearnings 'in her own *natural* kind' (l. 79).
[4] cp. *Hamlet*, I, i, 148–9,

> 'And then it started like a guilty thing
> Upon a fearful summons.'

The question that this kind of thing must suggest to anybody who is not a Wordsworthian is whether the clumsiness and the derivativeness do not go deeper. Are they perhaps the outward and visible sign of an inner spiritual factitiousness? Is the Ode pretending to be something more than it really is?

It will be advisable before attempting to answer this question to define what exactly the poem is about. A definition can perhaps be best approached by a consideration of its structure.

Structurally the outstanding features of the Ode are the detailed links (*a*) between stanzas I–II and XI, and (*b*) between stanzas III–IV and X. The opening lines of stanza X,

> Then sing, ye Birds, sing, sing a joyous song!
> And let the young Lambs bound
> As to the tabor's sound!

repeat almost verbatim the opening lines of stanza III:

> Now, while the birds thus sing a joyous song,
> And while the young lambs bound
> As to the tabor's sound.

And the reader, having been thus instructed to make the reference back, will note *inter alia* the following connections:

(i) the 'heart of May' (l .32), with which the country-side is welcoming the spring, on 'This sweet May-morning' (l. 44) and ll. 174–5,

> Ye that through your hearts to-day
> Feel the gladness of the May

(ii) the 'thought of grief' (l. 22) temporarily relieved ('I again am strong' (l. 24)) and ll. 180–1,

> We will grieve not, rather find
> Strength in what remains behind.

(iii) the 'meadow, grove, and stream' of l. 1, and their echo in the 'Fountains, Meadow, Hills, and Groves' (l. 188) which the last stanza of the poem begins by invoking.

Between the six interconnected opening and closing stanzas, all of which can be described as autobiographical, Wordsworth has inserted five stanzas that are not linked verbally or by the imagery to the rest of the poem. These central stanzas expound the 'myth' (using the word in the Platonic sense of a parable that is more than mere allegory) of the soul's pre-existence with God. The evolution of the Ode is therefore, at least in intention, (i) a statement of Wordsworth's personal problem (stanzas I–IV), (ii) an exposition of the theoretical solution (stanzas V–IX), and (iii) the application of the solution to Wordsworth's own case (stanzas X, XI). The *problem* may be said to be Wordsworth's distress at discovering that his response to sensuous experience (sights in stanzas I, II, sounds in III, IV) is becoming less keen. The theoretical *solution*—that growing older inevitably dulls the freshness of the senses' reactions—relieves Wordsworth of any personal responsibility for what is in fact inherent in the nature of things. And the application sees Wordsworth resigning himself to a decay of the senses in the consolations of 'thought'[1] and emotion recollected in tranquillity.[2]

---

[1] 'We in *thought* will join your throng' (l. 172),
  'the soothing *thoughts* that spring
  Out of human suffering' (l. 185),
  'the philosophic mind' (l. 187),
  '*Thoughts* that do often lie too deep for tears' (l. 204).

[2] This is the prose sense of the imagery of ll. 162–8. Provided there is 'a season of calm weather' (tranquillity), even adults ('Though inland far we be') can recapture in memory ('Our Souls have sight') the mystical ecstasies of childhood ('And see the Children sport upon the shore, And hear the mighty waters rolling evermore').

Wordsworth's overt intentions are clear enough. The poem is *meant* to be the record of a process of psychological stocktaking that results in a final mental readjustment. The Wordsworth that is *supposed* to emerge is a wiser if sadder man than the sentimentalist of the opening stanzas. But is this, in fact, the impression that the poem leaves? Is not the reader finally left with a feeling that the Philosophic Mind of middle age is decidedly a second-best? *Nothing* can bring back the 'splendour in the grass'! The 'glory' has departed! All that is left is 'the light of common day'! Even the sunset clouds now 'take a sober colouring'!

The contradiction between what the Ode is meant to say and what it actually says is acute. And it is implicit in the central myth. If the process of growing up is essentially a growing *away* from God, what is there for the middle-aged man to live for? In Henry Vaughan's poems—where Wordsworth probably found his myth[1]— there was the ultimate prospect of reunion with God, but Wordsworth had not the same conviction of personal immortality. (For Wordsworth middle age was simply a half-way stage to the final *exit*

From sunshine to the sunless land.)

And even recollection in tranquillity, though nothing 'Can utterly abolish or destroy' it as long as life lasts, necessarily becomes fainter and feebler as the time-interval increases between the remembering mind and the remembered experience.

[1] A copy of Vaughan's *Silex Scintillans* was found in Wordsworth's library after his death. At what date he acquired it is not known, but the parallels between the Ode and 'The Retreate' are so striking that he must at any rate have known Vaughan's poem when he wrote stanzas V–IX. Although many partial parallels have been cited from the Neoplatonists and Christian mystics nowhere but in Vaughan is there to be found the inch-by-inch regression that is the essence of Wordsworth's myth.

But before convicting Wordsworth of mental dishonesty it will be desirable to restore the poem to its contemporary setting. Whom was it written for? When was it written? Why was it written?

An entry in Dorothy Wordsworth's *Journal* establishes that the poem was *begun* on 27 March 1802 ('Wm. wrote part of an Ode'). Years later Wordsworth told Isabella Fenwick that 'two years at least passed between the writing of the four first stanzas and the remaining part,' and as the complete poem was certainly in existence in March 1804 (when Coleridge was given a copy to take to Malta) it has been assumed that stanzas I–IV date from March 1802 and stanzas V–XI from March 1804.[1] In fact, however, only the *termini a quo* and *ad quem* and an interval of undefined length between them can be considered certain. The 'myth' and the concluding stanzas are more likely, in my opinion, to have been written in 1803 than in 1804, and it is probable, I think, that the opening stanzas were expanded as early as May 1802.[2] Wordsworth would not have written 'This sweet May-morning' (l. 44) if it had really been a March morning. And the curious reference in ll. 22–3,

> To me alone there came a thought of grief;
> A timely utterance gave that thought relief,

is less likely to be to the lines beginning 'My heart leaps up,' as H. W. Garrod has suggested, than to 'Resolution and Independence.' Both of these poems were in process of composition at the time, the former having been drafted on 26 March and rewritten on 14 May, and the latter having been begun on 3 May and finished on 9 May

---

[1] See *The Poetical Works of Wordsworth*, ed. E. de Selincourt and H. Darbishire, vol. iv (1947), pp. 464–5.

[2] He was still tinkering with the poem in June. Dorothy noted in her *Journal* for 17 June, 'Wm. added a little to the Ode he is writing.'

(some changes were made later). But 'My heart leaps up' cannot have given Wordsworth the relief he describes. His trouble was that his heart would *not* leap up! On the other hand 'Resolution and Independence' is a dramatization of exactly the psychological state described in the Ode. Wordsworth summarized his intentions in 'Resolution and Independence' in a revealing letter to Sara Hutchinson:

> I describe myself as having been exalted to the highest pitch of delight by the joyousness and beauty of Nature and then as depressed, even in the midst of those beautiful objects, to the lowest dejection and despair. A young Poet in the midst of the happiness of Nature is described as overwhelmed by the thought of the miserable reverses which have befallen the happiest of all men, viz. Poets—I think of this till I am so deeply impressed by it, that I consider the manner in which I was rescued from my dejection and despair almost as an interposition of Providence.[1]

Here at any rate, whichever the poem was that 'gave that thought relief,' is the mood out of which the Ode grew. And here too is a hint of the personal problems of Wordsworth and his circle—the Ode's 'human suffering' productive of 'soothing thoughts'—that were clamouring for a solution in the year 1802. Wordsworth's use of the word 'dejection' was probably without *arrière pensée*, but it is worth noting that the original version of Coleridge's 'Dejection: An Ode' had been addressed to this same Sara Hutchinson as recently as 4 April[2] and had been 'repeated' to the Wordsworths by Coleridge himself on 21 April.

[1] 14 June 1802.
[2] The MS. (which was printed by E. de Selincourt in the English Association's *Essays and Studies* for 1937) is headed 'A Letter to ——.' A shorter version that was printed in the *Morning Post* on 4 Oct. 1802 seems to be the first with the familiar title.

Sara and Coleridge were in love (a tragic idyll in Coleridge's career that his early biographers did not know about), and the poet whose 'miserable reverses' Wordsworth's words must at once have turned her mind to would not be Chatterton or Burns, as in the poem, but Coleridge. Unlike Wordsworth, who had been temporarily rescued from his dejection by Providence (he had now become formally engaged to Sara's sister Mary), Coleridge was 'Past Cure, and past Complaint':

> A Grief without a pang, void, dark and drear,
> A stifling, drowsy, unimpassion'd Grief
> That finds no natural outlet, no Relief
> In word, or sigh, or tear—
> This, Sara! well thou know'st,
> Is that sore Evil, which I dread the most,
> And oft'nest suffer!

There could be no question of a 'timely utterance' relieving *this* grief.

But, though Coleridge's case was worse than Wordsworth's, their diseases were really the same, as their accounts of their separate symptoms demonstrate. Wordsworth's case-history is to be found in Book XI of *The Prelude* (Book XII in the 1850 text), which supplements the evidence of the Ode. His first crisis, according to his own diagnosis, had come when he was twenty-one or twenty-two. Before going to Cambridge, he still retained

> The first diviner influence of this world (l. 232),

and this *uncritical* love of all created things persisted until the last Long Vacation of his university career:

> through the gorgeous Alps
> Roaming, I carried with me the same heart (ll. 22–41).

The change apparently came during his residence in
France. He became a rationalist, a perfectibilist and an
æsthete. Like Coleridge ('I see, not feel, how beautiful
they are'), Wordsworth then allowed the eye to become
'master of the heart' (l. 172). And if Annette Vallon is to
be associated with 'this degradation' (l. 244), as she may
have been, her rôle must have been parallel to Mrs.
Coleridge's.[1] In 1795, under the influence of his sister
Dorothy, Wordsworth returned to the nature mysticism
of his youth, and it was at this period, according to his
own account, that he worked out the technique of an
emotional recollection of early childhood. Childish
incidents seem to have had a particularly 'vivifying
Virtue' (l. 260), replenishing his 'power' and 'strength.'
Coleridge, the lover of living children, laid less emphasis
on memories of his own childhood, though in 'Dejection'
a recollection of 'sky-gazing' at Christ's Hospital has
unconsciously relieved him:

> The Weight was somewhat lifted from my Breast.

That the process was not a purely passive one is made
clear by Wordsworth:

> this I feel,
> That from thyself it is that thou must give,
> Else never canst receive (ll. 332–4).

And here the parallel is particularly close with 'Dejection':

> O Sara! we receive but what we give,
> And in *our* life alone does Nature live.

---

[1] It may not be a coincidence that Wordsworth had written to Annette, the
first letter for a great many years, on 26 March, the day before he began the
Ode. The Peace of Amiens, which temporarily restored normal communication with France, was not formally signed until 27 March. Wordsworth's
seizing of the very first opportunity that had occurred to write *finis* to the
Annette episode is surely significant.

More therefore was involved than an act of memory. According to Coleridge what was primarily required, the 'beauty-making Power,' was joy, the spontaneous happiness of the innocent, like Sara. Wordsworth is less clear on this point. 'Joy,' 'bliss,' 'gladness,' 'delight,' 'glee,' and 'happiness' are words that recur again and again in his poems, but they are apparently the *effect* of recollection rather than an essential constituent of it. For both, however, their own joylessness ('grief'), or at least the intermittent character of their joy, is the real problem. Coleridge called Wordsworth's trouble 'hypochondria'; 'a hypochondriacal graft in his nature' is the way he put it to Richard Sharp in 1804. And during their Scotch tour of 1803 he complained in a letter to his wife that 'Wordsworth's hypochondriacal feelings keep him silent and self-centred.' But the real name for the disease from which both of them were suffering was Romanticism. Wordsworth and Coleridge were among the first victims of that *mal du siècle* which derived from the attempt to prolong adolescence artificially. The interest of their two Odes is the different ways in which the two friends react to what is fundamentally the same phenomenon.

For Coleridge the temptation was always to self-pity. But in 'Dejection' he was able to emerge out of his own self-pity, walk round it and record it objectively:

> For not to think of what I needs must feel,
> But to be still and patient all I can;
> And haply by abstruse Research to steal
> From my own Nature, all the Natural man—
> This was my sole Reserve, my wisest plan!
> And that, which suits a part, infects the whole,
> And now is almost grown the Temper of my Soul.

There is a clinical completeness about this poem that is

most satisfying. The moon, the larch, the sky with 'its peculiar Tint of Yellow Green,' and the suspension of his own 'shaping spirit of Imagination' (the romantic *sine qua non*) are all observed with the same inclusive detachment. Coleridge has made a moving poem out of the failure to prolong his own Golden Age, when

> The Joy within me dallied with Distress;
> And all Misfortunes were but as the Stuff
> Whence Fancy made me Dreams of Happiness.

It had been lovely while it lasted, but it had had no basis in reality. That happiness was only a dream—and not a real dream but one that was the creation of fancy, a dream of a dream.

If 'Dejection' is a confession of failure, Wordsworth's Ode is, superficially at any rate, a claim to success. He has solved the problem of prolonging the excitements of adolescence by his technique of emotional recollection! But the tone of voice in which the claim is advanced at once throws doubt upon its validity. Can what is so clearly felt to be only a second best be considered a success at all? And there is one piece of deliberate falsification. It is contained in ll. 193–4:

> I love the Brooks which down their channels fret,
> Even more than when I tripped lightly as they.

It is quite impossible to accept this statement at its face-value. All the evidence of the other autobiographical poems confirms the account of his development that Wordsworth gave in the 'Lines composed a few miles above Tintern Abbey.' There *was* a time when the cataract had haunted him 'like a passion,' but that was from about 1786 to 1793. By 1803 the 'Nature's Priest' had become the 'Man' living in 'the light of common day.' The two lines are in reality the merest wishful thinking. They are almost the first indication of the indifference to *fact* in the later Wordsworth that was to startle Hazlitt and Shelley.[1]

The explanation of Wordsworth's self-deception is that by 1803 it had become essential to his self-esteem. The whole basis of his life had been that he was to be the Great Poet, the modern Milton. Hitherto, with the help of his sister Dorothy and Coleridge, he had been training himself for the rôle, working out a style, elaborating a philosophy. The *Lyrical Ballads* of 1798 were only 'experiments' (the 'Advertisement' says so), but by 1803 he might be forgiven for thinking that he had 'arrived.' The *Lyrical Ballads* were already in a third edition, his admirers included great men like Charles James Fox, and in John Wilson of Glasgow University, who had written to him on 24 May 1802, he had found the first of the Wordsworthians. It was a pardonable mistake to think he could now marry and 'settle down'; his contemporaries like Crabbe and Scott had done so with eminently beneficial results. The antipathy between respectability and Romantic poetry was then still an undiscovered psychological law. Wordsworth found it out for himself —and then tried to save the situation by bluff. Hence perhaps the special importance that he assigned to the Ode. He was cheering himself up! The rhetoric was so good that he may almost have convinced himself.[2]

Wordsworth's self-esteem also demanded a moral to his Ode different from that of Coleridge's Ode. The two

[1] A curious example of this petty dishonesty is the section-heading in *Poems in Two Volumes*, 'Poems, composed during a Tour, chiefly on Foot.' Of the five poems in this section three were certainly composed at Grasmere and the other two may have been!

[2] Almost, but not quite. No. ix of the *Evening Voluntaries* (written in 1817) speaks of 'the light! Full early lost, and *fruitlessly* deplored.' and a prose note by Wordsworth specifically connects the passage with the Ode.

poems were closely associated in the intimate circle who were Wordsworth's real poetic audience at this time, and in elaborating his fragment he can hardly have failed to realize that he was entering into a sort of competition with Coleridge. When Coleridge wrote 'Dejection' he had just seen the embryonic first four stanzas of Wordsworth's Ode (all that was then written), as one or two passages in his own poem make clear. His 'I too will crown me with a Coronal' might even be interpreted as an acceptance of the implied challenge in Wordsworth's 'My heart hath its coronal.' As no MS. survives of Wordsworth's first draft it is impossible to say whether the metrical irregularity (inherited from Dryden and Cowley) is Coleridge's or Wordsworth's contribution; but *a priori* one would expect it to be Coleridge's, as this was Wordsworth's first ode. Wordsworth had certainly read 'Dejection' carefully—one MS. version is addressed to him, 'William' taking the place of 'Sara'—and his 'little Actor' (l. 103) and 'Mighty Prophet' (l.115) may be reminiscences of Coleridge's

> Thou Actor, perfect in all tragic Sounds!
> Thou mighty Poet . . .

In this domestic competition it may be assumed that Wordsworth won (he always did), but Coleridge's Ode is the better poem of the two. The variations of 'tone' are particularly admirable. Instead of the monotone of Wordsworth's 'egotistical sublime,' as Keats called it, Coleridge is in turn conversational, pathetic, rhetorical, analytic and descriptive. It is a human being who is speaking. And it is to Coleridge's credit that 'Dejection' was a junction, not a terminus. There were to be no more *Kubla Khans*, but on the wreckage of his youth Coleridge managed to build a second career as critic, philosopher and theologian. If he did not achieve the return to Manchester it was something to have been able to hold London spell-bound with the eloquence of his table talk. Wordsworth's Ode, on the other hand, *was* a terminus— or very nearly. After 1803 the man hardens and the style becomes clumsily Miltonic ('thick-ankled' was Tennyson's term for it). The lie had entered into the soul. Instead of the actuality and veracity of the early poems, the eye on the object, we get sermons in stones and sonnet sequences in the running brooks. Their Grasmere neighbours would soon be able to watch the Wordsworth family taking its daily walk, with William striding ahead, 'sayin' nowt to noan of 'em.' He had nothing left worth saying.

Wordsworth's case is a complicated one. He *was* a Lost Leader, but not in the vulgar sense imputed by Browning. It was rather that he had lost any sense of social direction. The good intentions of the *Lyrical Ballads* must be commended. They were intended, he says, to counteract the psychological effects of the Industrial Revolution:

> For a multitude of causes, unknown to former times, are now acting with a combined force to blunt the discriminating powers of the mind, and, unfitting it for all voluntary exertion, to reduce it to a state of almost savage torpor. The most effective of these causes are the great national events which are daily taking place, and the increasing accumulation of men in cities, when the uniformity of their occupations produces a craving for extraordinary incident, which the rapid communication of intelligence barely gratifies.[1]

Instead of the melodramatic excitements of the contemporary street ballads Wordsworth offered 'the middle

[1] Preface to second edition (1800).

P

and lower classes of society' a new kind of ballad containing 'a *natural* delineation of human passions, human characters, and human incidents.'[1] And it is clear that he had taken a good deal of trouble to learn the language of the popular ballad-writers. Most of the uncouthnesses and *naïvetés* of 'The Idiot Boy' and 'Simon Lee' are attributable to a deliberate attempt to reproduce the ballad manner rather than to any new theory of poetic diction. One of Wordsworth's ballad masters was Robert Anderson of Carlisle, whose song 'Lucy Gray of Allendale' was 'sung by Master Phelps, at Vauxhall, 1794.'[2] But it is only necessary to compare Anderson's Lucy Gray with Wordsworth's to realize why Wordsworth never became the poet of the nineteenth-century proletariat:

> O have you seen the blushing rose,
>   The blooming pink, or lily pale;
> Fairer than any flow'r that blows
>   Was Lucy Gray of Allendale. . . .

> 'Twas underneath the hawthorn shade
>   I told her first the tender tale;
> But now low lays the lovely maid
>   Sweet Lucy Gray of Allendale.

> Bleak blows the wind, keen beats the rain,
>   Upon my cottage in the vale:
> Long may I mourn a lonely swain,
>   For Lucy Gray of Allendale.

This is almost the exact opposite of the psychological realism of the *Lyrical Ballads*. But Anderson, in spite of his

---

[1] 'Advertisement' to first edition (1798). The italics are mine.

[2] See Anderson's *Poems on Various Subjects* (Carlisle, 1798), p. 149. Wordsworth's 'Lucy Gray; or Solitude' was written in 1799 and printed in 1800. Anderson's 'Ruth,' who went off 'wid a taistrel sowdger lad' (it is a song in the Cumberland dialect) also invites comparison with Wordsworth.

sentimentality and his technical incompetence, was writing in the tradition of English folk-poetry. The poet-reader relationship was definite and intimate. Words-worth, though immensely his superior in natural gifts, was reduced to fabricating, and even *faking*, a poet-reader relationship. And it was the failure of his social mission —for the middle and lower classes consistently refused to read the *Lyrical Ballads*—that drove Wordsworth in on himself. For a year or two the little group at Dove Cottage—Dorothy, Coleridge, the Hutchinsons—pro-vided an audience for his introspective recollections. It was Wordsworth's golden moment, the period of *The Prelude*, the Lucy poems, 'Michael' and 'Revolution and Independence.' But each member of the group was too closely attached emotionally to him and to its other members for the group to be able to persist as a harmonious and beneficent social entity. As it breaks up—the rejection of Dorothy implied in the marriage to Mary Hutchinson is the first fissure—the social basis of Wordsworth's poetry disappears. The process was completed by the quarrel with Coleridge in 1810. Wordsworth was only forty in 1810, but he had not the humility or the curiosity to attempt a new relationship with a new audience. Indeed, it would never have crossed his mind that such a thing was necessary. The disadvantage of Romanticism was that it discouraged self-knowledge and self-criticism. Wordsworth had never been certain why he wrote poetry or where it came from. The habit of composition persisted after 1810 and for him the fact of persistence guaranteed the quality of the products. It is true the emotions still overflowed spontaneously into words, but because they were not addressed to anybody in particular the result was no longer poetry.

III

Shelley seems to have been the first critic to mark the *stages* of Wordsworth's poetic decay. 'He was at first sublime, pathetic, impressive, profound; then dull; then prosy and dull; and now dull—O, so very dull! it is an ultra-legitimate dulness.'[1] It is an admirably accurate division, the first stage presumably ending in 1802 or 1803, the second in or about 1810, while the third is that of *The Excursion* (1813) and its successors. And what was right in the early Wordsworth (his 'Wakening a sort of thought in sense') and what was wrong in the later Wordsworth, 'A solemn and unsexual man,' are distinguished with equal felicity. Could anything be better than this summary of the second volume of *Lyrical Ballads*?

> Of lakes he had intelligence,
> He knew something of heath, and fell.

> He had also dim recollections
> Of pedlars tramping on their rounds;
> Milk-pans and pails; and odd collections
> Of saws, and proverbs; and reflections
> Old parsons make in burying-grounds.

Unfortunately Shelley's faculties of self-criticism were less acute. The accident of his place in the Romantic succession, the fact that he was twenty-two years younger than Wordsworth—an Assured Master rather than the Leader of a New Movement—saved him from the lapses of diction that are so frequent in Wordsworth and Coleridge. And his control of symbolic technique is more certain. The failure of the 'myth' in Wordsworth's Ode is largely attributable to the injudicious choice of symbols.

[1] *Peter Bell the Third* (Oct. 1819), 'Dedication.'

It was madness of the still semi-republican Wordsworth to equate the pre-natal glory with an 'imperial palace,' and it was equally rash to compare the corrupting influence of the world to the 'Yearnings . . . of a Mother's Mind.' In both cases the associations derived from Wordsworth's earlier poetry work *against* the intended meaning, the connotations cancelling out the denotations. This kind of mistake, the consequence of a failure to appreciate that the symbol is the basic unit of Romantic poetry, is hardly ever found in Shelley's poetry. Without being systematic (Yeats's attempt to unravel a symbolic system in Shelley's poems doesn't get very far[1]), Shelley's symbolism is remarkably self-consistent. But the internal contradiction that was a mark, as we have seen, of Wordsworth's declining power is discernible in even the best of Shelley's poems.

The 'Ode to the West Wind' is said to be 'the most symmetrically perfect as well as the most impassioned'[2] of Shelley's shorter poems. E. M. W. Tillyard has called it 'the most powerful' of all Shelley's lyrics because the most 'masterfully shaped.'[3] And N. I. White, Shelley's last and best biographer, thinks 'few poems, if any, have ever been written with a finer sense of structure than the "Ode to the West Wind".'[4] This emphasis upon the structural perfection of the Ode suggests that the fairest line of critical approach will be, as with Wordsworth's Ode, by a process of structural analysis.[5]

---

[1] See 'The Philosophy of Shelley's Poetry' in Yeats's *Essays* (1924).
[2] J. A. Symonds, *Shelley*, 'English Men of Letters' series, pp. 119–20.
[3] *Milton* (1934), p. 241.   [4] *Shelley* (1947), vol. ii, p. 453.
[5] In the remarkable depreciation of Shelley in *Revaluation* (1936), pp. 204 ff., F. R. Leavis has approached the Ode by way of the imagery. The confusions that he finds in stanza II—'the tangled boughs of Heaven and Ocean,' he says, 'stand for nothing that Shelley could have pointed to in the scene before him' —can be paralleled in stanza I, l. 4, 'Yellow, and black, and pale, and hectic red' *following* 'like ghosts from an enchanter fleeing' suggests that the ghosts have not been visualized. Ghosts are essentially colourless. In ll. 5–6 the

Structurally, then, Shelley's poem consists of three parallel invocations of the West Wind in its three fields of operation, on the land, in the sky and on the sea. The invocations are followed by a prayer to the Wind:

> If I were a dead leaf thou mightest bear;
> If I were a swift cloud to fly with thee
> A wave to pant beneath thy power. . . .

which resumes the invocations of stanzas I–III. The autumn leaf typifies the objects of the Wind's impact on land (stanza I); the cloud (conceived as the leaf of a sky forest, 'Shook from the tangled boughs of Heaven and Ocean') typifies the sky (stanza II); the wave typifies the sea, with its submarine 'oozy woods' and their 'sapless foliage' (stanza III). Shelley's prayer is for a similar impact of the Wind upon himself:

> Oh, lift me as a wave, a leaf, a cloud!
> I fall upon the thorns of life! I bleed!

The Wind, in other words, is to provide Shelley with a means of escape from the difficulties of everyday life. So far (stanza IV) his prayer is self-regarding only. In stanza V it becomes altruistic and there is a slight extension of the symbolism. The Wind is no longer conceived simply as the force that whirls leaves about; it is also, as it lashes the forest, the creator of a wild music. Shelley is now praying for a resurgence of poetic inspiration. With

---

metaphors are hopelessly mixed; a *chariot* containing *winged seeds* is proceeding to a *bed*. l. 11 ('Driving sweet birds like flocks to feed in air') compares the shoots of the spring flora to a shepherd driving his sheep, i.e., a vertical to a horizontal process. And so on. The significant thing, however, is that such defects are not noticed until one's attention is drawn to them. Shelley's images are not meant to build up a landscape or effect a comparison. Their function is simply to add to the kaleidoscope of associations which surrounds the central symbol. The ghosts, the enchanter and the bright colours are merely intended to enrich the *idea* of the West Wind rather than to define one of its spheres of action.

the Wind's help his poems will be whirled 'over the universe' and serve as 'The trumpet of a prophecy.' And there is a final return here to a theme originally broached in stanza I—the West Wind of autumn is only the precursor of the West Wind of spring.

Shelley's structural *intentions* are clear enough. In so far as they are carried out they are, of course, to his poetic credit. But a close examination raises one central difficulty. In stanza I the Wind is invoked as 'Destroyer and preserver' (it destroys the leaves and preserves the seeds), and Shelley appears to assign a similar dual function to his poetry in stanza V (as 'Ashes and sparks' it will destroy the dead heritage of the past; as 'withered leaves' it will fertilize the Utopia of the future). The connection is not altogether clear, but there can at any rate be no doubt that a socio-political implication is intended. Shelley wants his reader to see the West Wind as a symbol of the forces of progress. That is what the poem *ought* to be about.

But is it? Is not the real subject of the poem (i) Shelley's delight in natural violence, (ii) Shelley's self-pity, (iii) Shelley's consciousness of failing inspiration? It is surely extremely significant that the Wind's destroyer-preserver rôle, so essential to the political argument, is lost sight of entirely in stanzas II and III. The minute structural parallelism of stanzas I–III presumes an identity of content in them. But in fact in stanzas II and III the Wind is conceived simply as an irresistible natural force. What it symbolizes is not political reform but the instinctive energies of the subconscious mind. Its contemplation restores Shelley to his boyhood (the typical Romantic reversion);

> If even
> I were as in my boyhood, and could be

> The comrade of thy wanderings over Heaven,
> As then, when to outstrip thy skiey speed
> Scarce seemed a vision.

And the altruism of stanza V is only on its surface. Essentially the ageing Shelley ('my leaves are falling') is demanding the restoration of his own adolescent ecstasies:

> Be thou, Spirit fierce,
> My spirit! Be thou me, impetuous one!

And the spring that is not far behind is less a prophecy of the Reform Bill than the personal consolation that a Romantic poet is offering himself. Like Wordsworth in his Ode, Shelley is *primarily* cheering himself up!

This is not to accuse Shelley of conscious insincerity. Shelley's political interests were genuine enough but they were superficial. Their emotional basis was not a rational conviction of the desirability of political reform, but a boy's reaction against domestic tyranny. As he grew up, the interest in politics began to wane. In the 'Ode to the West Wind' it provided an *excuse* for a poem that is really only concerned with Shelley himself. By June 1822—over two and a half years after he had written the Ode—Shelley could write to Horace Smith:

> England appears to be in a desperate condition, Ireland still worse; and no class of those who subsist on the public labour will be persuaded that *their* claims on it must be diminished. But the government must content itself with less in taxes, the landholder must submit to receive less rent, and the fundholder a diminished interest, or they will all get nothing. I once thought to study these affairs, and write or act in them—I am glad that my good genius said *refrain*—I see little public virtue, and I foresee that the contest will be one of blood and gold, two elements which

however much to my taste in my pockets and my veins,
I have an objection to out of them.[1]

The retreat from politics, here explicit, had been
implicit in Shelley's poetry almost from the beginning.
If he had lived he would no doubt have followed Wordsworth and Coleridge into a non-political conservatism.
Romanticism and politics are inherently incompatible,
as even Blake eventually discovered.[2] The political façade
that Shelley's poems retain was a form of unconscious
hypocrisy—the tribute of the escapist to the social conscience. They are pretending to be more serious than they
really are. I am inclined to think Shelley's light verse his
best poetry. *Peter Bell*, *The Witch of Atlas* and the group of
lyrics addressed to Jane Williams ('Ariel to Miranda,'
'The keen stars are twinkling,' 'Best and brightest,' etc.),
though often carelessly written and always rather 'thin,'
are at any rate completely successful in what they set out
to be.

IV

Keats's 'Ode on a Grecian Urn' was written in the
early summer of 1819.[3] It therefore antedates the 'Ode to
the West Wind' by only three or four months. 1819 was
also the year of the Peterloo Massacre. Shelley's poem,
as we have seen, though explicitly political, is not really
political at all. The interest of Keats's poem is that,

[1] 29 June 1822. Shelley was drowned ten days later.

[2] Blake told Crabb Robinson that Christ 'should not have attacked the
govt. He had no business with such matters,' and that Dante was 'wrong'
in having 'political objects' (*Blake, Coleridge, Wordsworth, Lamb, etc.*, ed.
E. J. Morley (1932), pp. 3, 5).

[3] It is impossible to be more specific. Metrically the 'Grecian Urn' clearly
derives from the irregular 'Ode to Psyche' (included in the journal-letter of 30
April); it represents an intermediate stage between that poem—and perhaps the
'Ode to a Nightingale' which retains the occasional short lines of 'Psyche'—and
To Autumn (written at Winchester, 19 and 20 Sept.). Its Stanzas III, IV have
the same rhyme-scheme as the 'Ode on Indolence,' which had been completed
before 9 June.

though explicitly non-political, it is implicitly political. In spite of the Romantic trappings it is not at bottom a wholly Romantic poem.

The Urn, for one thing, is not a symbol in the sense in which the West Wind and Blake's Tiger and Keats's own Nightingale are symbols. There is no question here of an 'objective correlative.' The Urn really only provides an object lesson. By the use of analogies from the Urn Keats is able to make a number of points about the nature of poetry.

The Urn is introduced as comparable with but superior to poetry:

> Sylvan historian, who canst thus express
> A flowery tale more sweetly than our rhyme.

Endymion, it will be remembered, had opened with the claim that poetry provided 'A flowery band to bind us to the earth.' The Urn, then, can beat poetry at its own game. And what that game is is exemplified in the *motionless movement* of l. 9 of stanza I,

> What mad pursuit? What struggle to escape?

Stanza II elaborates the definition with examples of *soundless sound* ('ditties of no tone'), *stationary growth* ('Nor ever can those trees be bare'), and *timeless time* ('For ever wilt thou love and she be fair'). Stanzas III and IV draw certain pathetic and whimsical corollaries, and stanza V sums up the paradox of poetry. As Coleridge, with whom Keats had walked across Hampstead Heath as recently as the previous April, had taught his contemporaries, poetry 'reveals itself in the balance or reconcilement of opposite or discordant qualities.'[1] And Hazlitt, Keats's principal critical mentor, had made the same point even

[1] *Biographia Literaria*, chap. xiv.

more clearly when he attributed to Shakespeare 'the combination of the greatest extremes.' 'Shakespeare's imagination is rapid and devious. It unites the most opposite extremes.'[1] The Urn, in other words, in the terminology of Part One of this book, exemplifies the Synthetic Function of poetry and the Principle of the Semantic Gap.

The much-debated 'Beauty is truth, truth beauty' must be interpreted in this context. The Urn is a 'Cold Pastoral'; that is to say, like pastoral poetry (the only sense the noun *pastoral* had in the nineteenth century), it is allegorical.[2] Behind the particular unions of opposites depicted on the Urn (motion and immobility, growth and permanence, time and timelessness, etc.) a general synthetic principle is implied. This is the necessity for uniting Romanticism ('beauty') and realism ('truth'), the subconscious with the conscious mind, the feeling with the concept, poetry and philosophy. It is Keats's protest against the Romantic 'split man.' And the point of particular interest is Keats's *social* motive in propounding this generalization. The Urn is 'a friend to man.' The lesson that it teaches will be consolatory to the next generation as well as to Keats's.[3] Indeed, compared to the

[1] See J. R. Caldwell's admirable discussion of the poem in *Keats's Fancy* (1945), pp. 177, 183. Caldwell lists a number of eighteenth-century anticipations of Keats's 'Beauty is truth, truth beauty,' but has missed the closest of all. This is in Shaftesbury's *Sensus Communis* (1709), p. 111: 'For all *Beauty is* TRUTH . . . In Poetry, which is all Fable, Truth still is the Perfection. And whoever is Scholar enough to read the antient Philosopher, or his modern Copists, upon the nature of a Dramatick and Epick Poem, will easily understand this account of *Truth*.'

[2] Hazlitt discusses the English pastoral in the fifth of the *Lectures on the English Poets* (1818), stressing particularly its allegoric elements, e.g., 'Browne, who came after Spenser, and Withers, have left some pleasing allegorical poems of this kind.' Keats had heard Hazlitt deliver this actual lecture (letter to George and Thomas Keats, 14 Feb. 1818).

[3] Note that Keats speaks throughout in a representative capacity. In stanza I it is '*our* rhyme'; in stanza V the Urn teases '*us* out of thought,' and there is 'other woe Than *ours*.' Shelley would have written in the first person

need for psychological integration other social problems are of secondary importance:

> that is all
> Ye know on earth, and all ye need to know.

Keats oversimplified, of course, but to say, as Allen Tate has done,[1] that stanza V 'is an illicit commentary added by the poet to a "meaning" which was symbolically complete at the end of the preceding stanza' is to miss Keats's point. Stanza IV had been a relapse into Romanticism. The 'green altar,' the 'mysterious priest' and the 'little town' were alluring invitations to reverie. But Keats was too honest to leave it at that. The 'Ode to a Nightingale' had ended with the explicit admission that the 'fancy' is a 'cheat,' and the 'Grecian Urn' concludes with a similar repudiation. But this time it is a positive instead of a negative conclusion. There *is* no escape from the 'woe' that 'shall this generation waste,' but the action of time can be confronted and seen in its proper proportions. To enable its readers to do this is the special function of poetry.

Keats took the argument a stage further in the remarkable dialogue between Moneta and the poet in 'The Fall of Hyperion' (written some two months later):

> 'Art thou not of the dreamer tribe?
> 'The poet and the dreamer are distinct,
> 'Diverse, sheer opposite, antipodes.
> 'The one pours out a balm upon the World,
> 'The other vexes it.' Then shouted I

---

singular throughout. J. Middleton Murry (*Studies in Keats New and Old* (1939), p. 75) assigns 'that is all Ye know on earth and all ye need to know' to the poet. Obviously, however, this is also spoken by the Urn, the 'ye' being the *we* implied in '*ours*.'

[1] 'A Reading of Keats,' *New English Review* (Feb. 1946).

Spite of myself, and with a Pythia's spleen
'Apollo! faded! O far flown Apollo!
'Where is thy misty pestilence to creep
'Into the dwellings, through the door crannies
'Of all mock lyrists, large self worshippers
'And careless Hectorers in proud bad verse.
'Though I breathe death with them it will be life
'To see them sprawl before me into graves.'[1]

Here is Keats, at the end of his poetic career, repudiating
Romantic poetry at least as emphatically as he had
repudiated Augustan poetry at its beginning (in 'Sleep
and Poetry'). And more specifically. The objects of his
attack are, I think, easily identifiable. The 'careless
Hectorers' are presumably Byron and Shelley ('be more
of an artist'[2]). The 'large self-worshippers' are almost
certainly Wordsworth and Coleridge. And the 'mock
lyrists' must include Leigh Hunt, Tom Moore, Southey
and Rogers, who are grouped together in the journal-
letter of March 1819 as poets Keats did *not* admire. The
basis of the repudiation of these poets is that they are
'dreamers,' who only 'vex' the world. Put into modern
terms, Keats's criticism of the Romantic Movement is
that it represents a mere exploitation of the subconscious
mind without a satisfactory relationship with its audience.
The poetry that Keats admired—and that he was hoping
to write—was the exact opposite of this. Instead of the
irresponsible subliminal excitements of Romanticism
Keats wanted poetry to pour 'a balm upon the World,'
i.e. a soothing and healing influence. Its function was to
be social. In the last letter he wrote to Fanny Brawne he
gives an example of what he meant:

[1] At the last moment Keats decided to cancel this passage; not, however,
because he disagreed with its doctrine, but because he seems to have felt that
it complicated the argument unnecessarily.

[2] Keats to Shelley, 16 Aug. 1820.

If my health would bear it, I could write a Poem which I have in my head, which would be a consolation for people in such a situation as mine. I would show some one in Love as I am, with a person living in such Liberty as you do.

The poem—its heroine apparently was to have been the Sabrina of Milton's *Comus*—was never written, and *could* never have been written, even if his health had improved. The only consolation that poetry could provide in the nineteenth century, given the social setting and the contemporary condition of the English language, was the consolation of the daydream. Keats's Sabrina could only have been 'La Belle Dame Sans Merci' over again. In turning his back on that kind of thing—the 'vision' of the 'Ode to a Nightingale' *was*, he had decided, only 'a waking dream'—Keats had in fact condemned himself to poetic silence. It was not to be possible to write the sort of poetry that the mature Keats wanted to write for a hundred years. Eventually Wilfred Owen (for whom Keats was the poet of poets) was to take up the torch that Keats had kindled. 'Strange Meeting' (1918) can perhaps be said to carry on where 'The Fall of Hyperion' (1819) had left off.[1]

[1] The precocious maturity of Keats is a problem of its own. The turning-point seems to have been the winter of 1817–18. *Endymion* (finished Nov. 1817) is adolescent, *Isabella* (finished April 1818) is adult. I am inclined to connect the change with the moral shock that the syphilis contracted at Oxford in Sept. 1817 had given him. Amy Lowell tried to dispose of the tradition of Keats's syphilis, first recorded by W. M. Rossetti, by showing that the mercury referred to in the letter to Bailey of 8 Oct. 1817 might have been taken for a number of other diseases (*John Keats* (1925), vol. i, pp. 512–15). But she overlooked the information supplied by Keats's medical friend Henry Stephens (who must have known the facts): 'In the autumn of the same year, 1817, he visits a friend, Bailey by name, at Oxford, and in that visit runs loose, and pays a forfeit for his indiscretion, which ever afterwards physically and morally embarrasses him.' See Sir B. W. Richardson, *The Asclepiad* (April 1884), p. 143.

CHAPTER TWELVE

ROMANTIC SCHIZOPHRENIA:
TENNYSON'S 'TEARS, IDLE TEARS'

By its own Utilitarian criterion the Early Victorian Age must be accounted a failure. Never before in English history had so great a number of people been so acutely conscious of their own unhappiness. If the dominant social incentive was self-help, the dominant social fact was the accumulated misery of those who had not succeeded in helping themselves. And its consequence, as Léon Fancher, a Belgian observer who was here in the 1840's, noted, was that 'les diverses classes de la population, vivent non seulement séparées, mais hostiles, et où l'état de guerre semble être l'état naturel'[1]—an analysis that is confirmed by the sequence of riots and prosecutions, strikes and lock-outs, that preceded the Reform Act and accompanied the three Chartist Petitions. In addition to its intensity, there was one other feature that distinguishes the class-warfare of the 1830's and 1840's from earlier and later social antagonisms. This was its simplicity. As Marx and Engels pointed out in the *Communist Manifesto* (1848), 'Society as a whole is more and more splitting up into two great hostile camps, into two great classes directly facing each other—bourgeoisie and proletariat.' And, though their terminology is more naïve, the same conclusion had already been reached by such English social reformers as Thomas Arnold, Dickens, Carlyle and Disraeli. In one of his *Sermons Preached in the*

[1] *Etudes sur l'Angleterre* (Brussels, 1845) vol. i, p. 166.

Chapel of Rugby School (1832) Dr. Arnold accused his boys
of thinking that 'the rich and the poor are . . . two distinct
castes—I had almost said two distinct races.'[1] And in
Disraeli's *Sybil or the Two Nations* (1845), a brilliantly
objective social guidebook that only *pretends* to propound
a political philosophy, the two nations are specifically
defined in the same terms:

'This is a new reign,' said Egremont, 'perhaps it is a
new era.'

'I think so,' said the younger stranger.

'I hope so,' said the elder one.

'Well, society may be in its infancy,' said Egremont,
slightly smiling; 'but, say what you like, our Queen reigns
over the greatest nation that ever existed.'

'Which nation?' asked the younger stranger, 'for she
reigns over two.'

The stranger paused; Egremont was silent, but looked
inquiringly.

'Yes,' resumed the younger stranger after a moment's
interval. 'Two nations; between whom there is no intercourse and no sympathy; who are as ignorant of each other's
habits, thoughts and feelings, as if they were dwellers in
different zones, or inhabitants of different planets; who are
formed by a different breeding, are fed by a different food,
are ordered by different manners, and are not governed by
the same laws.'

'You speak of . . .' said Egremont, hesitatingly.

'THE RICH AND THE POOR.'[2]

The social skeleton in the Victorian cupboard looms
behind the poetry of Tennyson. As a young man he is

[1] Sermon xvi. As a small step in the right direction Arnold suggested that
the boys should stop using 'that contemptuous word by which you call the
poor.' Although the word itself is not specified by Arnold, *Tom Brown's
Schooldays* makes it clear that the 'insulting name' he had in mind was *lout*.

[2] Book II, ch. v.

reported to have said that the two great social questions impending in England were 'the housing and education of the poor man before making him our master, and the higher education of women.'[1] And an anecdote confirms his twinges of social conscience. In 1842, when the two-volume edition of his *Poems* had just publicly established his status as a poet, with other members of Edmund Lushington's house-party at Park House, Maidstone, he was in the walled garden, eating the peaches and the apricots. Many years later one of the younger members of the party recalled, in a letter to Tennyson's son, the conversation that took place that August. 'Some one made a remark about the fruit being liable to disagree with himself or others, to which another replied with a jocular remark about the "disturbed districts," alluding, of course, to some disorders apprehended or existing in the centres of industry. I remember being startled by your father's voice and accent, "I can't joke about so grave a question".'[2] But it was Tennyson the earnest citizen who was shocked; Tennyson the poet excluded such questions from his verse, except on the rarest of occasions, for the sufficient reason that he could not make poetry out of them. Between his conscience and his imagination there was a hiatus, a total lack of connection, that parallels the social gulf between the two nations. And the same psychic division is to be found *inside* his poetry. In 'Tears, Idle Tears' it can be shown, I believe, that two elements of his personality coexist without ever coalescing.

'Tears, Idle Tears' was written at Tintern Abbey, no doubt on some unrecorded excursion from Cheltenham, Tennyson's headquarters during the years immediately preceding his marriage. Though it cannot be dated

[1] *A Memoir by his Son* (1897), vol. i, p. 249.   [2] *Ibid.*, vol. i, p. 205.

Q

precisely it must have been composed at some time between the publication of *Sybil* (1845) and the commissioning of the *Communist Manifesto* by the Communist League (November 1847). It was published in the fourth canto of *The Princess* (1847). Unlike the songs added in 1850, 'Tears, Idle Tears' is an integral part of the story of that 'Medley,' and strictly speaking it should not be read, as it generally is, out of its dramatic context. There it is a song that is sung at the Princess's request:

> lightlier move
> The minutes fledged with music.

But the song proves less sedative in the poem than the Princess had anticipated, and she dismisses 'with some disdain' this reactionary plea for 'the moulder'd lodges of the past.' As a progressive feminist her motto is 'let the past be past,' and she asks the disguised Prince to sing instead a song about the republican future,

> Not such as moans about the retrospect.

The significance of these comments is the light they throw on Tennyson's own interpretation of 'the days that are no more,' the phrase that provides the poem's theme as well as its refrain. Apparently the days that are no more are the subject-matter of the history books. The unmotivated, incomprehensible tears must be taken, it seems, as a tribute to the glamour of the heroic past. A later comment by Tennyson himself seems to imply a similar interpretation: 'This song came to me on the yellowing autumn-tide at Tintern Abbey, full for me of its bygone memories. It is the sense of the abiding in the transient.'[1] The 'bygone memories,' in addition to those suggested by the Cistercian monastery, may also have included

[1] *The Works of Tennyson with Notes by the Author* (1913), p. 931.

memories of Wordsworth's *Lines Composed a Few Miles above Tintern Abbey*. It is at any rate curious that Tennyson characterized Wordsworth's line 'Whose dwelling is the light of setting suns' in almost identical terms as 'almost the grandest in the English language, giving the sense of the abiding in the transient.'[1] Another recorded comment makes it even more certain that the 'days that are no more' do not refer to Tennyson's (or the reader's) past:

> It was written at Tintern Abbey, when the woods were yellowing with autumn, seen through the ruined windows. It is what I have always felt as a boy, and what as a boy I called the passion of the past. And it is always with me now; it is the distance that charms me in the landscape, the picture and the past, and not the immediate to-day in which I move.[2]

Obviously, if the emotion that the poem records was felt by Tennyson as a boy, it cannot reside in the mature Tennyson's recollections of his boyhood. The days that are no more must belong to a public past.

But Tennyson's interpretation is certainly not the natural interpretation of the poem. And, as a matter of fact, most of his commentators have given 'the days that are no more' the personal sense that he consistently excluded. Sir Alfred Lyall has paraphrased the poem's mood as 'the tender melancholy of a feeling that life may be passing without love, of vague regrets and longings.'[3] W. M. Dixon's comment is on the same lines.[4] And more recently Cleanth Brooks, who describes the poem as an exploration of the nature of memory, has confirmed its

---

[1] *Memoir by his Son*, vol. ii, p. 288.
[2] W. M. Dixon, *A Primer of Tennyson* (1896), p. 134.
[3] *Tennyson*, 'English Men of Letters' series (1902), p. 57.
[4] Op. cit. p. 61.

subjective character.[1] It is almost impossible, indeed, to resist the impression that Tennyson's emotion is connected in some way with his own past. Nevertheless the poem *can* be given the meaning that he indicated. It is not the natural sense, but it is a possible sense. The one thing, in fact, that it is impossible to do is to give the poem both senses at once. *Either* the days that are no more are the objective past of kings and monasteries, *or* they are the subjective past of the poet's and reader's own earlier life. They cannot be both together.

There is a similar contradiction in the separate phrases and images. The clearest case perhaps is the phrase 'Dear as remember'd kisses after death.' This can be read in two ways. The natural sense is to take the person who remembers and the person who has died as one and the same. The meaning then will be that the dead man is remembering the kisses he exchanged when still alive— an effective if uncanny idea rather like the half-life of regret and reminiscence accorded to the Homeric hero after death. But, though this is certainly the sense that the grammar would suggest, the context makes it clear that Tennyson meant the person who remembers to be distinct from the person who is dead. Presumably it is the survivor who remembers the kisses exchanged with a loved one who is now dead.

An even more interesting example of this conflict between the natural interpretation and the intended meaning is provided by the lines,

> Fresh as the first beam glittering on a sail,
> That brings our friends up from the underworld.

Overtly Tennyson is here defining the retrospective vividness that attaches to episodes of the historic past. This

[1] *The Well Wrought Urn* (New York, 1947), ch. ix.

'freshness,' which derives from the absence of common-place associations, Tennyson compares to a visual sensation that must have been equally rare to the middle-class Victorian reader—the shimmer of sunrise on the sails of an East Indiaman on the horizon. But the comparison does not stop, as it ought to logically, at the visual image. This is not just a large sailing ship; the boat has passengers on board and the passengers are 'our friends' (yours, Gentle Reader, and mine!), who have returned from the antipodes. And with the addition the vividness of the image ('glittering' surely implies that the early morning dew is still on the sails?) is blurred by the emotional exalta-tion that the prospect of this reunion imposes. It is difficult to find anything especially 'fresh' in the senti-mental excitements of such an occasion. It looks as if, when he added the second line, Tennyson had forgotten about his simile and was simply surrendering to the subconscious suggestions of the imagery. Was he, in the depths of his mind, expecting to find Arthur Hallam—buried at Clevedon only twenty miles or so, as the crow flies, from Tintern—on board the incoming boat? The use of the word 'underworld' invites some such inter-pretation. Its overt sense here is certainly not its natural sense or its ordinary sense. Indeed, according to the Oxford Dictionary, Tennyson's use of 'underworld' as a synonym either for the antipodes or for 'the part of the earth beyond the horizon,' is the first occurrence of either sense in English. The *natural* sense of 'underworld' in this context is of a Hades, a world of departed spirits under the earth—a sense that goes back to the Elizabethans; and the natural interpretation of the line is to read it as a sort of nineteenth-century version of Charon's boat. The East Indiaman, in other words, is bringing back Hallam, a modern Eurydice, alive from the grave!

The poem's third stanza is also ostensibly a prolonged simile—one by means of which the peculiar combination of strangeness and sadness that the contemplation of the heroic past evokes is to be defined. But in fact, in a natural reading of the lines, is not the analogy—a somewhat forced one, in any case—almost immediately lost sight of and the whole of the reader's attention concentrated on the brilliantly recorded sense-reactions of the dying man?

> Ah, sad and strange as in dark summer dawns
> The earliest pipe of half-awaken'd birds
> To dying ears, when unto dying eyes
> The casement slowly grows a glimmering square;
> So sad, so strange, the days that are no more.

The dying man in this stanza is not, of course, in any literal sense Arthur Hallam, who died at midday on 15 September (not on a summer dawn) and in any case had no idea that he was dying (a blood-vessel near the brain suddenly burst). But the selection of this particular image, with its close connection both with the 'underworld' immediately preceding it and with the kisses 'after death' that follow it, is surely significant.

The last stanza of the poem seems to *demand* a personal interpretation:

> Dear as remember'd kisses after death,
> And sweet as those by hopeless fancy feign'd
> On lips that are for others; deep as love,
> Deep as first love, and wild with all regret;
> O Death in Life, the days that are no more.

The kisses are obviously not mere abstract poetic properties. And if they are not—and their strict relevance in this summing up of 'the passion of the past' is far from clear—may they not be the kisses that Hallam and Tennyson (and Emily Tennyson, Alfred's sister who was also Hallam's fiancée) did or did not exchange? It is at least *possible* that the 'first love' is Tennyson's for Hallam ('deep' because frustrated and repressed), and that the 'lips that are for others' are Hallam's lips—which were presumably reserved for Emily, with whom Hallam had fallen in love almost as soon as he and Tennyson had got to know each other.[1]

If the preceding analysis is not wholly misguided, it looks as if 'Tears, Idle Tears' was not really one poem but two. On the conscious level it is a poem about that feeling for the past that had been discovered by Carlyle and Froude, among the historians, in Tennyson's own generation, and by Scott in the previous generation. On the subconscious level, on the other hand, it is a poem about the relations between the living and the dead— and specifically perhaps those between the living Tennyson and the dead Hallam. It is possible, of course, that Tennyson was aware of the autobiographical elements in the poem, and that its incorporation in *The Princess* and his various expository comments upon it represent an elaborate attempt to put the reader off the scent. Or the censorship may have been subconscious—in which case we must envisage one subliminal layer in his mind covering up the indiscretions of an even deeper layer. But either hypothesis presupposes a purposiveness and a degree of integration of the psychic material that I cannot find reflected in the poem. Within the limits of his self-knowledge Tennyson's comments ring true to me. I doubt if there was any intention to deceive. And the poem too is, in its way, sincere—the authentic expression

[1] I would like to know more about Emily Tennyson and her brother's attitude towards her. She married Richard Jesse in 1842.

of an unintegrated personality. The morbidity lies in the absence of any effective connection between the two levels of statement. The days that are no more are at one and the same time the historic past and Tennyson's passionate. unhappy twenties. And between the two meanings no real link whatever is provided or apparently even felt necessary.

Tennyson was not the only Victorian poet who suffered from schizophrenia. It was the occupational disease of the period. The case of Browning. is notorious. Henry James wrote a short story about it ('The Private Life'). Clare Vawdrey—'the greatest (in the opinion of many) of our literary glories'—has a Mr. Hyde, a copiously commonplace talker, and a Dr. Jekyll, a lonely genius who sits up in his room and is never seen. James's preface explains that Vawdrey is Browning (whom he knew quite well): 'I have never ceased to ask myself, in this particular loud, sound, normal, hearty presence, all so assertive and so whole, all bristling with prompt responses and expected opinions and usual views . . . what lodgement, on such premises, the rich proud genius one adored could ever have contrived, what domestic commerce the subtlety that was its prime ornament and the world's wonder have enjoyed, under what shelter the obscurity that was its luckless drawback and the world's despair have flourished.'

James noted the contradiction, but was not able to explain it, or even to define it, except in terms of a fairy story. But the Victorian 'split personality' is clearly a reflection in some sense of the split in Victorian society. It would be to oversimplify to suggest that the psychic division that is revealed in 'Tears, Idle Tears' is the direct consequence of the coexistence of the two nations in the 1840's. But the two *traumata* are almost certainly related.

They can, I believe, both be attributed to the *inhuman* specialization (a specialization that repressed the full development of the human being, reducing, for example, the man to the 'hand') that the economic system encouraged. Physically it was the poor who suffered most, but the worst psychological victims were among the rich. The system, which assumed as its basic premiss that the prosperity of society depends upon the selfishness of its constituent individuals, discouraged at one and the same time social planning and individual integration. 'Each for himself' became as true of the separate elements in the personality as of the various competitors in the market. That at any rate was the trend. Its recognition should make for a fairer assessment of Victorian poetry than it has hitherto received.

CHAPTER THIRTEEN

FROM ESCAPISM TO SOCIAL REALISM: TWO POEMS ABOUT OXFORD

THE poetry of consolation that Keats projected and Wilfred Owen consolidated received its most memorable definition in the fragmentary Preface that was found among Owen's papers after his death. Familiar though it is, it is worth reproducing once more:

> This book is not about heroes. English Poetry is not yet fit to speak of them.
>
> Nor is it about deeds, or lands, nor anything about glory, honour, might, majesty, dominion, or power, except War.
>
> Above all I am not concerned with Poetry.
>
> My subject is War, and the pity of War.
>
> The Poetry is in the pity.
>
> Yet these elegies are to this generation in no sense con-solatory. They may be to the next. All a poet can do to-day is warn. That is why the true Poets must be truthful.

The true poets must be truthful. Owen's variation on Keats's 'Beauty is truth, truth beauty' might be taken as the battle-cry of modern English and American poetry. Its application provides the acid test at any rate between modern poetry and modern pseudo-poetry, such as that of Edith Sitwell. Their failure by its standards is what consigns most of the later Romantic poets to unreada-bility to-day. Once the singing robes were on, the Pre-Raphaelites and their successors could not or would not tell the truth.

Lionel Johnson's 'Oxford' is a typical specimen of Romantic poetry in its Polished Craftsman and Decadent phases.[1] (Its representativeness is guaranteed by its inclusion in *The Oxford Book of Victorian Verse*.) Here is the kind of thing that modern poetry was in reaction *against*:

Oxford

Over, the four long years! And now there rings
One voice of freedom and regret: *Farewell!*
Now old remembrance sorrows, and now sings:
But song from sorrow, now, I cannot tell.

City of weather'd cloister and worn court;
Grey city of strong towers and clustering spires:
Where art's fresh loveliness would first resort;
Where lingering art kindled her latest fires!

Where on all hands, wondrous with ancient grace,
Grace touch'd with age, rise works of goodliest men:
Next Wykeham's art obtain their splendid place
The zeal of Inigo, the strength of Wren.

Where at each coign of every antique street,
A memory hath taken root in stone:
There, Raleigh shone; there, toil'd Franciscan feet;
There, Johnson flinch'd not, but endured alone.

There, Shelley dream'd his white Platonic dreams;
There, classic Landor throve on Roman thought;
There, Addison pursued his quiet themes;
There, smiled Erasmus, and there, Colet taught.

And there, O memory more sweet than all!
Lived he, whose eyes keep yet our passing light;
Whose crystal lips Athenian speech recall;
Who wears Rome's purple with least pride, most right.

[1] From *Collected Poems* (1915).

That is the Oxford strong to charm us yet:
Eternal in her beauty and her past.
What though her soul be vex'd? She can forget
Cares of an hour: only the great things last.

Only the gracious air, only the charm,
And ancient might of true humanities,
These nor assault of man, nor time, can harm:
Not these, nor Oxford with her memories.

Together have we walk'd with willing feet
Gardens of plenteous trees, bowering soft lawn;
Hills whither Arnold wander'd; and all sweet
June meadows, from the troubling world withdrawn;

Chapels of cedarn fragrance, and rich gloom
Pour'd from empurpled panes on either hand;
Cool pavements, carved with legends of the tomb;
Grave haunts, where we might dream, and understand.

Over, the four long years! And unknown powers
Call to us, going forth upon our way:
Ah! Turn we, and look back upon the towers
That rose above our lives, and cheer'd the day.

Proud and serene, against the sky they gleam:
  roud and secure, upon the earth they stand.
Our city hath the air of a pure dream,
And hers indeed is a Hesperian land.

Think of her so! The wonderful, the fair,
The immemorial, and the ever young:
The city sweet with our forefathers' care:
The city where the Muses all have sung.

Ill times may be; she hath no thought of time:
She reigns beside the waters yet in pride.

> Rude voices cry: but in her ears the chime
> Of full sad bells brings back her old springtide.
>
> Like to a queen in pride of place, she wears
> The splendour of a crown in Radcliffe's dome.
> Well fare she—well! As perfect beauty fares,
> And those high places that are beauty's home.

The first reflection that a reading of Johnson's poem suggests is how easily they got away with it in Good Victoria's Golden Reign! No modern poet would dare to risk such slovenly writing as

> Chapels of cedarn fragrance, and rich gloom
> Pour'd from empurpled panes on either hand;
> Cool pavements, carved with legends of the tomb;
> Grave haunts, where we might dream, and understand.

The reader should surely not have been allowed to think, even momentarily, that the gloom is *poured on* the visitor's hands. And the use of the adjective *grave* immediately after *tomb* is unfortunate.[1]

A more serious matter is the metaphoric incompetence. The trope 'There, Raleigh *shone*' is obviously meant to be 'poetic.' That Johnson could have imagined anybody would think it poetic is a measure of his verbal *naïveté*. The 'crystal lips' he assigns to Newman (who is apparently the answer to the conundrum in the sixth verse) are another example of the same defect. And the metaphoric poverty is not compensated, as in Augustan poems, by solidity of structure. Johnson has only two devices by which to achieve poetic progression (i.e. the linking of line with line and verse with verse). The first is verbal

[1] Equally unfortunate are the city's 'pure dream' (as opposed to an impure dream?), the 'Rude voices' of Oxford's critics, and the identification of the Thames valley with 'those *high* places that are beauty's home.' The sublime should not be quite so near the ridiculous.

repetition. (In the first verse *now*; in the second *city*, *where*, *art*; in the third *when*, *grace*, etc.) The second is verbal antithesis. The antitheses are normally *merely* verbal, as

> The city sweet with our forefathers' care:
> The city where the Muses all have sung.

(No contrast is intended between the poets' Oxford and the Oxford the forefathers had cared for.) Occasionally, however, as in the following lines, a real antithesis seems to be intended, though on inspection it is not clear what the point of the opposition is:

> Proud and serene, against the sky they gleam:
> Proud and secure, upon the earth they stand.

Sky is opposed to *earth*, and the *gleaming* of the towers is opposed to their *standing*. But why? There is no incompatibility in the towers simultaneously gleaming in the sky and standing on the earth. The reader, slightly irritated, realizes at this point that the antithesis is a mere literary gesture, and that Johnson is only using it to diversify his descriptive catalogue.

Such technical dishonesty is the appropriate accompaniment of the mental dishonesty of the poem. It is intended to be a tribute to the University by a literary undergraduate who is 'going down' for the last time. The tribute is a *personal* one. Johnson begins by referring to the mixed pleasures and pain of the four years' residence. Later he describes the walks he and his friends had taken in and around Oxford. Now 'unknown powers' are calling him to a career of free-lance journalism in London. But as soon as one asks what Oxford had done for Johnson, as a human being, to deserve the tribute doubts begin to intrude themselves. Instead of the truth—the thrill of having Walter Pater as a tutor, the charms of alcohol and Catholicism, the titillation of literary vanity—we get a versified extract from the Oxford guidebook. Apart from a single reference ('Together have we walk'd') to the friend to whom the poem is dedicated, the only people who come into the poem are the architects and writers of the past. One would imagine that Johnson's time in Oxford had been passed in cloistered solitude, whereas in fact he was a popular figure with many intimate friends. And this misrepresentation of his own debt to the University is accompanied by an equally gross caricature of Oxford's place in the national life. Johnson's case for Oxford against the crying of the 'Rude voices' is based entirely on 'her beauty and her past.' ... escapist's paradise—'from the troubling ...drawn.' This was written in 1890, when ...ity's grip on the governmental, educa-... ...ous machine was perhaps more complete than at any time before or since.[1]

Like most of his Oxford contemporaries Lionel Johnson professed a profound admiration for Matthew Arnold. The year before 'Oxford' he had written a long elegiac poem on Arnold's grave ('Laleham'), and in 'Winchester' there is an earlier tribute. But the object of this admiration was Arnold the poet, the 'Prince of Song,' whose Romantic *juvenilia*, such as 'Empedocles on Etna' and 'The New Sirens,' the mature Arnold did his best to disavow. Johnson can have had little sympathy with the prose Arnold with his constant harping on the importance of seeing the thing in itself as it really is. To the æsthetes of the 1890's the thing was to be seen as it wasn't. Oscar

[1] It is true Johns... ...son was only twenty-three in 1890, but he was as mature then as he was ever ...aring Cross' was written in 1889. There is an amusing ... to be. His best and most familiar poem 'By the Statue of King Charles at Ch... Oxford in Arthur Waugh's *Tradition and Change* (1919). account of Johnson at ...

Wilde deplored 'The Decay of Lying.' And in his private life, according to his friends, Johnson himself excelled in the gratuitous and unmitigated lie.

.   .   .   .   .

W. H. Auden's 'Oxford' is the fifth poem in the collection *Another Time* (1940). It was perhaps written in 1937, when Auden judged a verse-speaking contest in Oxford. Like Johnson's poem it is essentially a report on the University, where the poet had been educated, and both poems contain many of the same 'properties' (e.g. the rivers, the architecture, the college gardens, and the neighbouring countryside). But t_____ matter are at least as striking as the _____ method.

An analysis of some of these diff_____ a more satisfactory approach to _____ modern poetry than the usual generalizations.

Oxford

Nature is so near: the rooks in the college garden
Like agile babies still speak the language of feeling;
By the tower the river still runs to the sea and will run,
    And the stones in that tower are utterly
    Satisfied still with their weight.

And the minerals and creatures, so deeply in love with their
    lives   10
Their sin of accidie excludes all other:
Challenge the nervous students with ___,
    Setting a single error   careless beauty,
    Against their countless faults.

O in these quadrangles where Wisdom honours herself
Does the original stone merely echo that praise
Shallowly, or utter a bland hymn of comfort,
      The founder's equivocal blessing
      On all who worship Success?

Promising to the sharp sword all the glittering prizes,
The cars, the hotels, the service, the boisterous bed,
Then power to silence outrage with a testament,
      The widow's tears forgotten,
      The fatherless unheard.

Whispering to chauffeurs and little girls, to tourists and dons,
That Knowledge is conceived in the hot womb of Violence
Who in a late hour of apprehension and exhaustion
      Strains to her weeping breast
      That blue-eyed darling head.

And is that child happy with his box of lucky books
And all the jokes of learning? Birds cannot grieve:
Wisdom is a beautiful bird; but to the wise
      Often, often is it denied
      To be beautiful or good.

Without are the shops, the works, the whole green county
Where a cigarette comforts the guilty and a kiss the weak;
There thousands fidget and poke and spend their money:
      Eros Paidagogos
      Weeps on his virginal bed.

Ah, if that thoughtless almost natural world
Would snatch his sorrow to her loving sensual heart!
But he is Eros and must hate what most he loves;
      And she is of Nature; Nature
      Can only love herself.

R

And over the talkative city like any other
Weep the non-attached angels. Here too the knowledge of
  death
Is a consuming love. And the natural heart refuses
     The low unflattering voice
     That rests not till it find a hearing.

Auden's poem is much better written than Johnson's.
Instead of the stock epithets like *weather'd* cloister, *worn*
court, *grey* city, *strong* towers, *clustering* spires, Auden
provides the unexpected word—*agile* babies, *nervous*
students, the *boisterous* bed, the *talkative* city. The range
of the diction is also much wider. Johnson confines himself to the 'poetic diction' of the Decadent Romantics.
Periphrases and elegant variations provide him with
cushions against reality. (He has written sixty lines on
Oxford without once introducing the words *undergraduate, student, don, fellow, university, college, quadrangle,
hall* or *library*.) Auden, on the other hand, has no verbal
inhibitions, and technical terms like *accidie* (Chaucerian
English for *sloth*), *the original stone, Eros Paidagogos* (a
'joke of learning' on the analogy of Hermes Psychagogos)
and *non-attached* jostle with the colloquialisms.

There is a similar inclusiveness in Auden's range of
social reference. Instead of reducing Oxford to its
architecture and the Illustrious Dead, as Johnson had
done, Auden brings in the townspeople, the tourists and
the employees of Morris Motors as well as the undergraduates, the dons and the founders of the colleges.
Instead of Johnson's uncritical adulation of the University,
Auden sees it as an anomalous, because uncoordinated,
part of the modern world. The poem is the dramatization
of a human problem, a particular application of E. M.
Forster's golden rule 'Only connect.'

Where Johnson was personal (in 'Oxford' he is deliber-
ately running away from his own private experiences at
the University),[1] Auden generalizes. (Auden's poem
might be described as a miniature sociological treatise.)
The difference is one that distinguishes the characteristically
Romantic poem from the characteristically modern poem.
For the Romantics the direction of interest is always
away *from* the generalization *to* the personal statement.
This is not to suggest that Romantic poetry is primarily
autobiographical, in the ordinary sense of the word.
Although there is some only slightly disguised autobiography in English Romantic poetry—in Shelley's *Epi-
psychidion*, for example—the personal element more generally finds its expressoin in the objective correlatives of
wild nature and other related symbols. The towers and
spires of Oxford were perhaps intended to have some such
function in Johnson's poem. Auden's poem, on the other
hand, is typical of the modern trend to poetic generalization. Not one detail in it leads back to Auden himself.
It is significant that the Oxford college suggested by his
opening lines is Magdalen, whereas Auden's own college
was Christ Church. The image of the tower is an
example of the conscious symbolism—made and not
found—that seems to provide the basic poetic unit of the
modern school. In contrast with Johnson, who tries to
dissolve Oxford into 'a pure dream' and 'a Hesperian
land,' Auden insists on the solidity of his self-conscious
tower:

> And the stones in that tower are utterly
> Satisfied still with their weight.

[1] Ezra Pound, who edited Johnson's *Poetical Works* (1915), notes in the Preface
the omnipresent 'fear of life, a fear that he was not afraid of, but which he
openly acknowledged.'

Until Hardy's and Hopkins's experiments this particular extension of the 'pathetic fallacy' was a device not often used by the English poets. Its characteristic flavour is a cool *unpretentiousness*. There is no suggestion here that the poet is tapping the deepest terrors and desires. All that he is doing is providing the reader with an analogy which will vivify and enlarge the stock response to the object of the comparison. 'Let's pretend,' Auden is saying in effect in this passage, 'that Magdalen tower is a big fat man. It's not true, of course, but it will help you to appreciate the impression of complacent solidity that the tower leaves.' The device relieves the underlying symbolism—the tower is clearly a symbol of the University—of portentousness. The symbolism too, it is implied, is a conscious convention, a way of saying something that could not be said in any other way.

Whom was Auden writing for? Or, putting the point more generally, who is the ideal reader in the particular poet-reader relationship that constitutes modern poetry?

The attitudes that Auden has taken for granted in contemporary readers of his 'Oxford' can be divided into the political, the intellectual, and the emotional. Politically Auden assumes an anti-capitalist bias. Unless you can join him in detesting the kind of success that money brings—'The cars, the hotels, the service, the boisterous bed'—you will not be able to make much of his poems. And this detestation of the rich and the powerful must be accompanied by the ability to identify oneself with the poor and the unsuccessful. You must be able to see the point of view at least of the thousands who 'fidget and poke.' Intellectually Auden assumes an interest in psycho-analysis, a religious scepticism, and a wide range of historical and literary information. ('Eros Paidagogos' would stump most readers.) There is no pretence that his poetry is easy, and he demands the complete intellectual co-operation of his reader. 'Oxford' must be read slowly, carefully and several times. It cannot be rushed. Emotionally the presuppositions are anti-sentimental. Auden's readers must be at once hard-boiled and emotionally adventurous.

If Auden is indeed the Assured Master of modern poetry, our Keats, our Pope or our Donne, there should be a close relationship between his ideal readers and the socially dominant class to-day. It should be possible indeed to identify the latter by reference to the former. A reading of him seems to me to confirm the tentative conclusion reached at the end of Part One that the socially dominant class in England to-day is that of the 'managers' or 'planners,' i.e. the men and women, of varying social origins, who sit on commissions and committees, the compilers of reports, with their allies in Parliament, the Civil Service, local governments and the trade unions. Auden's 'difficulty' and the undeniable obscurity of modern poetry generally, are partly explicable in terms of this poet-reader relationship. A society run by a minority of 'managers' presupposes a majority who are 'managed,' the non-ruling classes who are more planned against than planning. The success of such a system must depend on the extent to which the Managed are prepared to 'trust' the Managers. For the mass of the people to retain their confidence in the new *élite* they must look up to them as more intelligent and better informed than themselves. *Omne ignotum pro magnifico*, and the consciousness that the *élite* speak a different kind of English from theirs, more condensed, more allusive and with a much larger vocabulary, may act as a political reassurance. The danger, of course, is that the obscurity will come to acquire a value of its own. Some modern poetry, Dylan

Thomas's, for example (a compound at times of genius and perversity), sometimes seems to be putting on an 'act' simply to impress the crowd. There is a parallel here, socially and poetically, with the Pindaric Odes of the eighteenth century.

But the Managerial Revolution which Auden is the prophet of goes deeper than that of James Burnham. Burnham's Managers qualified as the new ruling class by virtue of their *expertise*. But what the quality or combination of qualities was that was responsible for their managerial efficiency Burnham did not inquire. His social order is without any dominant incentive. Although he has a chapter on 'The Managerial Ideologies,' he seems to regard such terms as 'the people,' 'collectivism' and 'planning' as a psychological smokescreen behind which the new rulers are imposing themselves on the community. The motive force in his Managers is apparently just the love of power for its own sake. But this cynicism is an oversimplification of the human factors involved. People only become managers because they are good at managing other human beings, and the essential qualification for this is not a lust for power but an intense interest in human nature, an ability to see things through other people's eyes, and a power of convincing people of one's own personal disinterestedness. Auden calls it 'love.' The word has always been a favourite of his. The most brilliant of his specifically political poems, the Prologue to *Look, Stranger*, began,

O love, the interest itself in thoughtless Heaven,

and the penultimate stanza of the profound 'September 1, 1939' (in *Another Time*) ended,

We must love one another or die.

'Love,' the supreme value for Auden, is social love, not sexual love. It is nearer to the 'friendship' of Pope than to the egocentric 'love' of the Renaissance poets or the Romantics.[1] To the extent that 'love' is at the creative centre of such measures of social reorganization as the Labour Party's nationalization programme, the Managerial Revolution receives Auden's qualified blessing. But 'All a poet can do to-day is warn,' and, as one lays the poems down, it is the warnings against managerial indifference to or oversimplifying of the human elements that remain and reverberate in the memory. 'In the end, human integration and social integration are complementary processes.' That is perhaps Auden's final message to us. The parallel with Pope and Gray is interesting. Their warnings were against the 'pride' that was corrupting the English aristocracy of the eighteenth century. Their society, like ours, was basically egalitarian because it was built upon a co-operative rationalism. But by the time it received its classic expression in such a poem as *The Rape of the Lock*, a process of social stratification had set in. Instead of the entry into the ruling class being determined by exceptional 'common sense' it was more and more being determined solely by birth. As Auden has seen, this is our danger too. The qualities required in a Manager are, I suppose, a scientific outlook and 'love.' The exceptional man or woman who possesses both these qualities in an unusual degree may come of any class, and complete equality of opportunity must therefore be the

---

[1] According to Josephine Miles, op. cit., *love* is the most frequently recurring major word in Shakespeare, Donne, Herrick, Collins, Coleridge and Tennyson. It comes second in order of frequency in Wyatt, Spenser, Wordsworth and Keats. The most frequently recurring word in Chaucer, Pope, Goldsmith and Cowper is *man*. These findings—which are limited to the poets for whom concordances exist—provide additional confirmation of the links between Chaucer and the Augustans, and the Renaissance and the Romantics. Pope uses *friend* more often than any of the poets examined by Miss Miles.

condition of survival of a Managerial Society. But, commendable though the progress has been since the Victorian Age, there is still not as much social equality in England as in most countries to-day, and as the inevitable consequence too few of our Managers possess more than the rudiments of the scientific point of view or of a social conscience.

CONCLUSION

CHAPTER FOURTEEN

THE RÔLE OF THE LITERARY HISTORIAN

IN an earlier excursion into the history of English poetry[1] I tried—not altogether successfully, as it seems to me now —to delimit the respective provinces of literary history and literary criticism. At that time the historian's rôle seemed to me to be confined, in its essence, to the exposition of literary change. His job, as I saw it, was to record the *differences* between one group or generation of poets and its immediate predecessors or successors, and to explain those differences causally. His data, the particular poems and poets he was to explore, would be provided for him, I assumed, by the literary critic, to whom I assigned the custody of literary values. The critic's job I took to be to tell us which the good poems were and what were the particular merits of the particular poems, poets and schools of poetry. Although my own field, as I imagined, was the humbler one of literary history no one could have been more respectful to the literary critics, that superior species.

It was with special disappointment, therefore, that I read a hostile review of my book in *Scrutiny* by F. R. Leavis.[2] Leavis was even then one of the best contemporary critics, and I had hoped my attempt at delimitation—

[1] *English Poetry and the English Language: An Experiment in Literary History* (1934).
[2] The review, my letter of rejoinder and Leavis's final comments have now been reprinted in *The Importance of Scrutiny*, ed. Eric Bentley (New York, 1948).

which was primarily aimed at the pure scholars, being intended to make them realize their precarious dependence upon the critics—would have interested him. But I was mistaken. Leavis admitted my good intentions but was completely unimpressed by my claims for literary history. The kind of history that I was trying to write 'could be successfully attempted,' he said, 'only by a critic and would then be essentially literary criticism.' The delimitation, in other words, was (in his opinion) artificial and unnecessary.

I am now inclined to agree that there are not two professions with a hard-and-fast boundary line between them. Literary history and literary criticism can only be differentiated, I now believe, in terms of trends and emphasis. The literary historian is *more* interested in poetic differences, though the detection of the differences depends upon appreciations of value. The literary critic is *more* concerned with poetic values (including the 'appreciation' out of which the values crystallize), though the basic values can only be estimated when the historical differences have been discounted. Whether the inclusive term should be 'history' or 'criticism' will perhaps depend upon the classifier's temperament. Leavis would like to reduce the whole field of literary study—excluding 'scholarship,' or 'mere statements of facts about works of literature'—to criticism. I wish now to suggest that a strong case can be made for incorporating 'criticism' within 'history.' I am tempted to add—*unless* criticism is 'statements of facts about works of literature,' is it worth having?

It will be best to begin by asking, What does criticizing a poem amount to? Surely it is only putting down on paper the experiences the critic has had in reading the poem. The critic's superiority to the rest of us can only lie in the greater completeness of his response to the stimulus of the poem, i.e. he is nearer being the ideal reader of the original poet-reader relationship. And this, as we have seen in Part One, involves: (i) the ability to effect an *intellectual* relation of the original words, speech-units, allusions, and the underlying social philosophy to their contemporary equivalents, their 'translation,' as it were, into modern terms; (ii) the capacity to undergo a *human* reaction (sensuous, emotional and intellectual) to the social situation 'synthesized' in the poem. If the first of these processes is primarily the historian's affair, the second is the one in which the literary critics have specialized. And its importance, and difficulty, must not be underestimated. But the literary critics can claim no special right of entry even into this province of experience. A discriminating interest in human nature, its motives and their disguises, is the mark of the effective member of any social group. The values that the critic prides himself on enforcing are not literary values, but general human values, reflected and embalmed in literature. Even the failures of communication, the poems that are 'technically' unsatisfactory, have their parallels in social intercourse. This indeed is the cardinal difference between poetry and the other arts. The 'medium' of poetry is not a non-utilitarian craft that has to be consciously learned but the language we grow up in, so that we all speak elementary poetry—as M. Jourdain spoke elementary prose—without realizing it and without being able to stop it.

The difference between the critic and the common reader, however diligent and sensitive, is the critic's greater self-consciousness. As he responds to the stimulus of the poem he *sees himself responding*. He is able to bring back a detailed report of his experiences precisely because one side of his mind has been watching the other side's behaviour. The danger of such self-awareness, once the critic is back at his desk, is the temptations it offers of self-dramatization. The good critic runs in continual danger of the sins of arrogance and condescension. Of the great English critics, from Ben Jonson to T. S. Eliot, have any altogether escaped the taint of arrogance? Matthew Arnold, it is true, professed humility, but how infuriating and insulting his nonchalance can be!

Arrogance is the first stage, however, in the relapse into subjectivity. Pride in the delicacy and purity of one's critical response soon leads to the response assuming in one's own eyes an existence largely independent of its source in the words of the poem. This was the trap into which Coleridge, Lamb, Pater and the other Romantic critics all tumbled. In the adventures of their souls among masterpieces the masterpieces were too often lost sight of altogether. Modern criticism, since T. S. Eliot, has given this kind of critical irrelevance a new turn. It can be called the cult of the bright idea. More or less innocent examples of the kind of thing I mean are to be found in almost every one of Eliot's earlier critical essays. 'Hamlet (the man) is dominated by an emotion which is inexpressible, because it is in *excess* of the facts as they appear.'[1] The *Jew of Malta* is a farce.[2] Othello in his last speech is 'cheering himself up.'[3] And Leavis, though less often, is also sometimes guilty of similar fatuities. The attempt in *Revaluation* to prove Pope a Metaphysical poet is perhaps the grossest. Almost the only evidence produced is six lines from the *Elegy to the Memory of an Unfortunate Lady*.[4]

---

[1] 'Hamlet and his Problems.'
[2] 'Notes on the Blank Verse of Christopher Marlowe.'
[3] 'Shakespeare and the Stoicism of Seneca.'
[4] Most souls, 'tis true, but peep out once an age,
  Dull sullen pris'ners in the body's cage:

The lines are not in the least typical either of that clever but unsatisfactory poem or of Pope's mature manner. Nor are they particularly Metaphysical. Almost any poet of the seventeenth century might have written them. It is significant that the editors cite parallel passages from Dryden and Cowley, but not from Donne or the Herberts. I find the irresponsibility of this pronouncement of Leavis's shocking. His 'hunch,' based upon the examination of a few lines in an uncharacteristic poem, is to outweigh the critical consensus of two hundred years that Pope, far from being in any sense a Metaphysical, is the *typical* English neoclassic poet. Of course, a critical tradition must not be accepted blindfold, but something more than the Great Man's *ipse dixit* is surely needed for its controversion.

The antidote to subjectivism is the discipline of fact. The literary historian, by virtue of his grounding in historical facts, is less liable to distort the objectivity of the poetic fact. And he should also be less liable to succumb to critical arrogance. The Thing in Itself is from its elusiveness a constant object-lesson in mental humility. It is so easy for the historian not only to be wrong but to be proved wrong. But there is another and a more important reason why the literary historian who is properly equipped is more likely to be a trustworthy reporter of the poetry of the past. It is, as we have seen, that he alone is competent to 'translate' the poem of another period or social group into our own terms; and the two processes of 'translation' and appreciation (response to the human experience) are inseparable. The emotional response, the poetic catharsis, *follows* the intellectual construction of the

---

Dim lights of life, that burn a length of years
Useless, unseen, as lamps in sepulchres;
Like Eastern Kings a lazy state they keep,
And close confin'd to their own palace, sleep.

situation embodied in the poem. The reader, in other words, must know what the sequence of words means before he can either laugh or cry. And the appropriate emotional response depends upon the intellectual meaning, the sense of the poem, being correctly apprehended. The kind of intelligence demanded in this process of meaning-construction is essentially the skilful balancing of probabilities that can be trained by historical investigation. It remains true, of course, that the historian cannot be guaranteed to respond emotionally or sensuously as completely as the inspired critic would. But there is this to be said for the emotionally arid historian: as far as it goes his report on the poem will be correct (objectively verifiable, publicly discriminable). The critics may *seem* to have responded more profoundly—I am thinking particularly of such contemporary figures as G. Wilson Knight, J. Middleton Murry, or H. I'A. Fausset—but it generally turns out that what they have responded to is a private poem created by their own misreading either of the text or of its socio-literary context. Such critics do more harm than good. Their misreadings tend to *vulgarize* the great poems. They have brought the poems down to our own level. But the refreshing quality of all poetry that is great, or nearly great, derives from the way in which it extends the range of our social horizon and raises us *above* our normal levels, enlarging and deepening our consciousness of our fellow men and women and of our relations with them. The critic is too apt to claim a special understanding of the whole meaning of the poem. If you have read his essay the implication is that there is no further need to read the poem it is about. The historian is more modest. At his best he can only offer you an introduction to the poem. Certainly nothing that he writes will be mistaken as a substitute for it.

It may be objected that, though arrogance and subjectivism are always dangers, the best contemporary critics have escaped them. Certainly E. M. W. Tillyard, L. C. Knights, John Crowe Ransom and Cleanth Brooks cannot be accused of either. William Empson, the most acute and profound of living critics of poetry, is sometimes the dupe of his own ingenuity, but his misreadings remain well this side of subjectivism. And the arrogance of T. S. Eliot and F. R. Leavis is more a matter of the tone of voice, the critical manner, than of a fundamental deep-seated self-complacency. But these admissions do not really affect the central issue, which is that literary criticism *by its nature* cannot achieve the finality of a demonstration unless it is supplemented by literary history or (in the case of a contemporary poet) literary sociology. The critic who is nothing but a critic may be interesting, stimulating, suggestive, but he can never be demonstrably *right* (or indeed *wrong*). It is always only his opinion against yours, one man's meat against another man's poison.

According to Eliot the Perfect Critic is one who builds his personal impressions up into laws. He quotes Rémy de Gourmont: 'Eriger en lois ses impressions personnelles, c'est le grand effort d'un homme s'il est sincère.'[1] But the proposition is clearly self-contradictory. A generalization by the critic of his own private perceptions can never become a *law*, because it can never be binding on anyone else. If he is to escape the quicksand of private preferences, the critic must integrate his perceptions with the social facts represented by the poem, i.e. the original poet-reader relationship in its historical complexity. He must look *out* as well as *in*. The personal impressions must be adjusted to the objective realities of space and time, a

[1] *The Sacred Wood* (1920), p. 1.

S

particular literary and social convention. It is the essential argument of this book that a good poem, properly read, constitutes a concrete social situation exactly comparable to the familiar 'facts' of the history-books, like the Battle of Hastings or the Execution of Charles I. Meaning is indivisible. You would not expect to understand what happened at Hastings simply by re-enacting within yourself the emotions and calculations that William and Harold are likely to have gone through. Your historical imagination must have the political and military facts to work on. And it is the same with the reading of poetry. Unless you know what the words mean, and the social implications of their meanings, you will not understand the poem. The vivid sympathetic imagination is not enough. Indeed, unless supplemented by an equally vivid factual curiosity, it is likely to be a positive handicap, because it will tempt you to create your own sentimental day-dream in place of the poem.

There is a related point that is worth making. It is that the historical-sociological approach alone provides the critic with a factual structure to which he can attach his perceptions and generalizations. This provides a reassurance to the reader as well as a convenience to the critic. The reader has the satisfaction of feeling that the critic in his interpretation is concerning himself with something that is really there. The purely literary critic sometimes gives the impression of fluttering helplessly round the object under discussion without being able to make contact with it. There is apparently nothing positive or concrete that he can say. He is reduced to vague gestures of approval or disapproval, such as 'sensuous richness,' 'weak grasp upon the actual,' 'natural speaking stress,' or 'rhythmic deadness.' *Who would not weep if Atticus were he?*

CHAPTER FIFTEEN

TOWARDS A POETRY-READING *ÉLITE*

As W. H. Auden has pointed out, 'There is no biological or mathematical law which would lead us to suppose that the quantity of innate artistic talent varies very greatly from generation to generation. The major genius may be a rare phenomenon, but no art is the creation solely of geniuses, rising in sudden isolation, like craters from a level plain; least of all literature, whose medium is language—the medium of ordinary social intercourse.'[1] And, as far as the English poets are concerned, this *a priori* probability can now be confirmed statistically. *The Cambridge Bibliography of English Literature* (1940), a standard work of reference, has listed 196 poets who flourished during the seventeenth century, 275 poets who flourished in the eighteenth century, and 489 poets who flourished in the nineteenth century. In terms of the country's total population and allowing for the slight increase in the average length of life, this works out as follows:

1600–1700: one poet in every 61,200 souls.
1700–1800: one poet in every 58,900 souls.
1800–1900: one poet in every 63,800 souls.

The virtual identity of these ratios cannot be a coincidence. It is reasonable to conclude that under modern conditions there will be on the average one poet that posterity will be prepared to read in every 60,000 persons. On this basis some 800 poets will have flourished during the twentieth century in Great Britain.

[1] *The Oxford Book of Light Verse* (1938), Introduction.

The most interesting implication of these figures is that a predisposition to write poetry is apparently a regularly recurrent natural abnormality, like the tendency to have twins. Although the kind of poetry that the poet writes must be determined by the social environment, the capacity to write it, i.e. an unusual facility in verbal syntheses, is apparently inborn and therefore hereditary. The Wesley, Coleridge and Tennyson families are English examples of the fact that the poet has to be born as well as made. As the hereditary factors are outside its control a study of poetry must be primarily concerned with the environmental factors, which will determine whether the potential poets are to be relatively good, as in the early seventeenth century, or relatively bad, as in the later nineteenth century. But the part played by heredity, the complicated combination of genes of which the precise formula is likely to remain unknown, must not be overlooked. Something more is required in the poet besides a capacity for taking pains.

Similar considerations presumably apply to the readers of poetry. If poetry only exists in the poet-reader relationship and the mental processes of the reader are, as they seem to be, complementary to the poet's, it is likely that the natural poetry-reader will also be a regularly recurrent abnormality. This is not to deny that every sane human being should be able to get *something* out of poetry. But, as there is a dividing line between the mere versifier and the very minor poet, so there is an important difference between the good reader of poetry and the reader to whom poetry doesn't come naturally. I imagine no teacher of literature would deny these differences of natural aptitude.

In this book I have been primarily concerned with the minority who are born potentially good readers of poetry.[1] The objective that university lecturers on English literature like myself must have continually before our eyes is to ensure, as far as we can, that the potentialities are realized. A natural reader of poetry who is also a trained reader of poetry will normally be a social asset outside the world of literature. This is because poetry-reading is not a full-time occupation. (Poetry-writing shouldn't be either; the professional poet is in constant danger of degenerating into a mere verbal conjurer.) If poetry is, as I have argued, the particular social order at its point of maximum consciousness, both the poet and the readers he is addressing must be functional members of society for them to be able to co-operate in expressing its *idea*. Poetry-writing and poetry-reading should not be considered ways of life in themselves so much as the overspill of successful communal living in *any* profession. They are at once the result of successful social living and the preparation for further successes. The habits of synthetic thinking that poetry encourages are particularly desirable in those professions that are directly concerned with human beings. Hence presumably the number of teachers, clergymen, doctors, lawyers,

---

[1] Illiteracy or semi-literacy has restricted the numbers of even the casual readers of poetry. Until the middle of the nineteenth century more than half the population of this country lived and worked in the country. But the English countryman has never been a reader. Miss M. L. Campbell, who has made an exhaustive search into the wills and correspondence of English farmers *c.* 1590–1650, has found very few references to any books at all and only one case of a farmer who we can be certain owned a book of poetry (it was the *Canterbury Tales*; see *The English Yeoman* [New Haven, 1942]). Clare's poem 'The Cottager' shows that there had been little change by his time; 'prime old Tusser' (i.e. *Five Hundred Points of Good Husbandry*) is the 'only Poet which his leisure knows.' And Taine, whose *Notes on England* (translated by W. F. Rae, 1862) provides an excellent summary of the mid-Victorian scene, found a Bible in all the cottages he visited, and sometimes religious books, novels or treatises on the art of rearing rabbits, etc., but no poetry (p. 155). Of course, the ballads and folk-songs persisted; Clare's cottager could recite 'many a moving tale in antique rhymes,' including 'Chevy Chase.'

soldiers and sailors who have always written and read poetry. But these professions have in addition extra-human interests. The profession that is concerned *par excellence* with human nature in its communal aspects is politics, and it is the politicians, in the wider sense of the word, who have made some of the best English poets as well as some of the best readers of English poetry. I include among the politicians such men as Johnson, Goldsmith, Byron, Newman, Carlyle, Arnold, Bagehot, Belloc and Aldous Huxley, but even among the professionals the proportion of serious poetry-readers has always been higher than in other walks of life. Of the nineteen Prime Ministers of the nineteenth century, for example, at least eight belonged to the poetry-reading *élite* of their times. Gladstone was almost the ideal reader of Romantic poetry.[1] Lord John Russell was another. And the light verse of Canning, Palmerston and Disraeli, and Lord Derby's translations, were all admirable of their kind.

The poetry, however, that was read with most care and most affection at that time was not English poetry but the poetry of Greece and Rome.[2] Since 1920 or so the number of serious readers of the classics has decreased and there has been a corresponding increase in the number of readers of English poetry.[3] The classical sides at the schools and the classical departments at the universities have been thinning out, partly no doubt because of a slump in the snob-values of Latin and Greek, and English

[1] He was one of the first to appreciate the extraordinary merit of Wordsworth's *Peter Bell*. See Morley's *Life*, ch. vii.

[2] ' . . . of the eighteen Prime Ministers between 1837 and 1937 ten were good classical scholars and four others had learnt both Latin and Greek' (Sir Richard Livingstone, 'The Classics and National Life,' Classical Association, 1941). The four ignoramuses were presumably Lloyd George, Bonar Law, Ramsay MacDonald and Neville Chamberlain.

[3] Until the extinction of the *Westminster Gazette* in 1928 its Saturday supplement ran a weekly competition in Latin verse-composition!

literature has been one of the principal beneficiaries. The change is sometimes deplored, not on the ground that English literature is inferior to the classics—poet for poet it is obviously better—but because the reading of English poetry, or so it is asserted, does not provide the intellectual discipline of the classics. It must be admitted that English *as it is often taught* cannot compare with the old classical curriculum as an educational instrument. Struggling with an inflected language so unlike his own did teach the Victorian schoolboy to think. The institution of 'prep,' by which the following day's translation had to be prepared the night before, compelled him to puzzle out the exact meaning of every sentence by himself. And the next day he was either right or wrong.

Unfortunately it is now possible to get high marks in most school and university examinations in English literature without being either right or wrong. All that is often required in the students is the ability to reproduce a muzzy impression of what they have been reading and to quote indiscriminately. The English Books paper in School Certificate was essentially simply a test of verbal memory. Even to-day it is possible to get a good Honours Degree in English at almost every university in this country if you are fluent, a rapid writer of fairly grammatical English, and can quote sufficiently freely from the standard works of the standard authors.

But this state of affairs is as unnecessary as it is deplorable. To the modern boy or girl, whose natural English reading is prose, the meaningful reading of poetry will provide at least as intellectually arduous a discipline as the reading of an inflected language. And it will have the additional advantage of introducing the adolescent to situations that will interest him or her as a human being. The old classical treadmill claimed to be *humane*. But in fact until one reached the Sixth Form one never got beyond the surface sense; all that counted was the struggle to straighten out the grammar. Properly taught English poetry could hardly fail to be the modern *litteræ humaniores*. And it is *humanizing* above all that is needed by many members of our new ruling class of the Managers.

The notion that is so prevalent at the older universities that English literature is a 'soft option' that needs to be reinforced by linguistics derives indirectly from Decadent Romanticism. If poetry-reading *was* simply a matter of passive 'ecstasy,' and poetry-criticism could be reduced to variations upon the theme of 'magic,' obviously it would be absurd to give a degree in it. And so the syllabus was extended and extended until you had to read everybody—but so fast that it did you no good at all—and, to add a little honest work to the lotos-eating, the textual criticism of *Beowulf* was made compulsory. The first step, therefore, in a programme of educational reform must be the complete discrediting of Romantic poetic theory. In its humble way I hope this little book of mine may help to do this. The second step will be the elaboration of a new syllabus and a new system of examining based upon the *difficulty* of English poetry, if it is to be properly understood. Some suggestions of the essential reforms at the university level may be worth adding. I shall confine myself to the final examination in the Honours School. The problem of the syllabus has been discussed by F. R. Leavis in *Education and the University* with his usual competence, and I have little to add to his recommendations.

The principal defects in the existing examination system are (i) the emphasis on verbal memory (the ability to quote), (ii) the encouragement of a superficial fluency (the capacity to 'write against the clock'), (iii) the essential similarity of almost all the questions asked (the only aptitude tested is the ability to summarize contemporary critical opinion), (iv) the tendency for the examination to become an endurance test (the student's whole career may depend upon his ability to maintain a consistent level for six hours a day for a week).

As for (i), the premium on quotations, the solution would seem to be for the examining body to provide plain texts of the set books or authors for use during the examination. It should also be permissible for the examinees to make use of their own notes in answering the questions asked. The memorizing of their own notes and essays, to which the term before the examination is now devoted, is a completely artificial procedure. Such a concession would encourage the taking of *good* notes, and a habit would then be formed of enormous intellectual importance in adult life.

(ii), the too fluent pen, might be counterbalanced by the requirement of a short thesis, to be submitted a little before the examination proper, from all candidates for a First or Second Class. The training in logical exposition and the habits of accurate scholarship that thesis-writing imposes are of incalculable value. The burden upon the examiners could be reduced by a limit on the number of words allowed and by the setting of certain specified topics each year as the subject-matter of the theses.

(iii), the restriction of the questions asked to elementary critical 'appreciation,' is a legacy of Romantic criticism. To effect its cure it will be necessary to educate the examiners. More 'practical criticism' *à la* I. A. Richards should certainly be included, and I should like to see questions set on the poet's rejected readings and similar problems of particular poetic 'meanings.' I see no reason why most of the topics dealt with in this book should not

be included in university examinations, provided they
are presented in *particular* form. The fault with most of
the questions now set is that they are too ambitious.
Confronted with the request to write on Wordsworth
as a poet of nature what on earth can the poor examinee
do in an hour except summarize and generalize? But if
the question were restricted to Wordsworth's attitude to
nature *in one poem*, e.g. in 'A slumber did my spirit seal,'
there would be an opportunity for the detailed appreciation that can alone be critical.

(iv), the problem of the week's endurance test, would
be mitigated by the introduction of one or more theses
or dissertations into the examination. It should not be
necessary for anybody to do more than one three-hour
paper a day.

.   .   .   .   .

A reform of the examination system would go some
way to ensuring that the potential poetry-reader became
a trained poetry-reader. And it could no doubt be accompanied by a reform of the textbooks, anthologies and
editions of the English poets. But the essential reform is
the permeation of our modern managerial society with
a synthetic mental outlook.

That is a task that may well seem beyond the capacity
of a poetry-reading *élite*, even in conjunction with the
many talented poets who are now writing. In his rhetorical
exuberance even Shelley never claimed that poets could
be the *acknowledged* legislators of mankind. But, though
a complete success is unlikely, a partial success is worth
fighting for. In favourable circumstances a poem's
immediate influence can extend far beyond the limited
circle of its original audience. Three classes of readers can
perhaps be distinguished. They are (i) the poet's own

immediate friends, (ii) the enthusiastic strangers who often tend to turn the poet into a cult, (iii) the general poetry-reading public (Dr. Johnson's 'common reader'). The three classes supplement and reinforce each other, and their coexistence is necessary if the contemporary condition of poetry is to be healthy. Romantic poetry suffered, at any rate up to the Polished Craftsman phase (Tennyson and his contemporaries), from the absence of readers of the third class. Their second class of readers—the Wordsworthians, for example, and the Pre-Raphaelite group whose enthusiasms for Keats, Shelley and Blake were equally uncritical—should have acted as intermediaries between the poets (i.e. the first class) and the general public (the third class). In fact, until the 1890's, such advocates and interpreters of Romanticism as Rossetti and Swinburne did more harm than good.

The pattern of Augustan poetry-reading was somewhat different. The inner circle of intimates was almost as small as Wordsworth's or Shelley's. Rochester wrote 'for the private Diversion of those happy Few whom he us'd to charm with his Company and honour with his Friendship.'[1] Their names are to be found in his 'Allusion to the Tenth Satyr of Horace':

> I loath the Rabble, 'tis enough for me
> If Sidley, Shadwell, Shephard, Wicherley,
> Godolphin, Butler, Buckhurst, Buckingham,
> And some few more, whom I omit to name,
> Approve my Sense, I count their Censure Fame.

A similar list is provided by Pope in the 'Epistle to Doctor Arbuthnot.' The second class of Augustan readers is represented by such men as Joseph Spence—whose

---

[1] Robert Wolseley, preface to *Valentinian* (1685); reprinted in *Critical Essays of the Seventeenth Century* (1909), ed. J. E. Spingarn, vol. iii, p. 25.

attitude to Pope was not unlike De Quincey's to Wordsworth—but this class was of much less importance then
than during the Romantic period. It merged impercep-
tibly into the large third class of common readers, who
secured Pope's independence by their subscriptions to
his *Homer* and who welcomed in turn the unknown
Thomson, Johnson, Gray and Cowper.

It is towards the creation and consolidation of a similar
class of common readers to-day that the energies of the
friends of English poetry should be directed. The first
step, in my opinion, must be the conscious stimulation
of a poetry-reading *élite*, who can be the missionaries of
poetry in a world of prose. Such an *élite*, if its social
assumptions were those of modern poetry, might constitute a new second class of readers, different from and
more effective than those of the Augustans and the
Romantics. It is likely to be larger and more self-conscious than its eighteenth-century predecessor, and it is
certain to be more critical and more coherent than its
Victorian counterpart. Its most promising nucleus at the
present time, in spite of the occasional arrogance and the
deficiencies of scholarship, seems to me to be *Scrutiny*,
the remarkable critical journal that F. R. Leavis has
edited at Cambridge since 1932. In the preceding pages
I have more than once criticized this or that pronouncement by Leavis. But Leavis has in an outstanding degree
two virtues that have always been rare in the history of
literary criticism. One is total incorruptibility. The other
is the moral fervour that he brings to the study of English
literature. For Leavis the reading of poetry is something
that matters enormously. It informs his life, as a philosophy or a religion might do. If Matthew Arnold was
right, as he may well have been, when he said that 'most
of what now passes with us for religion and philosophy'

is in process of being replaced by poetry, it is to Leavis and men like Leavis that we must increasingly look for spiritual guidance and nourishment. In a world that is full of his detractors I choose to conclude this 'Conclusion' with a salute to his achievement.

INDEX

Abercrombie, Lascelles, 42 ff.
Addison, Joseph, 123
Adjectives, 21
Anderson, Robert, 210
Anglo-Scottish poetry, 93
Aristotle, 49
Arnold, Matthew, 41, 181, 194, 239
Arnold, Thomas, 223 f.
Atterbury, Francis, 165 f.
Auden, W. H., 240 ff., 259
'Augustan,' 166

Bagehot, Walter, 103
Baker, Sir Richard, 150
Blake, William, 217
   And did those feet, 7 f.
   Hear the voice of the Bard, 37 ff.
Bradley, A. C., 197
Brémond, Henri, 47
Bridges, Robert, 13, 26
Brooks, Cleanth, 155, 181 f., 227 f.
Browning, Robert, 232
Burke, Edmund, 123
Bush, Douglas, 96, 166 f.
Butler, Samuel, 73

Caldwell, J. R., 219
Cambridge University, 18
Campbell, M. L., 261
Chambers, Sir E. K., 133
Chaucer, Geoffrey, 45 f., 120, 121 f.,
   133 f., 148, 247
   The Miller's Tale, 134 ff.
Clare, John, 261
Coleridge, S. T., 41, 49 f., 66 f., 247
   Dejection, 202 f.
Collins, William, 192, 247
Communist Manifesto, The, 223
Congreve, William, 57, 176
Content of poetry, 79 ff.
Cooper, Elizabeth, 3
Coulton, G. G., 132

Daiches, David, 26
Dallas, E. S., 43 f.
Digby, Sir Kenelm, 105 f.
Disraeli, Benjamin, 224
Dixon, W. M., 227
Donne, John, 150, 247
Drummond, William, of Hawthorn-
   den, 55
Dryden, John, 68, 89

Edward VI, King, 147
Eliot, T. S., 29, 36, 48 f., 51, 89, 91,
   110 f., 158, 254
   The Waste Land, 126
Evans, B. I., 73
Examination system, 264 ff.

Fancher, Léon, 223
Fenton, Elijah, 168
Flecker, J. E., 68
Ford, F. M., 35 f.
Foster, John, 35
'Friend,' 247

Gamelyn, 133
Garrod, H. W., 183
'Genius,' 52 f.
Givler, R. C., 24 f.
Gladstone, W. E., 262
Goldsmith, Oliver, 167
Graves, Robert, 16, 69
Gray, Thomas, 181 ff.
Greville, Frances, 191 f.
Grigson, Geoffrey, 40

Hallam, A. H., 229 f.
'Happy,' 146
Hazlitt, William, 218 f.
Herrick, Robert, 20, 82 f., 247
   Upon Julia's Clothes, 46
Higden, Ranulf, 131, 132
Higgons, Sir Thomas, 165